"Sexual abuse is horrifying, pair abuse in one's life or in the life ful and difficult and, if not ha that has already taken place. T  this delicate issue with sensitivity without shying away realities one must face in the aftermath of sexual abuse. Sue and Maria draw from their own personal experiences and the wisdom gleaned from helping others who have come through sexual abuse. This book is primarily a comprehensive guide for two people to walk through together. The "Leading Friend" and "Learning Friend" walk down this Scripture-saturated path toward healing and restoration arm-in-arm. *Treasure in the Ashes* is a guidebook, an applied theology book, and a source of hope and healing all rolled into one. I pray this book finds its way into the hands of everyone who has undergone the wretched experience of sexual abuse."
—**Curtis W. Solomon**, Director, The Biblical Counseling Coalition

"Working through the heartache and pain of childhood sexual abuse is both deeply distressing and bewildering. How can we navigate the turbulent waters between defining ourselves by our abuse or pretending that it doesn't really matter? Is there a better way? Does the Bible actually speak to the woman or man who's suffered sexual abuse? And, most importantly where was God during the abuse? Did he see? Did he care? Nicewander and Brookins have coupled their own experiences with their deep understanding of Scripture in this very helpful book. This book makes it clear that while there are no easy, pat answers that will assuage the heart of the abuse victim, there are lasting and true ones that will certainly help. I'm thankful for this resource. I'm sure you will be, too."
—**Elyse M. Fitzpatrick**, Author of *Counsel from the Cross, Because He Loves Me,* and *Idols of the Heart*

"Sue Nicewander and Maria Brookins have written a highly readable book for those who have suffered under the shame and hurt of sexual abuse. They have a unique voice as they write from their experience as both victims and counselors. *Treasure in the Ashes* is real but redemptive, honest but always with humility, biblical but always balanced with grace. If you or someone you love has struggled with sexual abuse, this book will be a life-giving resource. I highly recommend it.

—**Garrett Higbee**, PsyD, President, Twelve Stones Ministries; Founding board, Biblical Counseling Coalition; Leader, Soul Care Ministries; Director, Pastoral Care for the Great Commission Collective

"This book addresses a very sensitive subject with compassion and clarity. The hardest questions are addressed with powerful, God-centered answers which focus upon God's attributes, the suffering of Christ, and the struggles of the psalmist. While this book will bless individuals who have suffered sexual abuse, it is especially designed to be used with a mentor for whom helpful instructions are provided. There are many women in our churches who have been afraid to face what has happened to them. This could be used of God for them to get the help they need."

—**Jim Newheiser**, Pastor and Director of the IABC

"What a rich, real, raw, and relational guide *Treasure in the Ashes* is for everyone who has ever suffered the horrors of sexual abuse. This is a comprehensive and compassionate manual for gospel healing that gives sufferers permission to grieve and lament, and then invites sufferers to journey with Christ to the place of healing hope."

—**Bob Kellemen**, Founder and CEO of RPM Ministries, Vice President of Institutional Development and Chair of the Biblical Counseling Department at Crossroads Bible College. Author of thirteen books including *Sexual Abuse: Beauty for Ashes*

"Sue and Maria offer to fellow sufferers of sexual abuse a compassionate, hope-filled, thorough, and biblical approach to taking the journey to restoration and healing. The study blends personal reflection opportunities, studies of biblical texts and principles, clear teaching, and much encouragement to remove the confusion that so often assaults hurting hearts."

—**Jim Berg**, Seminary Professor, Bob Jones University; Executive Director of Freedom That Lasts®; Director of Faith Counseling Institute

"The experience of sexual abuse does not affect little bits and pieces of our lives, but our whole being. It is a great evil overcome only by a greater good. It requires a kind of healing that reaches into the details of who we are, who God is, and how he makes us new. The road of recovery can be long. *Treasure in the Ashes* guides us delicately through the details. It ministers the gospel of Jesus Christ over the long haul. It offers words from God—real, substantial hope to those who have suffered the grave and dark effects of evil in our world."

—**John Henderson**, Board of Directors, Association of Biblical Counselors

"*Treasure in the Ashes* is an instrument of healing grace. Whether you are a victim or one called to help those who have been abused, this Christ-centered, Scripture-saturated, grace-infused labor of love will wisely lead you through your painful past to the compassionate heart of the Savior."

—**Paul Tautges**, Pastor at Cornerstone Community Church, Author of *Counseling One Another, Discipling the Flock, Pray About Everything*

"Some of the hardest counseling I have done is helping people wrestle through the questions and pain of sexual abuse and the issues this creates in relationships. Sue and Maria are not afraid to hit these questions head on with the truth of Scripture. Even if you're not an experienced counselor, you can use this resource as a guide to walk beside your friend on the path to biblically processing this suffering."

—**Dr. Ernie Baker**, Pastor of Counseling and Discipleship, First Baptist Church Jacksonville; Chair of the online BA in Biblical Counseling at The Master's University. Author of *Marry Wisely, Marry Well*

"Sue and Maria have given the church one of the most practical and biblical resources available that address the problem of sexual abuse. Sue and Maria speak the truth in love and know how to both encourage the fainthearted and correct with gentleness. This book is a must read for all Christians who desire to please the Lord as they work through their own painful past or work with others who have experienced sexual abuse.

—**Joel Teague**, Pastor of Discipleship & Counseling, Faith Community Church in Woodstock, Georgia

COUNSEL
FOR THE
HEART

A RESOURCE for WORD-BASED
TRANSFORMATION and
PRACTICAL DISCIPLESHIP

Treasure
IN THE ASHES

*Our Journey Home from
the Ruins of Sexual Abuse*

Sue Nicewander
Maria Brookins

Shepherd Press
Wapwallopen, Pennsylvania

Treasure in the Ashes
© 2018 by Sue Nicewander and Maria Brookins

ISBN:
Print: 978-1-63342-139-4
ePub: 978-1-63342-140-0
Kindle: 978-1-63342-141-7

Published by Shepherd Press
P.O. Box 24
Wapwallopen, Pennsylvania 18660

Typesetting by JackofallTales.com
Cover Design by Andy Heckathorne · andyheckathorne.com

First Printing, 2018
Printed in the United States of America

B 24 23 22 21 20 19 18
 11 10 9 8 7 6 5 4 3 2 1

81NALC9NIVRI

Library of Congress Cataloging-in-Publication Data

eBooks: www.shepherdpress.com/ebooks

Dear Reader,

If your hands are trembling as you hold this book, we may share similar stories; we have been torn apart and tossed aside by lies and shame because of the sexual abuse we have suffered. Picking up this book may be one of the hardest things you have ever done. We are glad you have bravely come to join us here.

We are very sorry for your suffering. Someone has taken an intimate part of you that did not belong to them. God gave us our sexuality, not only to create children, but as a special way to express his desire for pure and beautiful unity and oneness to develop within a loving marriage. This intimate expression is meant to bond and unite two souls into one.

But being sexually abused, especially as a child, can bind us to lies and confuse our God-given design and desire for affection and love. This confusion stems from being manipulated and deceived into believing that this form of "affection" (the sexual abuse we suffered) is normal and okay. Before we could even begin to understand love, we were introduced to a very advanced and complicated distortion of it.

Are you feeling the rage? We are too! Sexual abuse can cause some of the most deeply destructive damage of any human experience and usually it is thoughtlessly overlooked. Our culture (including the church) has no idea what to do with us, so it remains painfully silent regarding matters of sexual abuse. This silence can hush even the boldest of souls and keep us locked away for years. The purpose of *Treasure in the Ashes* is to break the silence; to be the voice you've longed to hear and to equip you to begin your own journey home.

We write to you as fellow travelers, not as experts. We have sought long and hard after a God we weren't always sure we could trust, shed thousands (probably millions) of tears, and have found over and over again, that no matter how gut-wrenching the fight, Jesus, our gentle Healer, is always faithful and always good (Genesis 50:20; 1 Corinthians 1:9). Thank you for being courageous, and for reaching out. We welcome you to *Treasure in the Ashes*.

With sincere love,
Sue and Maria

Sue Nicewander, MABC, ACBC, BCC, has been counseling since 1994. She is founder and training coordinator of Biblical Counseling Ministries, Wisconsin Rapids, Wisconsin, and serves on the Council Board of the Biblical Counseling Coalition. Sue has her MA in biblical counseling from Central Baptist Theological Seminary, and is author of *Building a Church Counseling Ministry Without Killing the Pastor* and *Help! I Feel Ashamed,* and articles in the *Journal of Biblical Counseling* and *Baptist Bulletin.* Sue and her late husband Jim were married for 43 years. The Nicewander family includes two beautiful married daughters and six delightful grandchildren.

Maria Brookins has a BS in Biblical Studies/Counseling from Faith Baptist Bible College in Ankeny, Iowa. She and her husband, Corey, have been serving together in ministry since 2004. They enjoy God's gift of a full and vibrant life with four fabulous boys and two crazy dogs.

Contents

Part I

WELCOME TO THE JOURNEY

Welcome to the Journey

Treasure in the Ashes has been written because we are heartbroken by the number of women and men in our churches who suffer silently. For so many of us, the silence is deafening. Our hearts' desire is that *Treasure in the Ashes* will be a voice of hope for those who suffer (whom we call *learning friends*) and a means of equipping those who want to help (whom we call *leading friends*). This study is a way for local churches and Christian friendships to become places of refuge and healing as we learn to bear one another's burdens, not just emotionally, but purposefully.

We chose the subtitle *Our Journey Home from the Ruins of Sexual Abuse* for a few very special reasons.

- **Our**: We are walking together in unity and faith as God leads us (Psalm 133, Galatians 2:20, and Titus 2). We are not alone.

- **Journey**: Life is a process of learning and growing (Psalm 23). We are pilgrims here, called to fix our eyes on Jesus as we travel through this life (Philippians 3:20).

- **Home**: Home is a beautiful place of peace and safety in the presence of our good and merciful God, where we belong now and for all eternity (John 14:1–3, 23).

Treasure in the Ashes has been designed with the one-another relationships of the Bible in mind because we believe that hope and healing are found with God and his people. "Bear one another's burdens," Galatians 6:2 states, "and so fulfill the law of Christ." Ecclesiastes 4:9 tells us that "Two are better than one, because they have a good reward for their labor. For if they fall, one will lift up [her] companion.... And a threefold cord is not quickly broken."

Catching a Vision of Hope

The vision of *Treasure in the Ashes* is for a leading friend and a learning friend to learn to walk together to and with Jesus to examine the experience of sexual abuse, to wrestle through the hard questions and doubts we have about God, ourselves, the world, and to learn to identify lies, accept and embrace truth, and to find real and powerful hope,"… that you may proclaim the praises of Him who called you out of darkness into His marvelous Light" (1 Peter 2:9).

A Quick Overview

We have organized this study around six pivotal questions:

- **What's My Story?** *Exploring why our story matters*

- **Who Is God?** *Pursuing God in the context of sexual abuse*

- **Who Is Jesus?** *Discovering how Jesus makes all the difference*

- **Who Am I?** *Embracing our identity from God's perspective*

- **Who Are You?** *Building and maintaining healthy relationships*

- **Where Do We Go from Here?** *Finding meaning and hope in God's story of Redemption*

Working through these questions will help us identify destructive beliefs and lies and replace them with truth. The purpose of *Treasure in the Ashes* is to provide a biblical and Christ-centered framework to lean upon as we walk with Jesus and seek to heal from the devastating effects of sexual abuse.

Throughout this book there are places to fill in answers to questions. We recommend that you record additional thoughts in a private journal.

Format

- **Intended use** – This study can be used for individual or group use, but the heart of *Treasure in the Ashes* is to facilitate one-on-one discipleship relationships.[3]

- **Pace-flexible** – This book is designed to allow a healthy pace for each reader. The process should not be rushed.

- **Interaction/Discussion** – Throughout this book we have included talking points and a treasure. The talking points are meant to help the reader interact personally with the text. The treasure is a summary of the main idea of the section.

- **Voice** – We take care to include ourselves (the authors) as part of the vast group of sexual abuse victims/survivors. The word "we" refers to that group more often than it will refer to us as your authors.

- **Stories** – Along the way, we will share from our personal experiences, as well as from the fictional stories of Dylan, Shanae, and Rayna, who represent a broader experience and response to sexual abuse.

"I will give you the treasures of darkness and hidden riches of secret places, that you may know that I, the LORD, who call you by your name, am the God of Israel." —Isaiah 45:3

Preparing For Our Journey

If you've ever gone backpacking in the mountains, you will know that there is no substitute for good planning. The proper gear, a trustworthy guide, and a good map are essential for a successful trip. As we begin to face the reality of the evil we have suffered and how it has impacted us, we must be well equipped and prepared for what lies ahead.

---

[3] The Group Study Appendix contains suggestions for facilitating a group study using this workbook.

This journey can be complicated, so we will simplify our preparation by studying four essentials:

- Honesty

- Scripture

- Church

- Leading friends

Honesty

Did God leave me? Where was he? Did he look away? Is he evil? Why did God create us knowing we would sin? If God really loves us, then how could he allow such horror? "Why do You stand afar off O LORD?" (Psalm 10:1).

Questions like these arise from a heart desperate for understanding and peace. But feeling abandoned by God, among a host of other emotions, can evoke anger and an unwillingness to listen to him. This unrest can cause us to demand an explanation as to how and why a good and loving God could have allowed our suffering.

When Jesus arrived four days after the death of Lazarus, Martha cried out, "Lord if you had been here, my brother would not have died" (John 11:21). She didn't try to cover up what she really felt. She was honest. It may seem irreverent to even consider being that bold with God. But he already knows how we feel and lovingly invites us to approach him anyway (Hebrews 4:15-16).

Being respectfully honest with God positions us to be challenged, strengthened, and embraced (Gen. 32:28). As we turn to Jesus with all our heart, we will discover as Martha did, that he was there with us, but not in the way we thought was best.

Scripture

It can be difficult to trust the Bible, especially when wrestling with unanswered questions, doubt, and unbelief, but we must decide to believe that God's Word is trustworthy, right, and sufficient. Man's ideas and opinions are always changing and aren't fully dependable. Scripture is our only unchanging source of truth. No matter what we think or feel, we must fight the lie that Scripture is not enough (Ephesians 6:17). "Never doubt in the dark what you know to be true in the light" (Anonymous).

"The words of the LORD are pure words, like silver tried in a furnace of earth, purified seven times" (Psalm 12:6).

"He who heeds the word wisely will find good, and whoever trusts in the LORD, happy is he" (Proverbs 16:20).

Church

The traumatic effects of sexual abuse are far-reaching, making it crucial to invite and allow wise believers in Jesus to walk with us (Galatians 6:2; Ephesians 4:15-16). "And I pray that you being rooted and grounded in love, may have power, together with all the saints, to grasp how wide and long and high and deep is the love of Christ ... that you may be filled to the measure of the fullness of God" (Ephesians 3:17–19 NIV).

Leading Friends

"Bear one another's burdens, and so fulfill the law of Christ" (Galatians 6:2). God intends for us to help one another, so this study is built for a two-person team of leading friend and learning friend. The qualities of both friends contribute to progress, so the ability to interact well is important. Consider that a good leading friend is trustworthy and will demonstrate qualities of faithfulness, knowledge of God, wisdom, kindness, gentleness, and patience. Healthy relationships with godly believers can be an essential element in the healing process (Titus 2).

From Maria's Journal: Establishing Boundaries and Expectations

In my experience (Maria), I found it very difficult to know what to expect from Sue. In my deepest points of grief, I felt like a five-year-old and wanted her to function as a caring mother. But when I was doing well, I just wanted her to be my friend. I knew that my primary expectation should be in God (Psalm 62), but when I was angry with him and struggled to believe he was good, I found my emotions and affection for my friend to be complicated and exhausting.

We will talk more in depth about navigating relationships in Parts VI and VII, but for now, remind yourself over and over again that your leading friend is a companion, not a savior. Your friend has human limits. Though she desires to help you, she may tire and be unsure of how best to help. She may disappoint you, but don't give up or push her away. She, like you, is frail and desperate for Jesus. She cannot remove your sorrow or heal your wounds, but she will share her faith with you when you have none, and she will pray! Be patient with one another and make sure to place your hope and expectation in God. This relationship can be healthy and bring healing, but only when surrendered to the hands of our great Redeemer. "My soul, wait silently for God alone, for my expectation is from Him. He *only* is my rock and my salvation" (Psalm 62:5–6).

Committing to the Journey

Treasure in the Ashes is intended to be a marvelous journey of faith. But like backpacking, it may not always feel marvelous; it may feel quite brutal. Dry and suffocating valleys, treacherous storms, and heavy bags of shame, anger, and fear can make even the bravest of souls consider retreat. But God, in all his amazing love, is faithful to walk with us one step at a time. He will never take us anywhere he isn't willing to go.

Life in a fallen world can be messy and difficult, so learning to "fail and recover" is part of the process. Facing the reality of our suffering and the sins we have committed is painful but extremely necessary.

When we allow God access to the hidden places in our hearts, he carefully redeems truth for lies, hope for despair, and faith for unbelief.

Please care for your physical and spiritual needs on this pilgrimage. As you journey home, our prayer is that you will discover Jesus to be light in your darkness, comfort in your sorrow, treasure in your loss, a friend in your loneliness, and hope in your despair. "For He Himself is our peace" (Eph. 2:14).

The LORD upholds all who fall, and raises up all who are bowed down. The eyes of all look expectantly to You [the Lord], and You give them their food in due season. You open Your hand and satisfy the desire of every living thing. The LORD is righteous in all His ways, gracious in all His works. The LORD is near to all who call upon Him, to all who call upon Him in truth. He will fulfill the desire of those who fear Him; He also will hear their cry and save them. He preserves all who love Him, but all the wicked He will destroy. My mouth shall speak the praise of the LORD, and all flesh shall bless His holy name forever and ever. —Psalm 145:14–21

But may the God of all grace, who called us to His eternal glory by Christ Jesus, after you have suffered a while, perfect [mature], establish [firmly stabilize], strengthen, and settle you. —1 Peter 5:10

Part II

WHAT'S MY STORY?

The Cracked Pot

A water bearer in India had two large pots, one hung on each end of a pole, which she carried across her neck. One of the pots had a crack in it. While the other pot was perfect, and always delivered a full portion of water at the end of the long walk from the stream to the mistress's house, the cracked pot arrived only half full.

For a full two years this went on daily, with the bearer delivering only one and a half pots full of water to her master's house. The perfect pot was proud of its accomplishments, perfect to the end for which it was made. But the poor cracked pot was ashamed of its own imperfections, and miserable that it was able to accomplish only half of what it had been made to do.

After two years of what it perceived to be a bitter failure, it spoke to the water bearer one day by the stream: "I am ashamed of myself, and I want to apologize to you." "Why?" asked the bearer. "What are you ashamed of?" "I have been able, for these past two years, to deliver only half my load because this crack in my side causes water to leak out all the way back to your mistress's house. Because of my flaws, you have to do all of this work, and you don't get full value from your efforts," the pot said.

The water bearer felt sorry for the old cracked pot, and in her compassion she said, "As we return to the mistress's house, I want you to notice the beautiful flowers along the path." Indeed, as they went up the hill, the old cracked pot took notice of the sun warming the beautiful wild flowers on the side of the path, and this cheered it some.

But at the end of the trail, it still felt bad because it had leaked out half its load, and so again it apologized to the bearer for its failure. The bearer said to the pot, "Did you notice that there were flowers only on your side of the path, but not on the other pot's side? That's because I have always known about your flaw, and I took advantage of it. I planted flower seeds on your side of the path, and every day while we walk back from the stream, you've watered them. For two years I have been able to pick these beautiful flowers to decorate my mistress's table. Without you being just the way you are, she would not have this beauty to grace her house."[4]

---

[4]Shaun Patterson, *The Little Cracked Pot* (Ontario: Big Fox Creative Technologies.com, 2013) http://amazing-womenrock.com/the-story-of-the-cracked-pot-for-anyone-whos-not-quite-perfect. .

Chapter 1

Our Journey

From Maria's Journal: **Choosing to Forget**

In high school, after being confronted by a Christian friend for being too "needy," I decided that I should just "forget those things which are behind" (Philippians 3:13). Having heard this verse used in this way, I thought forgetting my past was the spiritual thing to do.

For seventeen years, I tried to forget. And for several of the less stressful years, I did a fine job. But when life became overwhelming, forgetting became impossible.

If you looked at my life from the outside, you might have thought I had it all. God had blessed me with a cuter-than-Brad Pitt husband and four healthy baby boys. I am athletic, musical, and most people think I'm sweet. But my story (and maybe yours, too?) was hidden deep beneath the surface of my "she-has-it-all" life. Even with all my blessings, I ached with a deep longing for some kind of redemption. I wanted my life and my suffering to matter. As hard as I tried, forgetting my past never worked. I ended up feeling like everything I suffered was wasted.

After a miscarriage and a crushing physical diagnosis, I began to question God. I was angry. The pain from all my forgotten experiences overwhelmed me. Forgetting was no longer an option, but remembering seemed unbearable. I never wanted to share my story because I knew how "needy" I had become. I was afraid I'd begin to cry and never stop. I felt like a failure in the eyes of God.

But because God is kind, he began to teach me that the forgetting of Philippians 3 was not a command to forget the pain in my life. God never wanted me to forget my past. He actually wanted me to choose to remember it, so he could **redeem** it! [3] But I had to be willing to break the silence.

What Is Sexual Abuse?

Sexual abuse has been defined as *"any type of sexual behavior or contact where consent is not freely given or obtained and is accomplished though force, intimidation, violence, coercion, manipulation, threat, deception, or abuse of authority."* [4]

The spectrum of sexual abuse is broad and our responses differ widely. We may not consider our suffering to be significant. On the other hand, we might be overwhelmed by the magnitude of our experiences. Either way, this truth remains: any form of sexual contact outside of marriage—wanted or unwanted—is destructive and needs to be addressed.

Unlike physical abuse, sexual abuse may leave no visible wounds, but it can cause untold damage to the soul. Children who have been abused have no idea how to handle what has happened to them, and most cannot process the trauma until well into adulthood. Dealing with the consequences of being sexually abused is a process, even after the abuse stops.

Where to Begin?

God has been kind to give the two of us the rich experience of sharing our own journey as we have learned to walk together in friendship. We, like you, have suffered deeply because of the abuse we have experienced. You are not alone. Let's begin our journey together by finding our voices.

"Blessed be the God and Father of our Lord Jesus Christ, the Father of mercies and God of all comfort, who comforts us in all our tribulation that we may be able to comfort those who are in any trouble, with the comfort with which we ourselves are comforted by God" (2 Corinthians 1:3–4).

---

[3] See "Lord, Do I Need to Remember?" in Journal tab at www.strugglingwell2gether.weebly. com.

[4] Justin S. and Lindsey A. Holcomb, *Rid of My Disgrace* (Wheaton, Il: Crossway, 2011), 28..

Sue's Story

I was five years old when a high school boy offered to help me move a heavy bucket of sand into my sandbox. As I stood with a friend at the ledge, panting from exertion, she whispered, "My mom told me to stay away from that guy." I shrugged off her words because the pail was heavy and I wanted help. My friend ran away, and the teen easily lifted the bucket into the box. Smiling, he turned to me and suggested we walk to the garage. There he molested me. If my mother had not called me home for supper, I am certain now that he would have raped me. Then, I was clueless as to what was going on. I only knew I didn't like being touched like that.

When I went home, my mom asked what I had been doing, and I simply told her. My parents were appropriately alarmed and immediately called the police. I was asked to identify the boy from a high school yearbook, then to point him out in the hallway at school. I was not scared; it all seemed puzzling to my five-year-old mind. And then it was over. No one spoke of it again. It wasn't until many years later when I was summoned for jury duty in a rape case that I even thought of my experience in the garage.

My story is not as awful as some, so I seldom see the need to tell it. We aren't often given a window into God's reasons for what he allows. But now many years later, as a biblical counselor, I clearly see that God was preparing me to reach out with compassion to Maria and others (perhaps to you?) who suffer long in agony because of a painful past.

Maria's Story

Childhood? What childhood? I felt like someone took mine and tossed it aside. There was a lot of love in my family but also a lot of pain. Divorce, abuse, and unbelief clouded my view of Jesus. We knew about him and some of us had even been saved, but our lives seemed so different from the people at church. It was hard to bridge the gap between life and God. He didn't seem very big.

I was three or four years old the first time I began to be sexually abused. My memories are sketchy, but I do remember being held down on a blue, damp, smelly rug, and finding it very difficult to breathe.

During many of the summers of my childhood, I was abused by a much older boy in the neighborhood. He was mean and rough, and found it entertaining to see how far he could push me or how willing I was to accept his advances. At first I liked the attention he gave to me, but eventually I became very afraid of him. I was probably about seven the first time I told my parents. They called the police twice during those years; the second time he was questioned, the abuse stopped.

My response to the abuse I suffered was not good. During my elementary years, I willingly participated in sexual exploration with kids from my neighborhood. Even our fun and innocent adventures included a game of truth or dare. By the time I was eight years old, my soul was full of shame.

But the most destructive abuse occurred during the summer before sixth grade. I met a man and his daughter while playing at the beach. We had a lot of fun together that day and became fast friends. One day, while playing at their house, he said that he had a movie for us to watch. We cuddled up on the bed and started the video, which at first seemed boring and odd. Then the content turned unexpectedly sexual and was uncomfortable to watch, but shamefully, I found it physically exciting. He offered us a special drink. I asked him what it was and he said brandy. I was eleven. He undressed in front of us and told us he'd pay us each five dollars if we would pleasure him. I remember laughing and feeling scared, but I hesitantly did what he asked. He gave us the money and when my mom asked where I got it, I told her we did some chores for him.

On another occasion, while I was spending the night with his daughter, he got into bed with us. He moved close to me and began to touch me. He started to fondle me and I became very afraid. I believe God gave me the insight to know that I was in danger. This man was preparing me for intercourse and that, I knew, was wrong. I reacted with fear and disgust and told him to stop. He did.

The morning after that incident was very uncomfortable and I told him to take me home. He yelled at me and said what had happened wasn't a big deal. When we got to my house, I ran inside and told my parents. The man spent two years in jail for his crimes against his daughter and me.

Jesus saved me when I was nine and I believe he began to do his healing and sanctifying work in my heart, but I had no clue what it meant to follow him. I continued to make horrible choices. When I was fifteen, I chose to have sex with a boy from the neighborhood. Immediately afterward, I felt deep loss, and the guilt and shame overwhelmed me. My heart was broken. I fell on my knees and begged God to help me. I began to realize that I needed Jesus to save me, not only from my sin, but also from myself. I knew I would ruin everything good he had for me if I didn't submit to him.

This turning point was good in a lot of ways. I ended up immersed in Scripture and church and eventually found myself at a Bible college. I married a pastor, and we looked forward to a promising future. I turned my back on my past and figured that God had allowed it to make me more compassionate. But I had no idea how deeply my soul had been affected by the abuses I suffered.

Because God is kind, he did not allow me to continue to live in denial. He took me deep into the valley of brokenness, and I am so very glad he did. He has begun to slowly and gently heal my heart as he teaches me about the power of the Cross and the value of deep and meaningful relationships.

Throughout my journey, I have struggled to believe that God is good and even wondered if he loved me. But he knew that I would struggle, and has given me the freedom to cry and to ask my tough questions. I am learning to trust him, even when I don't get the answers I want. He is becoming my answer, and as I rest in who he is, my "whys" become less important.

This journey can be really hard. Even today, it's hard. But the gifts I have received from the hands of God have become invaluable. I am glad that you have begun the journey too. I am praying for you, that you would see that God is truly good, and that he really does love you. A clearer view of Jesus will soften the ache in your heart and the sorrow in your soul. Seeing that our stories are part of God's grand story of redemption brings purpose and meaning to everything we have suffered.

Our Journey Together

Sue

Maria got to know me very carefully. She seemed shy and uncertain of herself, but once her story came out I realized that she was uncertain of me.

At first, we weren't sure we liked each other, being from different walks of life and different generations. She was my pastor's wife, which colored the nature of our friendship somewhat. So she proceeded slowly, sharing her experiences little by little to test how I would react, to know whether she should trust me. She was also testing her own memory, which came out in little pieces along our journey together. Emotionally she was a tinder box, very tender of heart and raw.

We met sporadically at first, until Maria realized that she could share her whole story (as much as she remembered at the time). At that point our relationship deepened and more trust was established. We began to go on walks together every week and to email almost daily, trying to understand one another better and to give Maria room to heal. As memories began to surface, she often felt out of control, with days where she couldn't stop crying. But she was finding her footing. She asked lots of hard questions and searched Scripture incessantly. We talked about her uncertainties about God, herself, her family, and the nature of her abuse. Our journey together has been challenging but oh so good for us both!

In all my years of counseling, I have met few people with the courage that Maria has exercised. She has never stopped trying, even when her struggle was at its most intense. She grappled fiercely with God's goodness in the face of her dark experiences, and struggled to shake free of her demand for an explanation. Even when all she could do was cry, she didn't give up. She pursued freedom—in Christ.

And God has rewarded her. After several months, Maria turned an important corner in her faith and began to find the freedom she had sought. [5]

---

[5] To read more about Maria's journey to freedom, go to her website at www.strugglingwell-2gether.weebly.com and look at blog post "Bleeding Grace."

Our journey has been significantly impacting me as her mentor and advocate. I'm no longer just a helper; God has truly taught us to be there for each other, to point one another to Christ. Maria's insightful spirit has prompted me to question my understanding of love and how to express it as Jesus does. I have become insatiably hungry to learn how best to help her, diving into Scripture and reading book after book.

But I have found that this journey is not one-sided. When my husband had a stroke in 2013, Maria's compassionate prayers and presence threw me desperately upon God, increasing my understanding of faith, humility, and grace from her example of patient unspeakable grief. What joy to witness the unveiling of her shy intelligence, her creative musical abilities, and the beauty of her written expressions as she has found freedom from the oppressions of her past!

As our journey continues, we are meeting more men and women who have been sexually abused. Most have suffered silently, feeling misunderstood and lost, with nowhere to turn. But the God who brought us here is fully able to rescue the abused and broken soul.

Maria

I am Sue's pastor's wife. My desire, from the first time we met, was to breathe refreshment and encouragement into her life. She is a busy counselor who spends and is spent for those she counsels. I believed the best way that I could relate to her was by offering her a safe place to be herself.

God blessed us with an abundance of time to get to know each other. We grew to appreciate one another's spiritual depth and found that we shared a deep love for Jesus and each other. As time progressed, the weight of my hidden sorrow and unanswered questions began to make life painfully unmanageable. In an attempt to find help, I began to test how she would react to my doubt and questions. Time after time, she received me with grace and patience.

One night during a Bible study, with tears in her eyes, Sue asked for prayer for all women who had been sexually abused. She acknowledged the very pain that I had been denying in my own life. She actually said, "sexual abuse." She said it out loud.

Asking for help tore my heart deeply. I hated to be needy and never wanted to burden anyone. But I saw no other options. I could no longer deny reality. I was a broken mess. In answer to a desperate email, Sue agreed to walk with me one step at a time, however long that took. She even assured me that it would be an honor.

As Sue and I began to walk into the wreckage of my past, we found our journey to be messy and, at times, very difficult. But oh, how beautiful it has been to walk with her to the Healer. I have found the freedom to share my pain and to begin my own journey home. Our relationship continues to be a healing tool in our Redeemer's capable hands. She will forever be etched upon my heart. I am so grateful that Jesus prepared my friend to walk with me out of my darkness into his marvelous light.

An Invitation

Sexual abuse can leave deep and unattended wounds in our souls, leaving us feeling lost in a storm of emotion. It may seem as if no one understands the depths of your pain. Please take heart. Jesus knows, because he was wounded too, in unspeakable ways; and because he is a Man of Sorrows and acquainted with grief, Jesus invites us to tell our stories just as he has told us his. Your story matters. In God's plan of redemption, nothing is wasted.

Fear of vulnerability, exposure, and shame can keep us locked away for years. But making the choice to remember our story can free us to begin our journey from darkness into the healing light of Jesus Christ (1 Peter 2:9).

"Bring my soul out of prison, that I may praise Your name" (Psalm 142:7).

Talking Points: Begin with prayer and then discuss the following questions with your leading friend.

   1. In what ways have you tried to forget your story?

2. What kind of redemption do you want to see in your life?

3. What would make your suffering meaningful?

4. What are some reasons you don't want to share your story?

5. What reasons do you have for wanting to share your story?

Treasure: My story matters. In God's plan of redemption, nothing is wasted.

He [Jesus] is despised and rejected by men, a Man of sorrows and acquainted with grief. And we hid, as it were, our faces from Him; He was despised, and we did not esteem Him. Surely He has borne our griefs and carried our sorrows; yet we esteemed Him stricken, smitten by God, and afflicted. But He was wounded for our transgressions, He was bruised for our iniquities; the chastisement for our peace was upon Him, and by His stripes we are healed. —Isaiah 53:3–5

He [God] has sent Me [Jesus] to heal the brokenhearted, to proclaim liberty to the captives, and the opening of the prison to those who are bound…to comfort all who mourn … to give them beauty for ashes, the oil of joy for mourning, the garment of praise for the spirit of heaviness, that they may be called trees of righteousness, the planting of the LORD, that He may be glorified. —Isaiah 61:1–3

Chapter 2

Surveying the Damage

"We do not wrestle against flesh and blood, but against principalities, against powers, against the rulers of the darkness of the age, against spiritual hosts of wickedness." —Ephesians 6:12

We live in a culture that devalues sex and treats it as casually as going out for ice cream. Even so, nearly everyone agrees that sexual abuse causes unspeakable harm. In order to understand God's good and loving heart toward us as victims, we will carefully define what sin is and why the sexual abuse we have endured is a serious crime.

Defining Sin

Scripture gives us two basic categories of sin:

1. *Transgression*—to go beyond God's boundaries (Genesis 1:26–27; 2:18-24; Psalm 51; Hebrews 13:4; Romans 3:9–20).

2. *Miss the mark*—to fall short of God's glory/standards (Rom 3:23).

Why Is This Important?

God designed sex to be experienced exclusively within a loving marriage. Sexual abuse is destructive because it transgresses, confuses, and distorts God's design for sex. Rather than being a beautiful expression of unity between a man and woman, sex becomes repulsive, transgressing God's design and missing the mark of his flawless character—falling very short of his glory. Your abuser is to blame for sexually using you. The abuse isn't your fault!

"Why do the wicked renounce God? He has said in his heart,
'[God] will not require an account.' But You [God] have seen, for
You observe trouble and grief, to repay it by Your hand. The helpless

commits himself to You; You are the helper of the fatherless" (Psalm 10:13-14).

Sinful Responses

Our culture treats sex casually, as though it has no impact on our souls. But when dealing with sexual abuse most people offer silence, denial, accusations, confusion, avoidance, anger, ignorance, repulsion, and injustice. The sinful responses of those around us can compound and intensify the already tragic consequences of being sexually abused. Recognizing and rejecting these lies with the truths of God will be the help and healing we desperately need.

Our Abuser's Response

Abusers often accuse, intimidate, and blame their victims. But the sexual abuse you endured is not your fault. Another typical response of an abuser is to ignore and belittle their offenses. When I (Maria) told my abuser that I wanted to go home, he told me that I was over-reacting to what happened. He minimized the reality of what he had done to me and expected me to believe that it was no big deal. To this day, I still tend to question and minimize my own thoughts, feelings, and perceptions, but with God's help, I am learning to recognize the power in that lie.

Think through your story. How did or does your abuser respond to you? Is their response helpful and good? Why or why not?

"But my eyes are upon You, O God the Lord; in You I take refuge; do not leave my soul destitute. Keep me from the snares they have laid for me, and from the traps of the workers of iniquity. Let the wicked fall into their own nets, while I escape safely" (Psalm 141:8–10).

Our Family's Response

Imagine a little girl (Rayna) finds the courage to tell her mom that daddy has been coming into her bedroom at night. She tells Mommy that he touches her and she feels scared when he does it. Mommy responds by telling her that she misunderstood Daddy's love and that she doesn't need to worry about it. The next time Rayna tells her mom about the abuse, and her mom gets angry and tells her to stop lying, Rayna runs to her room in tears. While she lies on her bed, she wonders what she did wrong. After several more months of abuse, she once again finds the courage to tell her mom. This time Mom walks away with a look of disgust. Rayna is left reeling in pain and confusion.

Rayna's mom has contributed to her pain by not believing her, dismissing her, and accusing her of lying. This type of tragic response is comparable to the abuse itself. If Rayna doesn't get the help she needs, she will believe her mother and begin to identify herself as a neglected, incompetent liar.

Think through your story. How has your family responded to you? Is their response helpful and good? Why or why not?

> Do not hide Your face from me; do not turn Your servant away in anger; You have been my help; do not leave me nor forsake me, O God of my salvation. When my father and my mother forsake me, then the LORD will take care of me.... I would have lost heart, unless I had believed that I would see the goodness of the LORD in the land of the living. Wait on the LORD; be of good courage, and He shall strengthen your heart; wait, I say, on the LORD! —Psalm 27:9–10, 13–14

The Christian Community's Response

Many churches are unprepared to address sexual abuse, and so they continue in ignorance or turn away like Rayna's mom did. Sadly, in some cases abuse happens within the church itself, even from church leaders. This leads to unspeakable hurt and confusion. Because church leaders are supposed to represent God, victims may think that God is like their abuser. But nothing could be further from the truth! It grieves God's heart and angers him when he sees the injustice of such cruel responses.

If your church has been blind to your pain, it may be helpful to remember that the church is a group of messy and sinful people seeking God together. Everybody has a story. Sometimes in our pain we lose sight of that. We are praying that the leaders of your church will be moved by God's concern for you as a survivor of sexual abuse, and that they will come alongside you. If you do not find this to be the case, please don't give up. Hold on to hope in God and do not let the failures of human beings keep you away from him. We are sorry that you have suffered. Your story is real and it needs to be told.

Think through your story. How has your church community responded to you? Is their response helpful and good? Why or why not?

> For I am poor and needy, and my heart is wounded within me.
> I am gone like a shadow when it lengthens; I am shaken off
> like a locust. My knees are weak from fasting, and my flesh is
> feeble from lack of fatness. I also have become a reproach to
> them; when they look at me, they shake their heads. Help me,
> O LORD my God! Oh, save me according to Your mercy, that
> they may know that this is Your hand—That You, LORD, have
> done it! —Psalm 109:22–27

God's Response

God knows your story and has seen your suffering. It breaks his heart and fills him with wrath (Psalm 10; Isaiah 53; Romans 1:18). You matter to him! Because he is holy and just, he will not allow your abuse to go unnoticed or unpunished.

"But You have seen, for You observe trouble and grief, to repay it by Your hand. The helpless commits himself to You; You are the helper of the fatherless" (Psalm 10:14).

According to this verse …

God has seen our trouble and grief and will _____
it by His hand.

God is "the _____of the fatherless."

"LORD, You have heard the desire of the humble; You will prepare their heart; You will cause Your ear to hear, to do justice to the fatherless and the oppressed, that the man of the earth may oppress no more" (Psalm 10:17–18).

According to this verse ...

What has God done for the humble, the fatherless, and the oppressed?

Will he do that for us?

The pangs of death surrounded me, and the floods of ungodliness made me afraid. The sorrows of Sheol surrounded me; the snare of death confronted me. In my distress I called upon the LORD, and cried out to my God; He heard my voice from His temple, and my cry came before Him, even to His ears.... He sent from above, He took me; He drew me out of many waters, He delivered me from my strong enemy, from those who hated me, for they were too strong for me. —Psalm 18:4–6, 16–17

Considering My Own Responses

"God, grant me the serenity to accept the things I cannot change; the courage to change the things I can; and the wisdom to know the difference." —Reinhold Niebuhr [6]

A great preacher once said, "Life is 10 percent what happens to you and 90 percent how you react to it." [7] Our response matters. Sexual abuse is horrible, but responding to it in an unhealthy way can complicate an already difficult story. The chart below briefly illustrates some of the responses we may have, and suggests the reasons or motives that may be behind those responses. We will talk more in depth about our motivations later. For now, we will discuss several common responses to being sexually abused.

---

[6] http://www.beliefnet.com/prayers/protestant/addiction/serenity-prayer.aspx Accessed 7-1-2018
[7] Charles R. Swindoll. https://www.brainyquote.com/quotes/quotes/c/charlesrs388332.html. Accessed 5-17-2017

Response to being abused	Motivated by ...
Hiding, denying, and minimizing	Fear/helplessness/pride
Accepting and overcoming challenges	Faith or ambition
Railing and rebelling	Anger
Perpetual victim and/or using people	Sympathy/self-pity/ attention-seeking
Perfectionism/ self-sufficiency	Desire to control/anger

Victim Mentality

As a little girl, I (Maria) developed a strong attachment to the attention I received as a victim of sexual abuse. It felt good to be cared for and validated and I began to find my identity in the attention (good or bad). But the problem with finding our identity in this kind of attention is that we have to remain a victim in order to continue to get the attention we crave. This mentality cripples us and can cause us to reject any true and lasting help, leaving us in a cycle of self-pity and validation.

Living for the attention of others will always leave us empty and wanting more. Eventually, after being confronted by my friend for being too needy, I withdrew and began to hide. I discovered that God was the only One who would ever satisfy. I truly did have a great need. But no one in this world would ever be able to meet it. Accepting this truth was difficult; I had to stop needing the attention of others and let God begin to help me in his way and his timing. Craving attention as well as safety creates a tug of war inside us.

Hiding and Denial

Because of the shame associated with sexual abuse (or a strong determination to "get over it"), many of us hide our stories deep within our hearts, hoping never ever to reveal the truth. We may think that hiding will protect us, but, in fact, it only isolates us.

When I (Maria) learned that God had a good purpose for my story and that he wanted to bring light into the dark places in my heart, I began to find my voice. I knew it was time to stop hiding. God had prepared my heart and provided a friend I could trust. I had longed for redemption far too long to pass up the opportunity to tell my story.

Talking Point: Pray and discuss the following questions with your leading friend.

1. How have you responded to the abuse you have suffered?

   * *In your body: (example: overeating, cutting, over-exercising)*

   * *In your mind: (example: dwelling on the pain, bitterness, hatred)*

   * *In your spirit: (example: unbelief, depression, oversleeping)*

   * *In your relationships: (example: dishonesty, isolation, bitterness, distrust)*

2. Look at the previous chart. What may be motivating your responses?

3. Have your responses been helpful or hurtful?

We will talk more specifically about how to navigate the responses of others in chapters 21–23, but for now consider how your own responses might be contributing to the pain and heartache in your life.

Treasure: Being sexually abused was not my fault. But my response to it matters.

Chapter 3

Sharing My Story

Treasure in the Ashes has been written as a guide. We cannot know exactly how your story should be told, but we can give you some guidance. The following section includes some foundational truths to think through as you consider telling your story.

Why Talk About It?

The pain of sexual abuse defies description; even a distant memory can evoke an emotional surge. Why would we want to talk about that?

In the darkness of our experiences, it can be difficult to see God as he really is; in fact, sometimes it's hard to see him at all. But as we tell our stories, we begin to discover and discard the fear, lies, and false beliefs that distort a true and healthy view of God.

Telling our stories:

- Reveals the true condition of our relationship with God;

- Helps us to recognize that we are never alone;

- Helps us to process our experiences, thoughts, and emotions well;

- Builds genuine and enduring relationships;

- Encourages others to recognize and attend to the tragic effects of sexual abuse.

With a redeeming God, even the most painful journey can become a beautiful message of hope to others who are going through similar experiences.

Blessed be the God and Father of our Lord Jesus Christ, the Father of mercies and God of all comfort, who comforts us in all our tribulation, that we may be able to comfort those who are in any trouble, with the comfort with which we ourselves are comforted by God. —2 Corinthians 1:3–4

For you were once darkness, but now you are light in the Lord. Walk as children of light … finding out what is acceptable to the Lord. And have no fellowship with the unfruitful works of darkness, but rather expose them. —Ephesians 5:8–11

Whom Should I Tell?

- **God**

  Talk to God by expressing your sorrow and pain (a lament) as the psalmists did. "Trust in Him at all times, you people; pour out your heart before Him; God is a refuge for us" (Psalm 62:8). "O Lord my God, I cried out to You, and You healed me"(Psalm 30:2).

- **Leading friend, spouse, and trusted friends and family**

  Think carefully and pray about who you will tell. Look for those in your life who are trustworthy, wise, and kind. Wait on the Lord to guide you to one or two safe listeners. "Bear one another's burdens, and so fulfill the law of Christ" (Galatians 6:2). "Confess your trespasses to one another, and pray for one another, that you may be healed" (James 5:16).

How Should I Tell?

- **Tell the truth.**

  Think through your story and tell what you remember, even if the memory is incomplete. Be careful not to misapply "forgetting those things which are behind" (Philippians 3:13). We don't have to forget. God wants to redeem our stories and help us to grow (2 Corinthians 1:3–4).

- **With faith and hope.**

  God wants you to tell your story. Your shame was removed at the cross. [8] Believe that God will protect and guide you as you remember and journey back into your past.

How Much Should I Tell?

Every part of your story matters to God. When you speak with God, there is no need to withhold anything from him. He already knows you completely. But when you begin to consider who you will tell and how much, consider the testimony of Nicole Braddock Bromley. She writes about a teacher who helped her to talk about her experience of sexual abuse.

> Mrs. Bell told me that it would help me to really say it, to say everything, to tell the worst parts, and to use the right words for them. I hated that. I didn't want to say any "dirty" words; I just wanted to get each story out as fast as I could. But as we continued to meet and as my trust in her grew, I saw that doing what she suggested was helping, for my burden was being lifted.
>
> While I was telling her what I remembered, it felt as if I had a really heavy blanket on my head and shoulders; but afterward, the blanket didn't seem as heavy as before. As we continued to talk after school, every time I shared more details, I felt the blanket on me getting lighter. My burden was being lifted bit by bit, story by story. Once I told a memory, it was as if I didn't own it anymore. [9]

Holding back some information can be a good thing. But keeping the secret of sexual abuse only locks us away. Finding the courage to appropriately share the details of your story will free you from bearing those memories alone. Relief will come as you release your grip and carefully tell your story to those who are wise and trustworthy.

---

[8]Read about shame in Sue Nicewander, *Help! I Feel Ashamed* (Shepherd Press, 2016).
[9]Nicole Braddock Bromley, *Hush* (Chicago: Moody Publishers, 2007), 46.

- *Details are reserved.*

  You may find that some people want to help, but many are unprepared and will not handle your details respectfully. They may not know how to respond and will find it hard to relate to you. Don't put yourself in this position. Your details are reserved for your leading friend and (non-abusive) spouse.

- *Speak in general to other trusted friends and family.*

  People (church friends, family, children, strangers, etc.) do not need to know specific details to help you. You may say something like: "God is taking me on a difficult journey; I am dealing with some painful things from my childhood." If you are comfortable sharing that you were sexually abused, you may choose to do so. It may open opportunities for you to hear from others who have been abused. Seek God for wisdom as you share.

- *Tell only what you remember when you remember it.*

  God knows your frame. He will only allow you to remember what is necessary and helpful for your healing. Trust him to guide your memory. Don't rush the process. Use proper terms to describe what happened so that you will think honestly about the reality of what you have experienced.

- *Take care not to unload emotionally on the people around you.*

  When you tell your story you may feel vulnerable and become overwhelmed by emotion. Sharing your story is difficult for everyone, and it is important not to wound others in the process. If you are angry, know that God is furious about the abuse you have suffered, so furious that he poured out his wrath on Jesus as though he were your abuser. Go to God first with any overwhelming emotion that you feel.

What If It's Too Difficult?

Telling your story may awaken a storm of emotion, such as sadness, anger, fear, anxiety, shame, guilt, loneliness, bitterness, hate, and a strong desire to be understood and validated. Oftentimes, we are told to "just get over it and move on," but that is heartless advice. Instead of denying or indulging these intense emotions, we can learn to express and manage them well.

Expressions of Grief: Lamenting

The dictionary defines the word lament: *"To express sorrow about something … a song or poem that expresses sorrow."* [10] Laments are found throughout Scripture, but especially in the Psalms. Through the writers' prayers and laments, we can learn to express the intensity of our struggle with hope and faith.

> But You, O GOD the Lord, deal with me for Your name's sake; because Your mercy is good, deliver me. For I am poor and needy, and my heart is wounded within me, I am gone like a shadow when it lengthens; I am shaken off like a locust. My knees are weak through fasting, and my flesh is feeble from lack of fatness. I also have become a reproach to them; when they look at me, they shake their heads. Help me, O LORD my God! Oh, save me according to Your mercy, that they may know that this is Your hand—that You, O LORD, have done it!... For He shall stand at the right hand of the poor, to save him from those who condemn him. — Psalm 109:21–27, 31

> For we do not have a High Priest who cannot sympathize with our weaknesses, but was in all points tempted as we are, yet without sin. Let us, therefore, come boldly to the throne of grace, that we may obtain mercy and find grace to help in time of need. —Hebrews 4:15–16

---

[10]Merriam-Webster *Learner's Dictionary: English*, http://www.learnersdictionary.com/definition/lament. Accessed 9/30/2013 and 5/18/2017.

For He Himself has said, "I will never leave you nor forsake you."
So we may boldly say, "The LORD is my helper; I will not fear.
What can man do to me?" —Hebrews 13:5-6

According to these verses …

Does Jesus sympathize with our suffering?

What can we do when we need help?

What will we receive there?

Being honest with God will open our minds and hearts to receive the truth we so desperately need. As we journey through this life, we can acknowledge our thoughts and feelings, recognizing that Jesus understands completely and gives us not only a place to cry, but a safe and steady place to put our hope.

Talking Points: Pray and discuss these questions with your leading friend.

1. Are you aware of the spiritual (and emotional) battle in your life? If so, describe it.

2. Do you believe God loves you and wants you to draw near to him? (1 Peter 5:7; Hebrews 4:16)

3. Are you ready to pour out your heart to God (Psalm 62:8; Psalm 116:1–2)? Why or why not?

4. If so, find a Psalm that speaks closely to your struggle, such as Psalm 109, 9–10, 25, 37, 55, or 73.

From those examples and the list below, begin to write your own lament. It doesn't have to be perfect, just honest and respectful.

- Describe the struggle honestly to God (Psalm 10). Pour out your heart to him (Psalm 62:8).

- Look to Scripture for truth about God (Psalm 119:76–77).

- Write what you learn (Psalm 119:49–50).

- Praise God with thanksgiving based on what you learn (Psalm 30:4–5).

Treasure: God wants me to draw near. He knows the intensity of the battle and has invited me to cry out to him.

How long, oh Lord, will it be until my eyes open to see how much you really love me? I hurt and ache and cry inside; I drown in a sea of despair. Many have been the days of my life where all I have known is a hand of wrath. This, my Jesus, can it be? I know you cannot be God and one dimensional ... or even two. A God of love and wrath some say ... I know deep inside ... you are so much more. You are a multi-faceted jewel with prisms of wonder. I want to see you Lord. I want to see your many beautiful facets. Show me by your grace. Lord, release me from the lies and the anger; the mire and the pit. How long until I know I am free? How long until my eyes see the God I have longed for you to be? Even in the mist and the shadow and the pain, your love, O Lord, remains the same. You provide for me and hold me; You comfort me and clothe me. Ever will I sing and ever will I trust the One to whom the mountains bow and rocks cry out and all of heaven shouts. Great are you O LORD, my God, and most worthy of praise! —Anonymous

When Should I Tell?

If you are ready now to share your story in more detail, ask your leading friend if she is ready to hear your story. Give her time to pray and prepare for your talk. Discuss when and where this will take place and look for a quiet confidential place and some uninterrupted time. Be sure to pray together before and after you share.

Sometimes our stories come out in bits and pieces as the memories surface. This can make telling your story a bit challenging, but there is no need to rush this process. Take your time. However, if you are being abused now, please tell the proper authorities immediately.

Sharing My Story: Am I Ready?

The following questions will prepare and allow you to share your story very generally. Use a journal if you are uncomfortable writing here.

1. Who abused you? (If more than one person, feel free to write those details separately.)

2. How old were you when the abuse occurred?

3. How often did it occur?

4. Did you tell anyone? Who did you tell?

5. Did that person believe you?

6. How did that person respond? How did you respond?

7. In what ways has your story impacted you?

8. What people have been helpful to you, and how?

9. When have you seen God at work in your story?

10. How has your faith been challenged? How has your faith grown?

Chapter 4

After My Story's Been Told

Fear and Faith

In Matthew 14:25–33 we read that Peter and the other disciples were in the middle of a terrible wind storm on the Sea of Galilee. Jesus saw their need and ...

> ... went to them, walking on the sea. And when the disciples saw Him walking on the sea, they were troubled, saying, "It is a ghost!" And they cried out for fear. But immediately Jesus spoke to them, saying, "Be of good cheer! It is I; do not be afraid." And Peter answered Him and said, "Lord if it is You, command me to come to You on the water." So He said, "Come." And when Peter had come down out of the boat, he walked on the water to go to Jesus. But when he saw that the wind was boisterous, he was afraid; and beginning to sink he cried out, saying, "Lord, save me!" And immediately Jesus stretched out His hand and caught him, and said to him, "O you of little faith, why did you doubt?" And when they got into the boat, the wind ceased. Then those who were in the boat came and worshiped Him, saying, "Truly You are the Son of God."

Telling our stories is a huge step of faith. It can bring great relief but can also leave us feeling extremely vulnerable. If you find yourself feeling emotionally raw, sinking in a sea of pain and fear, please look up. Jesus is right there. Just as Peter put his faith in Jesus, you too have taken a great step of faith. You have left the unstable and unreliable "safety" of your boat and stepped out toward the only One who can truly save you. The overwhelming waves of this storm will not drown you. Because God is good, he will use the raging storm of your past to purify and heal you and redeem your suffering. Reach for him. He is there.

Painful Memories

After your story has been told it is common to face a series of painful memories. Certain smells, sights, sensations, sounds, and even tastes can trigger flashbacks and emotional upset. It is normal to feel overwhelmed and wonder if this burden is more than you can bear, but "God is faithful, who will not allow you to be tempted beyond what you are able, but with the temptation will also make the way of escape, that you may be able to bear it" (1 Corinthians 10:13).

From Maria's Journal: This Valley

> This valley; the one with so much confusion and the gut-wrenching pain is the kind that leaves me breathless. The memories overwhelm me. But this time I am breathing. I am walking. I am alive. This valley isn't like the others. In this valley there is lots of Light. The Light loves me. The Light has seen the darkness. The Light is my life and hope. There are beautiful pools here; pools with refreshing water. Sometimes, I am refreshed by simple pleasures. When the tears fall, I am grateful for healthy eyes. When my heart feels numb, I remember I don't have to feel. It's okay. Life—its valleys, mountains, and plateaus—takes everything out of me. Looking up from a tear-stained pillow into the night sky brings me Home. There is meaning to all of the pain. Accepting good and bad from the Sovereign One gives me some solid ground. It is safe to cry here. There is hope in Someone sure and stable. The words he speaks and his faithful love speak deeply to my broken soul. In some ways, I hope to stay broken. May pride and self-assurance stay far away. If valleys like this will keep my pillow tear-stained and my eyes fixed on Jesus, then I accept. "Where does my help come from?"... "The Maker of heaven and earth" (Psalm 121:1-2 NIV).

"When my heart is overwhelmed, lead me to the rock that is higher than I" (Psalm 61:2).

When Jesus suffered and died on the cross, you were on his mind (Psalm 139:1–3, 17–18). He knows your pain because he suffered in your place; for your sin and your sorrow (Isaiah 53:3–5). Your valley, with all its painful memories, is an invitation into the healing arms of our Savior. As you turn to him in faith, Jesus will tend to those dark and lonely places in your heart, and will lovingly bind up your wounds.

Talking Points: Pray and discuss these questions with your leading friend.

1. Have you told your story and, if so, to whom?

2. Describe how you are processing or handling your memories.

3. Do you believe that Jesus actually feels your pain? Why or why not?

4. Do you believe God wants you to be close to him? Do you trust him? Why or why not?

Treasure: Jesus bore my pain, my sin, and my sorrow. I can seek refuge in him. He is my Savior.

He has borne our griefs and carried our sorrows … [He was oppressed and afflicted] … the chastisement for our peace was upon Him, and by His stripes we are healed. —Isaiah 53:4–7.

He heals the brokenhearted and binds up their wounds.
—Psalm 147:3

Let us therefore come boldly to the throne of grace, that we may obtain mercy and find grace to help in time of need.
—Hebrews 4:16

Are We Making Too Much Of All This?

Sexual abuse is a sin against God, against our soul, spirit, and body, and against our relationships with other people. [11] In Mark 9:42–43, Jesus says that "it would be better for [the offender] if a millstone were hung around his neck, and he were thrown into the sea." Jesus takes our suffering very seriously. He had to die because of the sin that was committed against us. It really was that bad.

For some of us, the abuse we endured seems unspeakable and so repulsive that we find it nearly impossible to believe that God is loving or good. We may ask: Where was he? What was he doing when I was being abused? Why would I ever consider telling anyone my story? If God turned his back on me, how can I trust anyone?

These are important questions. As we find courage to say them out loud, God is faithful to listen with grace, and to answer truthfully (Psalm 61:1–4; 119:107). Asking hard questions like these is a vital part of the journey, but we must take care not to demand explanations. Regardless of how we feel or what we think in our anger and confusion, Christ alone is the answer we seek.

Perhaps that is hard to believe. But let's not lose hope. We will search Scripture in the coming chapters to see what God thinks about sexual abuse, and we will look at his nature and how he relates to us and to our abusers. We may be surprised at the extent of his presence and involvement in our lives, and the hope he can bring.

Treasure: God takes my suffering very seriously. He will not allow it to go unpunished.

---

[11] See Justin Holcomb's article "What does the Bible Say About Sexual Assault?" At http://biblicalcounselingcoalition.org/blogs/2013/08/28/what-does-the-bible-say-about-sex. Accessed 5/18/2017.

Part III

TO TRUST OR NOT TO TRUST

Chapter 5

Why Trust?

At the core of our nature is a desire to feel safe. A child runs to someone he trusts when he is afraid; even animals dash for cover when threatened. When someone is deceived and abused, finding the courage to trust anyone can be terribly difficult. Fear, anger, and sorrow can paralyze our willingness to be vulnerable. So why not just withdraw into safety, or fight back? What's so important about trust?

Rayna is the "perfect" wife and mom and an avid churchgoer. Although she leads an active life and appears to be fine, she is not. Years of unexpressed grief have begun to suffocate her. As a child, Rayna was repeatedly molested by her father and rejected by her mother. The weight of this tragic reality is crushing her. Rayna doubts God's sovereignty, thinking that if he is in control, he isn't very good at it. In fact, she doesn't believe God is good at all. Constant fear of rejection and abandonment make trusting anyone seem dangerous. To protect herself, she stays busy, overcommitted, and controlling. Her expectations of herself and everyone around her are high—too high! She seeks to control her world as perfectly as possible. She believes that she is her only hope.

Shanae, a victim of a neighborhood pedophile, is a reckless, risk-taking rebel who struggles to function on any level. She cuts herself out of anger and guilt, believing that she is irredeemable and damaged beyond repair. Because of the evil things she has suffered, Shanae has concluded that God is weak, cruel, and careless. She believes that he is mad at her, that he certainly doesn't love her, and neither does anyone else. As a result, she is manipulative and extremely defensive.

Shanae desperately longs for help but doesn't believe anyone is worth trusting. She is losing hope.

Emotions and Conclusions

When we suffer, it is only natural to draw some conclusions. Rayna feels abandoned, so she concludes that God is absent. Shanae feels damaged, so she assumes that God doesn't want her. Both women have formed beliefs about their experiences. Their conclusions reflect how their thoughts have flowed, and that leads to powerful emotions. Our feelings need to be informed and controlled by truth or we will be very unstable. No matter how nice Hollywood tries to make it sound, following our hearts usually leaves us exhausted, confused, and driven to live in unhealthy and destructive ways. Consider how beliefs have led to strong emotions in the following examples:

- Rayna believes that she is to blame for her abuse because she didn't take control. She hates men and is angry with God for failing to rescue her.

- Shanae feels damaged and believes she will never be more than a victim.

- Dylan's grandfather's longtime abuses left him with a deep sense of shame. When Dylan's grandpa fondled him, he had some physical pleasure; now he thinks he is disgusting to God. (We will hear more of Dylan's story later.)

Talking Points: Pray and discuss the following with your leading friend.

1. What are some of your strongest emotions?

2. In what situations do you find it hard to trust?

3. In light of your suffering and your responses to suffering; what conclusions have you drawn about God, yourself, and others?

It may be helpful to fill in the following blanks.

" I feel _____ about myself because _____."

"I believe _____ about God because _____."

"I think _____ about my abuser because _____."

The Need for Objective Guidance

As humans, it's impossible to have complete and accurate knowledge of everything. If we try to make sense of our experiences apart from a reliable source of truth, we have no way of knowing if our conclusions are correct. We may end up blindly believing something that is not true. Faulty conclusions based on lies and false beliefs will tragically color the rest of our lives, causing ongoing distress and a downward spiral of harmful choices.

Look at the picture below. Are the horizontal lines parallel or do they slope?

This is a simple optical illusion that uses black and white effectively to confuse our perceptions of what we are seeing. Because we are trying to rationalize either the black vertical lines or white vertical lines, we cannot make sense of the untidiness of the columns and, to our eyes, the horizontal lines are sloping downwards. Our eyes naturally follow the powerful vertical lines. In fact, the horizontal lines themselves are perfectly straight and measuring them would prove that they do not slope down at all. [12]

Were you fooled? The context made the lines look curved. Set a straight edge on the horizontal lines. You will see the truth that your eyes could not correctly conclude alone: the lines are straight. We all need help to see the truth. We can't discern it on our own.

Spiritually, we need help too. We can be easily deceived into believing lies because "the heart is deceitful above all things, and desperately wicked; who can know it?" (Jeremiah 17:9).

Consider three other factors that can deceive us:

1. **Our own thinking** is tainted and incomplete; we must not trust ourselves.

2. **Other people** can lead us astray; we must be careful whose voices we believe.

3. **Our experiences** in this fallen world can confuse us; we can't trust our conclusions.

What *can* we trust, then?

Trusting Scripture: Our Standard

We need a reliable source for truth. Using a straight edge helps us to see that the lines in the illusion above are actually straight, not curved. Scripture is our only trustworthy source of truth. The very words of God are the standard by which we discern truth from error and the basis on which we make our conclusions and form our beliefs.

"Great is our LORD, and mighty in power; His understanding is infinite" (Psalm 147:5).

---

[12]http://www.optics4kids.org/home/content/illusions/horizontal-lines/. Accessed 5/1/2017.

"Through your [Word] I get understanding ..." (Psalm 119:104).

"The entrance of Your Words gives light; it gives understanding to the simple" (Psalm 119:130).

> **From these passages ...**
>
> Where do we get our understanding?

Scripture: Our Map

We find truth and wisdom in Scripture when we allow the Holy Spirit to:

- **Teach us about the character of God** (Psalm 19:7–11)

  "The judgments of the LORD are true and righteous altogether" (Psalm 19:9).

- **Test our own thoughts, motives, and actions** (Proverbs 3:5-7)

  "For the word of God is living and powerful, and sharper than any two-edged sword, piercing even to the division of soul and spirit, and of the joints and marrow, and is a discerner of the thoughts and intent of the heart" (Hebrews 4:12).

- **Discern whether to believe other people** (Psalm 119:97–100; 146:3)

  "Beware lest anyone cheat you through philosophy and empty deceit, according to the tradition of men, according to the basic principles of the world, and not according to Christ" (Colossians 2:8).

- **Evaluate our experiences** (Psalm 143:8)

  "But as for you, you meant evil against me; but God meant it for good, in order to bring it about as it is this day, to save many people alive" (Genesis 50:20).

Scripture: Our Choice

Suffering cruelty and injustice can make trusting Scripture very difficult. Our emotions may insist that God is cruel while Scripture declares and defends his goodness. And this is war: a battle to believe what is true. Our ever-changing emotions are reactive. They are meant to drive us to seek truth, but we usually misunderstand their purpose. When our feelings say one thing and Scripture says another, we must make a choice: what will we believe?

From Maria's Journal

Facing the pain in my heart and my lack of faith in the goodness of God propelled me into the greatest fight of my life. Struggling in a raging fire of emotion, I found myself more out of control than I would ever want to admit. I wanted life to be easy. I was tired of Christianity. I wanted to chuck it all.

My suffering led me to believe that God was absent and mean. I started to question the trustworthiness of the Bible and even considered walking away from the church. But deep down I knew I was wrong. I just didn't know what to do. I knew that God couldn't possibly be that way. I had become desperate. It was time to make a decision. Would I continue to allow my emotions to rule me, or would I submit to God?

I began to search Scripture as though my life depended on it. I begged God to teach me and to show me his ways. The battle was intense, but I knew I couldn't quit. In time, I began to recognize and reject the lies I believed, and God gently taught me to replace those lies with truth.

Knowing God has become my treasure and his word is my treasure map (Psalm 119:162). I'm still searching. Finding truth and rejecting lies is a lifelong process that requires a great deal of hard work. But I am committed to the fight because the rewards far outweigh the sweat.

"If you abide in My word, you are My disciples indeed. And you shall know the truth, and the truth shall make you free." —John 8:31–32

Trusting People

We all live by faith. Without thought, we trust that the stoplights are working correctly, that the manufacturer didn't poison our food, and that our chairs will hold us up. But when considering who to trust, we need to be more intentional in discerning whether a person is reliable and trustworthy. Not everyone is safe. The following paragraphs will help us to trust wisely as we move forward in our relationships.

Who Should I Trust?

Because people can be evil and deceitful, we must be careful who we trust. We will talk about human relationships more fully in chapter 6, but for now the following list will be helpful to consider. While no one is perfect, a trustworthy person will consistently seek to develop and demonstrate these characteristics:

- **Honesty**: They tell the truth consistently and kindly, even when it's hard. They are wise and clear-minded, with pure motives.

- **Consideration**: They demonstrate concern for your well-being. They care about the things that matter to you. Before they act, they think about how their actions will affect you. They want to know what you think and what you have experienced, because they want what is best for you.

- **Dependability**: They do what they say they will do, without deception or self-centeredness, in a spirit of love. They act on your behalf and for your well-being, even if you don't respond very well to them.

- **Moral Character:** They consistently pursue what God says is right, good, noble, wise, pure, and beautiful, even if they are ridiculed or misunderstood. They stand up for justice and mercy, even if they have to stand alone. They are gentle and kind, but are also firmly rooted in biblical principles and reflect moral character described in Scripture.

Talking Points: Pray and discuss the following with your leading friend.

1. Name some trustworthy people that you know. Describe the qualities that make these people trustworthy.

2. How might it be helpful to trust one of these trustworthy people more fully? What might this kind of trust be like?

Who Shouldn't I Trust?

We already know that evil people can do a lot of damage, especially if they don't care about the harm they've caused. We can't trust them, and we shouldn't. They are not trustworthy. Even well-intentioned people are flawed and insufficient, but there is a difference between imperfection and wickedness.

- *Wickedness* is a willful embrace of things that are morally wrong and harmful to others.

- *Imperfection* is the frailty of being human, even those who sincerely seek to be good: "The spirit is willing, but the flesh is weak" (Matthew 26:41 NIV). Everyone is imperfect.

In the examples below, mark *imperfections* with an "**I**" and *wickedness* with a "**W**."

_____ You tell your friend your story, but she doesn't know what to say.

_____ You tell your friend your story in confidence and she tells your secrets to other people.

_____ Your friend is late because she got stuck at a railroad crossing.

_____ A woman steals something from your handbag.

_____ A woman bumps your handbag, spilling its contents on the floor.

_____ A man at work smiles and greets you with a handshake, then forgets your name.

_____ A man at work tells a dirty joke.

_____ Your friend doesn't sit with you in church.

_____ Your husband calls you names and hits you.

_____ A woman lies to you.

_____ Your friend is pleasant, but she doesn't make your emotional pain go away.

_____ A neighbor makes sexual advances toward you.

_____ Your husband wants to have sex with you, and he asks in a way you don't like.

_____ A coworker is clumsy and not very good at her job, even though she tries.

_____ Someone at church seems too busy to notice you.

_____ A friend tells you something she thinks is true, but she is wrong.

Understanding the difference between outright wickedness and imperfection will help us to discern whether someone is trustworthy. We all need grace when we mess up. But when someone sins against us intentionally, it is wise not to trust them until they demonstrate a consistent and genuine change of heart.

Talking Points: Pray and discuss the following with your leading friend.

1. Name some untrustworthy people that you have trusted in the past. What qualities made them untrustworthy?

2. How might it be helpful to stop trusting them? What might this look like? (We will talk more about this in Part VI: Who Are You?)

Can I Trust the Church?

The local Church can be one of the most awkward and hurtful places to be for a survivor of sexual abuse, especially if the environment is stuffy and unwelcoming. But this isn't always the case. There are genuine believers who want to help; we just need wisdom to know who they are and how to find them. While looking for trustworthy people at church, we need to understand that people who claim to be believers don't always act in godly ways. Consider these two possibilities:

First, some people are not Christians though they say they are:

"Not everyone who says to Me, 'Lord, Lord', shall enter the kingdom of heaven, but he who does the will of My Father in heaven" (Matthew 7:21).

> **From this passage ...**
>
> A person may claim to be a Christian, but does that automatically mean he or she is?

"You will know them by their fruits.... every good tree bears good fruit, but a bad tree bears bad fruit" (Matthew 7:16a, 17).

> **From this passage ...**
>
> How will we know if someone is a Christian?

"But the fruit of the Spirit is love, joy, peace, longsuffering, kindness, goodness, faithfulness, gentleness, self-control ..." (Galatians 5:22–23).

> **From this passage ...**
>
> What kind of "fruit" will a true Christian have?

Second, real believers will bear good fruit, but no one is perfect. Some will respond well; others will not. Some Christians are unwise because they are young in their faith or don't put much effort into following Christ. Others may be more mature but have not yet learned how to be compassionate. In this context, survivors of sexual abuse find church to be uncomfortable. Our stories may be met with awkward silence—or unwelcomed. Feeling isolated and rejected, we may choose to say nothing, believing that God holds us at arm's length because he is uncomfortable with us.

As a pastor's wife, Maria began to wrestle with unanswerable questions. After a miscarriage, a difficult ministry, illness, and challenges with parenting, her ideas about God were completely uprooted: "I realized I was worshiping someone I didn't know." But she couldn't seem to find him. To her, God was absent and his people were a concrete wall. She was trapped and felt forced to remain silent at church. Frustrated and enraged, she believed God owed her an explanation: "You're going to have to convince me that you're good, or I'm done." She writes,

> Why all this doubt? Why do I continue to find the Bible difficult to trust? Is God really as good as everyone says he is? No matter how much Bible study and praying I do, I continue to wonder. Why would God create us knowing we would sin so horribly against one another? How can there be anything good about a child suffering unspeakable abuse? Where is the justice? Should I even be asking these questions? Am I being disrespectful or irreverent?
>
> I spent several months wrestling with God and even challenged my leading friend, my husband, and my mom with these questions, hoping for some answers. I wanted God to prove to me that he could be trusted. I wanted an explanation for all of the madness.
>
> When I had exhausted my list of questions, God began to teach me that answers and explanations would not satisfy my soul. He answered my why questions by revealing himself to me. I found great relief when I let go of my need for an explanation and stopped demanding answers.

Maria was desperate to know that God is trustworthy and good, but thought that she had to deny her questions and simply stay silent to conform at church. But after honest and genuine searching, she is learning that although there isn't always an explanation, God hears and understands. She is also learning that God wants her to express her questions with humility and a genuine desire to know him more. He is using Maria's story to awaken her church family to the desperate and silent needs of his people. And as they seek God together, they are learning to love and serve one another in light of the true character of God.

Keeping People in Perspective

As we learn to walk with one another on this journey home, let's keep our eyes fixed on Jesus. Dark and unspoken suffering like sexual abuse can blur our view of God, making it difficult to trust him. But no matter what we feel or think, we can't allow human beings to define or replace God. It will only complicate and add pain to our story.

People will fail us, and we them, but our sinful actions and characteristics do not in any way define God. Scripture says that God never sins. He alone is perfectly holy and good. Always! And as hard as it may be, we must continue to seek him above all as we journey together.

"[God] satisfies the longing soul, and fills the hungry soul with goodness" (Psalm 107:8–9).

Talking Points: Pray and discuss the following with your leading friend.

1. In what ways have I allowed people's actions to define God? (i.e., the people at church don't understand me, so God must not understand either.)

2. Am I allowing other people to replace God? In what ways and why?

Trusting God

"But You, O GOD the Lord, deal with me for Your name's sake; because Your mercy is good, deliver me. For I am poor and needy, and my heart is wounded within me" (Psalm 109:21–22).

We have come to the most pressing issue in this entire study. Many victims of sexual abuse struggle to believe that God is actually trustworthy. We might not say it out loud, but we live as if he isn't. The following chapter will address many questions and concerns about his trustworthiness, but for now let's get a snapshot of our current conclusions about God's character in light of our suffering.

Write your most significant thoughts and feelings about God (i.e., distant, ineffective, loving...).	Read Psalm 103. List what God's Word says about him from that passage.

Look over the chart above again. Compare your thoughts and feelings to the truths listed from Psalm 103.

This exercise is designed to help us identify and assess our current view of God. Being honest about our opinion of God is necessary on this journey home. If we don't find him to be trustworthy, we have no hope of moving forward. As painful as it may be, we must "get real" with God. He is more than worthy of our trust; we must be willing to face the darkness that blinds us.

God is faithful to receive us in all our honesty because he is full of beautiful and redeeming grace. Be loved. Because you are! Seek him with all your heart and you will find him.

"And you will seek Me and find Me, when you search for Me with all your heart" (Jeremiah 29:13).

Choosing Well

At the beginning of this section we discussed our need for a trustworthy standard by which to measure our conclusions. If we neglect this standard and let our human evaluations and emotions determine our beliefs, life will be miserable. Trusting our *feelings* may seem like the easier way, but emotion was never meant to be our inner compass. Instead, emotion is like an indicator light on our dashboard, showing us that we need to pay attention to something important. God purposefully created those indicators to remind us to listen to what he says to us in his Word. When we choose to trust him, we will find in him the security, stability, and freedom we crave. And that's a promise!

"Trust in the LORD with all your heart, and lean not on your own understanding; in all your ways acknowledge Him, and He shall direct your paths" (Proverbs 3:5–6).

From this passage ...

I can trust God with _____ of my heart.

I can't lean on my own _____.

When I acknowledge *the LORD*, He will _____
_____.

Talking Points: Pray and discuss the following with your leading friend.

1. Am I willing to consider that my emotional responses may be causing me to believe lies?

2. Am I willing to trust God? If not, why?

3. What may be hindering my trust in God?

4. What are my questions for God?

Part IV

WHO IS GOD?

Chapter 6

Our View of God

God is not visible to our human eyes, but it's possible to know and trust him, even when life is perplexing and hard. Our last chapter encouraged trust, which endures and rests upon knowing someone well. But lots of nagging questions and demands arise from a heart devastated by sexual abuse. These concerns deserve serious attention and careful thought.

If God is in control of all things, then how is it possible for him to remain loving and good while allowing wickedness to prevail? Where is justice? Does God even exist? Is he cruel? Is he disgusted and repelled by my shame? Has he turned his face away? Does he hate me? Where was God while I was being abused?

He Leadeth Me

By John F. Chaplain

In pastures green? Not always; sometimes He
Who knows best, in kindness leads me
By weary ways, where heavy shadows be.
Out of the sunshine warm and soft and bright—
Out of the sunshine into the darkest night,
I oft would faint with sorrow and affright,
Only for this—I know He holds my hand;
So whether in the green or desert land
I trust; although I may not understand

And by still waters? No, not always so;
Oft-times the heavy tempests round me blow

and o'er my soul the water and billows go.
But when the storm is loudest and I cry
Aloud for help, the Master stands by
And whispers to my soul, "Lo, it is I."
Above the tempest wild I hear Him say,
"Beyond this darkness lies the perfect day;
In every path of thine I lead the way."

So whether on the hilltop high and fair
I dwell, or in the sunless valley where
Shadows lay—What matter? He is there!
So where He leads me, I can safely go,
And in the blest hereafter I shall know
Why, in His wisdom, He hath led me so.[13]

Being sexually abused can wreak havoc on our souls and deeply impact our view of God. By sharing our stories, we have begun to face the pain in our hearts and the questions that arise, but now we must search for truth, so we can learn to interpret our stories through a correct view of God.

The Importance of Our View of God

As the writer of the poem points out,[14] it matters what we believe, especially about God. Wrong thinking fuels doubt, overwhelming emotion, and bad decisions. This part of *Treasure in the Ashes* has been written to bring light to the questions and emotions that fill our hearts, but usually remain unspoken. We will dive headlong into the ocean of God's essential nature. We will brave some hard questions, but will find solid ground and build a bridge for hope and stability on the journey.

When we see God more clearly and seek to interpret our stories from his perspective, we will begin to experience his peace; stabil-

---

[13]John F. Chaplain, Bible Truth Publishers, http://bibletruthpublishers.com/he-leadeth-me-poetry-cards/john-f-chaplain/cheer-comfort-encouragement-and-sympathy/pd7962. Accessed 5/18/2017.
[14]See page 33.

ity, security, and joy. Let's explore God's essential nature and some reasons why these truths are important:

WHY IT MATTERS

God Is Holy   Psalm 107:8–9; Isaiah 6:3

"As you do not know what is the way of the wind, or how the bones grow in the womb of her who is with child, so you do not know the works of God who makes everything." —Ecclesiastes 11:5

The word *holy*—as used in the Bible—means *set apart*. God is not like us; his thoughts and ways are far above ours (Isaiah 55:8–9). As imperfect human beings, our understanding of the infinite God of the universe is very limited. God is infinite in every respect; he is perfect, knows everything, and possesses all power. His holiness sets him far above us and he cannot and will not be defined by our human reasoning. We will understand God only to the extent that he reveals himself to us in Scripture.

God's holiness matters because it means there is Someone bigger and better than our suffering, who can give us strength, purpose, and perspective on everything we see and experience in this world; Someone we can trust.

Write down a comment or question you have about God's holiness:

WHY IT MATTERS

God Is Good   Psalm 34:8

"Oh, taste and see that the Lord is good; blessed is the man who trusts in Him!" —Psalm 34:8

Goodness means full of loving-kindness and of excellent character, summarizing all of God's attributes. [15] Only God can make something

---

[15] See "Goodness," *Unger's Bible Dictionary, Regular Edition* (Chicago: Moody Press, 1966), 420.

beautiful out of the horror in our lives; only God can transform and redeem what is hopelessly broken. Sometimes he shows us what he's doing, but most of the time God asks us to wait, trust him, and take him at his Word.

From Sue's Journal

The agony of suffering is waiting for relief that never seems to arrive, while our circumstances scream hateful lies at us: "God does not care; he doesn't love you. He has turned away from you in disgust."

These deadly lies rob us of hope and cause us to curl up in despair or raise our fists in defiance. But they bring us no help because they claim that God is not good, when his goodness is what we need most.

God's goodness matters because it means God is for us and is available to us, no matter who we are. (See Romans 8:31.) This truth gives us hope in our helplessness and pain.

Write down a comment or question you have about God's goodness:

WHY IT MATTERS

God Is Love   1 John 4:7–11

"Yet in all these things we are more than conquerors through Him who loved us." —Romans 8:37

Contrary to popular opinion, love is not an emotion, although emotions are obviously involved. Love sacrifices for the well-being of the one loved, regardless of the loved one's worthiness or ability to repay, and is not based on performance.

Love is a fundamental need of every human being that is met perfectly by God. Human love is important, too, but it falls far short of perfection so it cannot fulfill another's need. God's love perfectly overcomes human imperfection and cruelty. We will talk about the profound nature of God's love throughout the rest of this study.

Write down a comment or question you have about God's love:

WHY IT MATTERS

God Is Sovereign   Genesis 1:1; Acts 17:24–25; Col. 1:16

"Trust in the Lord with all your heart, and lean not on your own understanding. In all your ways acknowledge Him, and He will direct your paths." —Proverbs 3:5–6

The *sovereignty* of God means he is in control and his plan will not fail. Because our sovereign God is loving and good, his plan is also good and executed out of love. This truth can be hard to grasp because evil exists, and evil contradicts God's goodness. [16] But it is important to wrestle with these difficulties.

God's sovereignty can bring confidence, security and peace when we believe that he has the power to cause a good result in his perfect timing, and that he will do so because he is good.

Write down a comment or question you have about God's sovereignty:

WHY IT MATTERS

God Is Wise   Romans 11:33

"For the LORD gives wisdom; from His mouth come knowledge and understanding. He stores up sound wisdom for the upright; He is a shield to those who walk in integrity." —Proverbs 2:6–7 NASB

---

[16]For a more thorough discussion of God's sovereignty, we recommend *Trusting God Even When Life Hurts* by Jerry Bridges (Colorado Springs: NavPress, 1989).

Wisdom is the correct application of knowledge. God knows all things at all times, so he is able to see motives, outcomes, reasons, and consequences. The explanation of all things is clear only to him. He alone is able to take everything into account simultaneously and acts in harmony with that explanation. Because God is also loving and powerful, we can be sure that his wisdom is good and kind toward us, even when he allows us to suffer.

Because we are not able to know all things, we need God's wisdom to guide us. We can trust him because he is good and he knows how to take us where we need to go.

Write down a comment or question you have about God's wisdom:

WHY IT MATTERS

God Is Just   Isaiah 30:18; Acts 3:14

"Righteousness and justice are the foundations of Your throne; lovingkindness and truth go before You." —Psalm 89:14 NASB

Because God is infinite, he knows all things at all times and makes thoroughly perfect moral judgments. He will right all wrongs according to his perfect knowledge. No human being measures up to that standard, nor can anyone predict how God will bring justice to pass. But we can be sure that he will execute justice.

We cannot right the wrongs that have been done to us, so we need God to stand up for us and to apply perfect justice with our abusers. We are better equipped to overcome destructive anger and debilitating despair when we accept that God is just.

Write down a comment or question you have about God's justice:

WHY IT MATTERS

The Gospel Is Our Hope   Romans 8:24; Col. 1:27

First Corinthians 15:1-5 sums up the message of the gospel: "Brethren, I declare to you the gospel ... that Christ died for our sins according to the Scriptures, and that He was buried, and that He rose again the third day according to the Scriptures ..."

God freely and fully provides forgiveness and grace through the sacrificial death and resurrection of Jesus Christ for all who receive him (John 1:12). The gospel means that we can be sure of eternal life: there's more—much more—in store for us than our present suffering and sorrow. In Christ, we can experience his amazing grace in a vibrant relationship with our holy, good, loving, sovereign, just, gracious, and forgiving God—forever.

The reality of the gospel provides hope for today and all eternity, giving us eyes to see purpose beyond the evil in this world.

Write down a question you have about the gospel:

Soul-Deep Questions

Attempting to acknowledge the soul-deep questions that arise from a sufferer's heart is risky, especially because the wounds are tender and deep. Answering the question *"Who is God?"* is not to be considered lightly and we (your authors) will not offer heartless platitudes.

If you are deeply wounded and you struggle to believe that God is good, please take heart. Our journey will take time, and you may have to wrestle with your beliefs. But that's normal; like a butterfly fighting to be free of its cocoon, it's worth the battle.

Just a Glimpse: Seeing God

"I love those who love me, and those who seek me diligently will find me" (Proverbs 8:17).

"And you will seek Me and find Me, when you search for Me with all your heart" (Jeremiah 29:13).

From these passages ...

When we search for God diligently and with all of our hearts what does he promise?

"I will lift up my eyes to the hills ... my help comes from the LORD, who made heaven and earth" (Psalm 121:1–2).

From this passage ...

Where does our help come from?

Where do you go for hope and help? Why do you go there?

What do you receive from that source? How long does it last?

"Ask, and it will be given to you; seek, and you will find; knock, and it will be opened to you" (Matthew 7:7).

"But You, O Lord, are a God full of compassion, and gracious, longsuffering, and abundant in mercy and truth. Oh, turn to me, and have mercy on me! Give Your strength to your servant ..." (Psalm 86:15–16).

Treasure: Biblical faith does not ignore evil or the questions it raises. Faith seeks and accepts what God says, leaning on him for strength to endure, believing that he is good.

Chapter 7

Wrestling

The Character of God
in Light of Hard Questions

"Oh, the depth of the riches both of the wisdom and knowledge of God! How unsearchable are His judgments and His ways past finding out! For who has known the mind of the LORD?"
—Romans 11:33-34

In our last chapter we explored aspects of the essential nature (character) of God:

- **God is holy and good:** He is bigger and better than our suffering. He is for us. We can trust him.

- **God is love:** He cares for our well-being. His love overcomes human imperfections and cruelties.

- **God is sovereign:** By his power and control, he will bring a good result.

- **God is wise:** He knows perfectly how to lead us.

- **God is just:** He will make all things right.

- **The gospel is our hope:** God freely gives forgiveness, eternal hope, and grace in Jesus Christ.

This chapter will examine his character more fully as we begin to address some hard questions.

From Maria's Journal

In my desire to glorify God, I would often minimize or deny my questions or concerns about his character. If I came across a passage of Scripture that challenged my view of God, I would ignore it or assume I had misunderstood its intent. This approach did not help me, nor did it glorify God. It became my own way of handling my unbelief and kept me locked away.

Hard Questions

Many of us shiver at the thought of questioning the almighty God. But in reality, we question him often. Every time we make choices based on fear, we have concluded and testified that God is absent, doesn't care, or is unable to help. Saying our questions out loud will begin to break the powerful darkness of silence, expose the reality of our spiritual condition, and invite the Holy Spirit to do his healing and sanctifying work in our hearts.

Is God the Author of Evil? Does He Encourage Evil?

God's Word describes him as holy, which means he is perfectly good and pure (1 Samuel 2:2). God does not cause evil and he never views it lightly. He never overlooks, ignores, excuses, applauds, entices, or condones wickedness.

"Let no one say when he is tempted, 'I am tempted by God'; for God cannot be tempted by evil, nor does He Himself tempt anyone" (James 1:13)

According to this passage …

Since God cannot be tempted by evil, does he tempt or cause people to abuse one another?

God Hates Evil

"For You are not a God who takes pleasure in wickedness, nor shall evil dwell with You. The boastful shall not stand in Your sight; You hate all workers of iniquity. You shall destroy those who speak falsehood; the LORD abhors the bloodthirsty and deceitful man" (Psalm 5:4–6).

According to this passage ...

What is God's response to:

... Wickedness and evil?
... The boastful (proud and arrogant)?
... Workers of iniquity (sin)?
... Liars?
... The bloodthirsty and deceitful man?

While it may seem that evil has free reign, this is not so. We may not understand why God allows evil, but we do know that he promises to redeem [17] our suffering by bringing all things together for his good and divine purposes. We see this clearly in the story of Joseph, who was sold into slavery by his brothers but later became second-in-command in Egypt (Genesis chapters 37–50).

"[Lord,] You are good, and do good ..." (Psalm 119:68).

But Why Does God Allow Evil to Exist?

God created human beings with the freedom to choose— not as robots or puppets— so that our relationship with him would be genuine rather than forced or programmed. So that people could freely choose to love God, he made it possible for us to reject him.

---

[17] To buy back. Consider how we redeem a coupon: exchanging a relatively worthless scrap of paper for something of value. The store pays the price of the coupon on the customer's behalf. Through his death, Christ paid the price for humankind's sin. We "redeem" His "coupon" when we bow to exchange our sin for his forgiveness and eternal life. This redemption impacts us forever, bringing value to our suffering. We will talk much more about redemption, suffering, and the gospel later.

In the beginning God created a perfect world. He breathed life into a man and woman and gave them one command: "Of every tree of the garden you may freely eat; but of the tree of the knowledge of good and evil you shall not eat, for in the day that you eat of it you shall surely die" (Genesis 2:16–17).

From this passage ...

What condition did God set?

Think about God's requirement for a moment. Out of scores of perfect trees, Adam and Eve could eat from all but one. Does this seem difficult to you? God gave them a clear opportunity to choose to love him, just as they were created to do.

"If you love Me, keep My commandments" (John 14:15).

From this passage ...

Would they eat the "forbidden" fruit if they truly loved God?

"So when the woman saw that the tree was good for food, that it was pleasant to the eyes, and a tree desirable to make one wise, she took of its fruit and ate. She also gave to her husband with her, and he ate" (Genesis 3:6).

From this passage ...

What choice did they make?

God set the conditions, but who made the choice—people or God?

"Therefore, just as through one man [Adam] sin entered the world, and death through sin, and thus death spread to all men, because all had sinned" (Romans 5:12).

From this passage ...

When Adam ate the fruit, what were the consequences?

How widespread were those consequences?

Scripture reveals that Adam and Eve chose to believe lies. Their sinful choice brought many consequences, including the entrance of sin and death into the world. God warned them this would happen (Genesis 2:16-17). But they didn't listen.

God gave us real choices. When we express our will selfishly and rebelliously, evil is born.

"In returning and rest you shall be saved; in quietness and confidence shall be your strength. But you would not ..." —Isaiah 30:15

Since God Gave Us Freedom to Choose, Isn't Evil His Fault?

"If God is so good and loving, why did he create us knowing we would sin? What's the point? It seems cruel."

Even the best theologians can't give a fully satisfying explanation as to why God created things the way he did, but we can explore and hold fast to some basic truths to help settle the stormy waters in our souls.

Cause and Effect

From our perspective, God created the world to function according to cause and effect. Everything except God is the result of some kind of action. Consider this: if I plant corn, then if conditions permit, corn will grow. Similarly, if I've built a sound foundation under my house, it will stand even during a heavy rainstorm. Scripture says that we experience consequences (effects) based upon decisions we have made (causes), including factors we personally did not cause (Matthew 7:24-27). Everyone functions according to cause and effect. Even if we deny this principle, we cannot escape it. God created the world so that we reap what we sow.[18] What we do matters!

People sin (the cause), so there is suffering (the effect)

God created us in his image with an intellect, emotion, and will. Because we have freedom to make choices, we can choose to do good,

---

[18] Galatians 6:7

78

but often we choose to sin, and so do other people. Sin causes terrible suffering. Our abuser's evil choices have brought unspeakable agonies to us. But the sins of people neither define nor hinder God. The horrors caused by people do not stop God from being good, holy, and loving.

God is love (the cause), so there is hope (the effect)

Scripture makes it clear that the almighty and Holy God wants to have a relationship with us because he loves us. This truth is astounding. First John 4:8 tells us that love isn't just something God does, it's who he is. He loves us because he is good and kind, not because we deserve it. That gives hope!

These truths can be terribly hard to swallow when such deep wounds bleed unattended. But the words you read on these pages are written by hands and hearts that hear the gentle pleas of our Savior on your behalf. The source of our suffering flows from the world, the flesh, and the devil, not God. Because God is holy and good, he never does anything evil. He always does what is best; he acts on our behalf and does so continually. He is for us, never against us! [19]

God's Expression of Love

God is fully aware of the gnawing tension and the myriad questions that bind us. "As a father pities his children, so the LORD pities those who fear Him. For He knows our frame; He remembers that we are dust" (Psalm 103:13–14). He knows how desperate we are for peace and redemption. But how does he show us this love? Let's look at some specific ways:

"God so loved the world that He gave His one and only Son ..." (John 3:16).

From this passage ...

Since God loves us, what did he do? "He gave His_____."

---

[19] Romans 8:31

"In this the love of God was manifested toward us, that God has sent His only begotten Son into the world, that we might live through Him. In this is love, not that we loved God, but that He loved us and sent His Son to be the propitiation [wrath-removing sacrifice] for our sins" (1 John 4:9-10).

From this passage ...

How did God show us his love? "In this the _____ of God was manifested toward us ... that He _____ us and sent His Son ..."

Jesus died to remove God's wrath from us. If you have put your faith in Jesus, is God angry with you?

"God demonstrates His own love toward us, in that while we were still sinners, Christ died for us" (Romans 5:8).

From this passage ...

Christ died for us even while we were still_____.

"But God, who is rich in mercy because of His great love with which He loved us, even when we were dead in trespasses, has made us alive in Christ (by grace you have been saved)" (Ephesians 2:4-5).

From this passage ...

God is rich in_____. "Because of His great _____ with which He loved us."

Our greatest need, even above emotional, spiritual, and physical healing, is for the gospel. Jesus Christ is the greatest expression of God's love for us. In the coming pages we will look more fully into why this is absolutely and wonderfully true, not just for the distant future but also for today.

Our Expression of Love

In gratitude to God for his amazing love and mercy, we can respond by seeking to know and love him even more. As we grow in the knowledge of our Lord and Savior, the nagging questions and doubts begin to quiet down: "... and the peace of God, which surpasses all understanding, will guard [our] hearts and minds through Christ Jesus" (Philippians 4:7).

"We love Him because He first loved us" (1 John 4:19).

According to this passage:

Why do we love God?

"Jesus said to him, 'You shall love the LORD your God with all your heart, with all your soul, and with all your mind. This is the first and great commandment. And the second is like it: 'You shall love your neighbor as yourself'" (Matthew 22:37–39).

According to this passage:

A believer in Jesus seeks to love God, but who else does he want us to love?

If the entire world obeyed God, there would be a lot of love everywhere. But we know this isn't reality. God isn't to blame for the evil around us. He has stepped into time, in the form of a swaddled baby named Jesus, and set the world and its darkness ablaze with the light of his love. He is here. He is our hope!

From Maria's Journal

God does not owe me love. It was out of his kindness that he used my sin and the sin committed against me to draw me near to him and open my eyes to my utter need for him. He doesn't have to redeem anyone, but he does. That is love.

But I don't know why or how some of us are chosen and others are not. Or do we choose God? This is where I feel torn apart by tension. How can I rest? Are some people purely and intentionally evil? Do they freely choose to sin, or are they destined to it? Are they given the same opportunity for belief? In the face of these doubts we may not know all the answers, but we do know that: God is in control, God is good, God is just, and people are responsible for their evil actions. After that we must leave this tension in God's hands.

Talking Points: Pray and discuss the following with your leading friend.

1. Do you believe that God can remain good and loving while allowing evil? Why or why not?

2. Is it possible to trust God while questions remain unanswered?

3. Do you believe that God loves you personally? Why or why not?

4. Do you believe you must somehow earn his love? Read Titus 3:5–6 and 1 John 4:9–10. Write your thoughts here.

In your journal write fifteen to twenty-five things for which you are thankful. We'll help get you started: the ability to read, chocolate cake, a phone call from a friend, the Bible, music, a beautiful sunset ... It might be difficult to see, but God is the giver of every one of those good gifts (James 1:17). The good things on your list are just a few of the amazing ways he genuinely loves and cares for you (1 Peter 5:7).

Treasure: Evil exists because we are free to make choices, not because God is evil. God is the answer, not the problem. Faith chooses to believe that God is good, even when reason demands that he isn't.

Chapter 8

Where Was God?

"O LORD, how long shall I cry, and You will not hear? Even cry out to You, 'Violence!' and You will not save. Why do You show me iniquity, and cause me to see trouble? For plundering and violence are before me; there is strife, and contention arises. Therefore the law is powerless, and justice never goes forth. For the wicked surround the righteous; therefore perverse judgment proceeds." —Habakkuk 1:2–4

Psalm 10

"Why do You stand afar off, O LORD? Why do You hide in times of trouble?" —Psalm 10:1

Where is God when someone is being raped? What is he doing? Why doesn't he stop it? Wrestling with these questions, especially considering the horrors of sexual abuse, can be some of the darkest moments we may ever face.

Read Psalm 10. Let's walk through that psalm as outlined in the chart below to see how David expressed some of his own hard questions about God's presence during his suffering. The chart analyzes the passage into three separate sections.

David cried out to God with all his heart. He asked questions, made requests, and reminded himself of God's promises to rescue him and redeem his suffering. When we cry out to God the way David did, we too can find hope in the midst of our dark circumstances.

Questions (from Ps. 10)	Concerns/demands	Hope
Why do You stand afar off?	The prideful wicked persecutes the poor … catch them!	Your judgments are far above …
Why do You hide in times of trouble?	The wicked in his pride, doesn't seek God … but his ways seem to prosper. He gives to the greedy.	But you have seen, for You observe trouble and grief, to repay it by Your hand.
Why do the wicked renounce God?	The wicked is smug and his mouth is full of cursing, deceit, and oppression.	The helpless commits himself to You, for You are the helper of the fatherless.
	The wicked is sneaky, his eyes are fixed on the helpless, in secret places he murders the innocent, and he lies in wait to catch the poor!	The LORD is King forever.
	The wicked doesn't think he'll get caught.	LORD, You have heard the desire of the humble; you will prepare their heart.
	Arise, O LORD! You have seen the trouble and grief… Break the arm of the wicked and the evil man; seek out his wickedness until You find none.	LORD, You will cause Your ear to hear, to do justice to the fatherless and the oppressed, that the man of the earth may oppress no more.

Before we move on, take a few minutes to draw a chart like the one above and write out your own lament, using a psalm to structure your thoughts (such as Psalm 10, 27, 35, 55, 73, or 143). Include questions, concerns, and requests, and be sure fill up your hope section with promises from God's Word. Ask for the Holy Spirit's help as you pray, and you may be astounded by his healing and strengthening presence.

Let's return to the big questions at hand: Where was God? Why didn't he stop the abuse?

Did God Turn Away Because He Is Angry or Disgusted with Me?

Shanae's behavior is far from acceptable. She is promiscuous and outright angry. But in her heart, she wonders if God is punishing her. Did she deserve to be abused? Is she the reason for all of her suffering? Would life get easier if she would just straighten up?

Suffering Is Not Punishment

Because of God's grace, suffering is not punishment. We know this is true because Jesus suffered horribly even though he was perfect. God was not angry with Jesus. In fact, God was pleased with the way his Son handled hardship.

Suffering itself is not God's expression of condemnation or displeasure. However, it does arise from various sources of evil, as a natural consequence of our own sin, the sins of other people, and from living in a fallen world where physical pain and death occur. Later we will look more closely at God's purposes for suffering, but for now we need to remember that evil does not come from God (Isaiah 24:5–6; Matthew 5:45; Romans 8:19–22; Galatians 6:7–9). We all suffer because we live as sinners among other sinners in a corrupted world.

But we have a redeeming God who loves us and provides for our needs by his grace.

God's Response to Suffering Is Compassionate

"I drew them with gentle cords, with bands of love, and I was to them as those who take the yoke from their neck. I stooped and fed them" (Hosea 11:4).

85

"He heals the brokenhearted and binds up their wounds.... Great is our Lord, and mighty in power; His understanding is infinite. The LORD lifts up the humble; He casts the wicked down to the ground.... The LORD takes pleasure in those who fear Him, in those who hope in His mercy" (Psalm 147:3b, 5, 11).

From this passage ...

What will God do for those who are brokenhearted and wounded?

What will God do for the humble?

What will God do to the wicked?

What does the Lord take pleasure in?

Where does he want us to look for hope?

"For we do not have a High Priest who cannot sympathize with our weaknesses, but was in all points tempted as we are, yet without sin. Let us therefore come boldly to the throne of grace, that we may obtain mercy and find grace to help in time of need" (Hebrews 4:15–16)

From this passage ...

Christ, as a sinless human being, was tempted like we are and he _____ with our weaknesses.

In our time of need, where does Christ invite us?

Why should we go? What will we find there?

Do we have to be afraid? How can we go to the throne of grace?

"Happy is he who has the God of Jacob for his help, whose hope is in the LORD his God, who made heaven and earth, the sea, and all that is in them; who keeps truth forever, who executes justice for the oppressed, who gives food to the hungry. The LORD gives freedom to the prisoners. The LORD opens the eyes of the blind; the LORD raises those who are bowed down; the LORD loves the righteous. The LORD watches over the strangers; He relieves the fatherless and widow; but the way of the wicked He turns upside down" (Psalm 146:5–9).

From this passage ...

What will God do for ...

... the oppressed (abused)? _____

... the hungry? _____

... the prisoners? _____

... the blind? _____

... the bowed down? _____

... the strangers? _____

... the fatherless? _____

... the widows? _____

What will God do to the wicked?

Who Gets the Blame?

"A good man out of the good treasure of his heart brings forth good things, and an evil man out of the evil treasure brings forth evil things" (Matthew 12:35).

From this passage ...

Where does evil come from?

"For out of the heart proceed evil thoughts, murders, adulteries, fornications [sexual sins], thefts, false witness, blasphemies. These are the things which defile a man ..." (Matthew 15:19–20).

From this passage ...

Where do evil thoughts, murders, adulteries, fornications, thefts, false witness, and blasphemies come from?

Can a victim cause her abuser to sin?

Is a victim of sexual abuse defiled by her abuser?

The two passages above tell us that an evil heart is what defiles a person. Our abuser's evil heart may have caused our suffering, but he cannot stain or defile us. He doesn't have that much power.

"But each one is tempted when he is drawn away by his own desires" (James 1:14).

"... an evil man out of the evil treasure of his heart brings forth evil" (Luke 6:45).

From these passages ...

> Who is to blame for your abuse? Write the person's name(s) here.

"But if a man finds a betrothed young woman in the countryside, and the man forces her and lies with her, then only the man who lay with her shall die. But you shall do nothing to the young woman; there is in the young woman no sin deserving of death ..." (Deuteronomy 22:25–26).

From this passage ...

> Who does God say is at fault: the abuser or the victim?

People abuse others because of their own sinful desires. The evil actions from those sinful desires are the oppressor's fault, *never the victim's fault.* Even if we, as victims, know that we contributed to the situation, we cannot cause an abuser's heart to be evil, and that evil heart is what caused our abuse.

Talking Points: Pray and discuss the following with your leading friend.

1. Summarize why suffering isn't punishment for a believer in Jesus.

2. Who is to blame for the abuse you endured? Why?

Treasure: Being sexually abused was not my fault.

God *did not* turn away while we were being abused, and he does not blame us. He was there. He heard our cries and saw what happened. But he was not passive. Our all-powerful and wise God was and is active on our behalf.

In What Ways Was God *With* Me?

"For He has not despised nor abhorred the affliction of the afflicted, nor has He hidden his face from him; but when he cried to Him, He heard" (Psalm 22:24).

Let's look for specific ways God was present and active in our defense during our suffering.

"But now, thus says the LORD, who created you ... 'Fear not, for I have redeemed you; I have called you by your name ... when you pass through the waters, I will be with you; and through the rivers, they shall not overflow you. When you walk through the fire, you shall not be burned, nor shall the flame scorch you. For I am the LORD your God, the Holy One of Israel, your Savior ...'" (Isaiah 43:1–3).

According to this passage ...

What does God promise?

Does He promise to keep us from suffering?

Who does God claim to be?

Who shall separate us from the love of Christ? Shall tribulation, or distress, or persecution, or famine, or nakedness, or peril, or sword? ...Yet in all these things we are more than conquerors through Him who loved us. For I am persuaded that neither death nor life, nor angels nor principalities nor powers, nor things present nor things to come, nor height nor depth, nor any other created thing, shall be able to separate us from the love of God which is in Christ Jesus our Lord. —Romans 8:31–39

According to this passage ...

Can anything separate us from the Love of Christ?

Because even in the most horrific of suffering "we are
_____ through Him who loved us."

"God is our refuge and strength, a very present help in trouble"
(Psalm 46:1).

In all these things (even the horrors of sexual abuse) we can be
more than conquerors through Jesus, who loves us! If you are already
a believer in Jesus, this may be a good time to ask him to walk with
you through your darkest and most painful memories. When we
bring our details to God, he walks with us through those experiences
and his Spirit helps us to see how he was and is with us in the midst
of our suffering.

Talking Point: Pray and discuss the following with your leading
friend.

Talk through your story and consider in what ways God might have
been working on your behalf. I (Maria) will share a few of mine. (A
word from Sue: Notice how Maria acknowledges her abuse but also
expresses gratitude for the good things God has done—a beautiful
result.)

God was present in my (Maria's) suffering in these ways:	In what ways was God with you?
God gave me loving parents. They believed me when I told them I was being abused.	
When the abuse I endured became too intense and scary, God gave me the courage to yell and pull away from my abuser. The man stopped hurting me.	

God was present in my (Maria's) suffering in these ways:	In what ways was God with you?
When I thought some of what I was experiencing was dangerously exciting, God prevented me from accepting abuse as normal. He forgave me for my own sin and rescued me from a life of promiscuity.	
God placed people in my life who demonstrated faithfulness, kindness, and love. I knew the difference between right and wrong.	
I was invited to a children's Bible club. They made the gospel very clear to me. Jesus saved my soul in the midst of my suffering.	
God gave me musical and athletic talents. These were healthy ways I was able to express myself, even while I was confused and struggling internally.	

Suffering: Reality and Hope

"What is the point of life if we all just suffer? I don't get it! God, I think your plan is bad. But I know I'm wrong! Please help me."

From Maria's Journal

Sue would often remind me (Maria) that we live in a fallen world and until we see Jesus face to face, suffering is part of reality. "Welcome to the real world!" she would say. Ouch! Really? Is life all about suffering? What's the point? But I am learning that God is much bigger than our suffering, and although I don't understand him, I can trust that he is doing something good. He is redeeming all of this mess; yours and mine. And I am beginning to see it! I still find myself lost in a sea of questions but my Rescuer is with me. And when I turn to him, he sets me on solid ground once again (Psalm 61:1–5).

"[Jesus said] These things I have spoken to you, that in Me you may have peace. In the world you will have tribulation; but be of good cheer, I have overcome the world" (John 16:33).

Chapter 9

Resting

Finding Peace in God's Justice

"He will bring justice to the poor of the people; He will save the children of the needy, and will break in pieces the oppressor."
—Psalm 72:4

Where Is Justice?

"Although you say you do not see [God], yet justice is before Him, and you must wait for Him." —Job 35:14

> Deep within her heart, Rayna wonders if God really cares. Her dad never owned up to his sin against her. When he died, her sorrow eventually changed into anger. Why didn't God restore their relationship? Why didn't her dad apologize? Where is he now? She feels isolated and paralyzed by her questions. Where is God in all of this? Will there ever be any justice?

The Bible claims that God's actions are completely just. He is morally upright, perfectly good, and completely correct. He is flawlessly wise and powerful and knows exactly what to do and when to do it. God knows all things all the time, and he sees the end of all things from the beginning. He knows exactly what you have endured and will bring your abusers into full judgment. And although God allows evil to exist for the present time, ultimately, evildoers will not get away with their sin. God promises to make all things right. But these truths seem to fly in the face of our dark experiences. Does God care? Can he really be just while evil seems to have the upper hand?

"They do not consider in their hearts that I remember all their wickedness; now their own deeds have surrounded them; they are before My face" (Hosea 7:2).

According to this verse ...

The wicked don't think God sees their evil deeds, but what does God say?

"Though they join forces, the wicked will not go unpunished; but the posterity of the righteous will be delivered" (Proverbs 11:21).

"Though a sinner does evil a hundred times, and his days are prolonged, yet I surely know that it will be well with those who fear God, who fear before Him. But it will not be well with the wicked; nor will he prolong his days, which are as a shadow, because he does not fear before God" (Ecclesiastes 8:12–13).

According to these verses ...

What does God promise to the wicked and to the righteous?

Scripture assures us that God executes perfect justice; it's just hard to discern exactly when and how. We know that God, the Righteous Judge, sees the hearts of all people and will not dismiss or overlook any evil. He will mete out perfect justice in his good and perfect time. But waiting for justice can be terribly difficult.

One of the greatest paradoxes of the Christian faith is that God's mercy exists with justice. But how is it possible for God to be both merciful and just? Is God being merciful toward our offenders while we suffer? Should we simply grit our teeth and painfully wait for justice?

Scripture says that God is holy—his ways are infinitely higher and wiser than ours. Therefore, we are called to faith rather than doubt. God's justice will be carried out. Although we struggle to understand, we can count on him. Let's see what the Bible says:

"The LORD executes righteousness and justice for all who are oppressed" (Psalm 103:6).

From this passage …

What will God do for those who are abused?

How many oppressed people will he do this for?

Does God say when he will do this? Will you trust him for that?

"Whoever digs a pit will fall into it, and he who rolls a stone will have it roll back on him" (Proverbs 26:27).

"Do not be deceived, God is not mocked; for whatever a man sows, that he will also reap. For he who sows to his flesh will of the flesh reap corruption, but he who sows to the Spirit will of the spirit reap everlasting life" (Galatians 6:7–8).

From these passages …

Although it may seem that our abusers got away with sin, what is their true fate?

But in accordance with your hardness and your impenitent heart you are treasuring up for yourself wrath in the day of wrath and revelation of the righteous judgment of God, who will "[give] to each one according to his deeds": … to those who are self-seeking and do not obey the truth, but obey unrighteousness—indignation and wrath, tribulation and anguish on every soul of man who does evil … —Romans 2:5–9

From this passage …

When someone is hardhearted and impenitent (doesn't change), what does God give to every soul who does evil? "_____ and _____ on every soul of man who does evil".

Because a person's soul is not visible, will you necessarily see the tribulation and anguish that person is experiencing?

- **When Justice Is Painful**

  If our abuser is someone we love, his fate may not be comforting. While we cannot change our abuser's heart or God's justice, we can pray for him and trust that God will forgive him if he truly puts his faith in Christ. We can also act wisely to discourage our abuser from hurting us or anyone else again.

- **When Justice Meets Mercy**

  Because God is merciful, he offers even the vilest of offenders grace and forgiveness. Jesus endured the punishment for sin. The gospel of Jesus Christ means that both the sinner and the sinned-against can be rescued. But if our abuser does not receive the gift of Christ's sacrifice, he will suffer God's wrath. Either way, justice is served. "'Come!' And let him who thirsts come. Whoever desires, let him take the water of life freely" (Revelation 22: 17).

- **The Government and Justice**

  Justice is also served through the governmental system that God has put in place to reward good and to punish evil. Romans 13:1–4 explains that human government "executes wrath on him who practices evil." Everyone is subject to the law, regardless of their spiritual condition or beliefs. Therefore, it is appropriate to report abuse to law enforcement so that God's purposes for government are served.

Sexual abuse is an act of violence, in which one leverages power to sexually violate the helpless. The resulting aftermath is not just a guilty conscience awaiting judgment on the part of the perpetrator, but a victim who has been assaulted. Sexual abuse is not just a sin but also a crime, not just a matter of personal unrighteousness on the part of the perpetrator but also a matter of public justice.

This means that sexual abuse in the context of the church must be handled by the institutions that hold authority—both the church and the state. The state has been given the sword of justice to wield against those who commit crimes (Romans 13:1–7); the church has no such sword (Matthew 26:51–53). This means that the immediate response to allegations of sexual abuse is to call the civil authorities, to render unto Caesar the responsibility that belongs to Caesar to investigate the crime. The church may or may not know the truth of the allegations, but it is the God-ordained prerogative of the civil authorities to discover such matters and to prosecute accordingly. When faced with a question of potential sexual abuse, call the authorities without delay. [20]

Treasure: God is just. He knows exactly what happened to me. I can trust him to execute his justice in his good timing.

Why Should I Accept All of This?

"So you've said I need to know God and respond according to truth rather than to my questions or emotions. Why should I believe you?"

We simply have to make a choice. *Am I going to believe what I want to or will I submit to God, the good Creator of this vast universe?* God loves us too much to leave us to ourselves, so he gives us his Word to inform and guide us. Here are some reasons why we must not demand more of an explanation than God gives:

- *We are not God*

  God tells us not to elevate ourselves and our desires above him because it is not good for us. Life is about him, not about us. If we made our own planet we could make our own rules.

  * "I am the LORD, that is My name; and My glory I will not give to another" (Isaiah 42:8).

- *Only God knows the whole truth, and he never makes a mistake*

  We can neither understand truth, nor live by it, apart from God. We are too flawed and finite.

---

[20] Russell Moore, "Moore to the Point: What Should the Duggar Scandal Teach the Church?" http://www.russellmoore.com/2015/05/22/what-should-the-duggar-scandal-teach-the-church (Ethics and Religious Liberty Commission of the Southern Baptist Convention, 2015). Accessed 7-13-2015.

* "… without Me you can do nothing" (John 15:5).

* Sanctify them by Your truth; Your word is truth" (John 17:17).

* Jesus said to him, "I am the way, the truth, and the life. No man comes to the Father except through Me" (John 14:6).

- **Only God is perfectly wise and good**

  We are not. Without him, we make a mess of everything we touch.

  * "You [God] are good, and you do good; teach me Your statutes" (Psalm 119:68).

  * "They have all turned aside; they have together become unprofitable; there is none who does good, no, not one" (Romans 3:12).

- **We were designed by God to serve his purposes, not our own**

  As created beings, we are to follow our Creator, never the other way around.

  * "Know that the LORD, He is God; it is He who has made us, and not we ourselves; we are His people and the sheep of His pasture" (Psalm 100:2–3).

- **To go our own way is not good for us**

  * "There is a way that seems right to a man, but its end is the way of death" (Proverbs 14:12).

  * "All we like sheep have gone astray; we have turned, every one, to his own way; and the LORD has laid on Him the iniquity of us all" (Isaiah 53:6).

- *We cannot survive apart from God*

  * "… without Me you can do nothing" (John 15:5).

  * "For by Him all things were created that are in heaven and that are on earth, visible and invisible, whether thrones or dominions or principalities or powers. All things were created through Him and for Him. And He is before all things, and in Him all things consist [hold together]" (Colossians 1:16–17).

Without God, our lives are hopelessly messy. We need him. He is the only One who gives us life, purpose, and direction. God wants us to turn to him because he loves us and wants what is best for us. But within his sovereign will he also allows us to refuse to follow him because he wants our faith to be genuine.

Choosing Well

Once again, we are asked to trust God even when we can't figure out what he is doing. To do that, we must read Scripture, choose to believe it, and actively seek God for the faith, knowledge, and strength we need to continue moving forward.

In light of our many unanswered questions, God may still seem confusing and even frightening. Rest assured that he understands our desperate struggle to believe and understand him. He is not limited or frustrated by our doubts and failures. God loves us and wants us to journey with him, not to drift on our own. Every time our experiences and feelings tell us that God is cruel or hateful, we have to choose to believe what Scripture says about him; God is always good, always holy, and always just. We can trust him.

"It is time to seek the LORD, till He comes and rains righteousness on you" (Hosea 10:12).

Talking Points: Pray and discuss the following with your leading friend.

1. Think through the following characteristics of God:

- **God is holy and good.** He is bigger and better than our suffering. He is for us. We can trust him.

- **God is love.** He cares for our well-being. His love overcomes our sin as well as the cruelties we suffer.

- **God is sovereign.** By his power, he will bring a good result.

- **God is wise.** He knows everything all at once, so he knows exactly what to do.

- **God is just.** He stands for everything that is right.

2. Do you believe God's claims about himself?

3. Consider how God intersects with your story. Take a few moments to fill in the chart on the next page.

Truth Claim	Applied to Sue's Story	Applied to My Story
God is holy and good. He is for me. I can trust him.	My abuser's actions do not speak for God. He is nothing like that. God is always for me, never against me, even during abuse. I can fully count on God to be good. When I lift up my eyes, I see his signature in countless beautiful things and kind people that he puts in my path.	
God is love. He cares for my well-being. His love overcomes our sin as well as the cruelties we suffer.	God cares for me, so he will cause this abuse to turn out for my well-being. He is with me all the time—even when I am alone, emotionally undone, or in trouble. He loves me even though I'm a mess. His love doesn't depend on me. He loves me because he is good.	
God is sovereign. By his power, he will bring a good result.	God's power overcomes my helplessness. He gave me parents who shielded me from further harm and law enforcement that worked. Even all these years later, he is using that abuse for good purposes as I reach out to Maria and we write this book together.	

Truth Claim	Applied to Sue's Story	Applied to My Story
God is wise. He knows everything all at once, so he knows exactly what to do..	I can't figure out much of anything. My life has been full of perplexing and troubling situations, but I know that God has been guiding me to someplace good. He knows what it will take to get me there. I can't trust my own mind—certainly not my emotions. But I can trust in his wisdom and guidance on this hard journey, especially when nothing seems to make sense.	
God is just. He stands for everything that is right. He defends me when I am wrongly treated.	Even though I have been blamed for going with that boy into the garage, I know that God does not condemn me. He stands up for me and condemns the evil that was done to me. He gave me parents who pursued justice; evil did not go unpunished.	

Talking Points: Pray and discuss the following with your leading friend.

4. How is your suffering affecting your view of God?

5. Is your view of God changing? In what ways?

6. How have you seen God working in good and just ways?

7. Read 2 Samuel 22. Notice how the writer expresses his confidence in God. List three or four things that God did for David. Has God done some of these things for you? List those as well.

Undoubtedly, we still have many unanswered questions and concerns. You may want to spend some additional times of discussion with your leading friend, but don't be surprised if she is unable to answer everything. Answers feed our minds, but they aren't going to satisfy the ache in our souls. What we really crave is God himself.

"God is our refuge and strength, a very present help in trouble … Therefore we will not fear … be still and know that I am God" (Psalm 46:1-2, 10).

Chapter 10

The Gospel

Good news

"As many as have received Him, to them He gave the right to become the sons of God." —John 1:12

What Is the Gospel?

1 Corinthians 15:1–8 summarizes the gospel of Jesus Christ beautifully and clearly. "Moreover brethren, I declare to you the gospel … that Christ died for our sins according to the Scriptures, and that He was buried, and that He rose again the third day according to the Scriptures."

What's so important about that?

The gospel of Jesus is "the power of God to salvation for everyone who believes, for the Jew first and also for the Greek. For in it the righteousness of God is revealed from faith to faith" (Romans 1:16–17). The gospel of Jesus is not only our source of hope and relief, it is our salvation. Let's spend some time pondering what the gospel is and why it is so important.

Hard News

The existence of evil has brought terrible consequences for all of us. When sin came into the world, death and suffering entered, causing problems in three realms (Romans 3:10–12 and 5:8, 12; Genesis 2:16–3:24):

- **Inside us:** Inner conflict, guilt, confusion, foolishness, acceptance of lies, turning our hearts to lesser things, etc.

- **Between people:** Mistreatment, anger, bitterness, rejection, neglect, abuse, misunderstanding, lying, evil thoughts and actions, etc.

- **In our fallen world:** Death, pain, illness, disease, pestilence, deterioration, dangerous weather, etc.

Because God is good, there is an amazing solution for evil. But first we have to hear some hard news. Take a moment to ask God to help you learn and accept what you need to know. This is the hard part of the gospel, but it's too important to skip.

All Have Sinned

"Therefore, just as through one man sin entered the world, and death through sin, and thus death spread to all men, because all sinned" (Romans 5:12).

From this passage …

How many people sin?

Does that include you and me?

The truth is we're all a mess. We go our own way instead of God's way (Isaiah 53:6) and we're definitely not innocent of wrongdoing. Sin corrupts everything. "The wages of sin is death …"—physical and spiritual death, death of relationships, hopes, wisdom, and goodness (Romans 6:23). That is why there is so much suffering in the world. And that is why you have suffered.

Sin Is the Problem

"For all have sinned …" (Romans 3:23).

Yes, our abuser's sin is obviously heinous. But ours is too. This is difficult to hear, especially if you have been told you are "slutty" and worthless. Let's be really clear that our abuser's sin does not make us guilty; that guilt belongs to him. But God wants us to admit that our own sin makes *us* guilty (not the sins we have been accused of but the sins we actually commit). This is really important and it ends with very good news.

We're All Guilty

"For whoever shall keep the whole law, and yet stumble in one point, he is guilty of all" (James 2:10).

From this passage ...

How many sins does it take to make a person guilty?

Have you committed one sin?

Are you guilty?

Please remember that we are not guilty of the sins that other people commit (Romans 14:12; Ezekiel 18:20). But our own sin contributes to the problems in the world. That's very hard news.

Love Meets Justice

Now, here's a paradox. God not only loves us, but he is also just. That means he can't brush off, ignore, or minimize our sin. He will not overlook or excuse what we have done. A good and righteous judge declares guilty people guilty and sets an appropriate sentence. Scripture says the penalty for sin is death (Romans 6:23). This is tragic. But God is perfectly just. He has to declare us guilty and carry out a just sentence. It's the right thing to do.

Imagine that you have labored for hours creating an exquisite cake. It has five beautifully crafted layers, intricately iced to look like a castle. When you graciously invite your guests to enjoy a piece, they laugh at it, spit on it, knock it over, and stomp on it. How would you react? Hurt? Enraged? God made a perfect world, full of beauty and intricate design, into which he placed creatures made in his image. He invited us to share his creation with him, but instead of loving him we wrecked his creation and plunged everyone and everything into death (Romans 6:23a). Just as the cake can't be put back together, we can't fix the damage caused by our sin.

The Mercy of God

The Master Designer could have turned away in disgust and left us hopeless in our guilt and shame. He could have destroyed us all. But he didn't. Instead, he's made a beautiful way for us to be rescued. God is our merciful Redeemer. "The Lord is … not willing that any should perish but that all should come to repentance" (2 Peter 3:9).

The Very Good News

"Behold, the virgin shall be with child, and bear a Son, and they shall call His name Immanuel," which is translated, 'God with us'" (Matthew 1:23).

From this passage …

Who is Jesus Christ? "_____ with us."

"[God] made [Christ] who knew no sin to be sin for us …" (2 Corinthians 5:21).

"… Christ also has loved us and given Himself for us, an offering and a sacrifice to God …" (Ephesians 5:2).

From these two passages …

What did Christ do for us?

"… who Himself bore our sins in His own body on the tree, that we, having died to sins, might live for righteousness—by whose stripes you were healed" (1 Peter 2:24).

From this passage …

Whose sins did Christ bear?

Jesus came to die in our place, to pay the penalty for our sin. He took the punishment in order that we can have eternal life. Why?

Because God loves us. He wants what is best for us: forgiveness, new life, and hope (2 Corinthians 5:17; John 3:16; 10:10; 1 John 1:9).

"For the Son of Man has come to seek and to save that which was lost" (Luke 19:10).

"For God did not send His Son into the world to condemn the world, but that the world through Him might be saved. 'He who believes in Him is not condemned; but he who does not believe is condemned already, because he has not believed in the name of the only [unique] Son of God'" (John 3:17–18).

Finding Freedom and Life in Christ

Turning to Christ means embracing two truths:

1. **I am a sinner.** I cannot save myself or meet my greatest needs. My sin drives me to Christ. I need him. There is no hope if I rely on myself.

"There is none righteous, no, not one; there is none who understands; there is none who seeks after God. They have all turned aside; they have together become unprofitable; there is none who does good, no, not one" (Romans 3:10–12).

2. **Christ is the only Redeemer.** After he died to pay the penalty for my sin, he rose again to offer me eternal life. Everlasting life begins the moment I put my faith in him. Christ provides eternal hope and purpose.

"But God demonstrates His own love toward us, in that while we were still sinners, Christ died for us.... For the wages of sin is death, but the gift of God is eternal life in Jesus Christ our Lord" (Romans 5:8; 6:23).

"... not having my own righteousness, which is from the law, but that which is through faith in Christ, the righteousness which is from God by faith" (Philippians 3:9).

Receive Christ

"But as many as received Him, to them He gave the right to

become children of God, to those who believe in His name" (John 1:12).

From this passage ...

Notice that not everyone is a child of God. How does a person become a child of God?

Regardless of your past experiences or unanswered questions, in order to have eternal life and to become his child, you must receive Jesus. God won't force anyone to receive his gift of forgiveness and eternal life through Christ. We must willingly decide to put our faith in him.

... if you confess with your mouth the Lord Jesus and believe in your heart that God has raised Him from the dead, you will be saved. For with the heart one believes unto righteousness, and with the mouth confession is made unto salvation. For the Scripture says, "Whoever believes on Him will not be put to shame"... "Whoever calls on the name of the LORD shall be saved." —Romans 10:9–11,13

From this passage ...

What are the promises? If this ... then this.

If you haven't already placed your faith in Jesus and would like to do so now, this would be a great place to write out a prayer. Pour out your heart to God and thank him for his amazing love and forgiveness. And then make sure to share your wonderful news with your leading friend and your pastor too! Welcome to the family!

"I would have lost heart, unless I had believed that I would see the goodness of the Lord in the land of the living" (Psalm 27:13).

But God, who is rich in mercy, because of His great love with which He loved us, even when we were dead in trespasses, made us alive together with Christ (by grace you have been saved), and raised us up together, and made us sit together in the heavenly places in Christ Jesus, that in the ages to come He might show the exceeding riches of His grace in His kindness toward us in Christ Jesus. —Ephesians 2:4–7

Part V

WHO IS JESUS?

Chapter 11

Coming to the Light

"I am the Light of the world. He who follows Me shall not walk in darkness, but have the light of life." —John 8:12

Dylan is a quiet young man who never feels accepted. His grandfather's longtime abuses have left him with a deep sense of shame. He has no idea who he is and often wonders if he could ever really be loved. He condemns himself for the anger he feels toward his "big teddy bear" grandpa and insists that he is at fault, because everyone seems to love Grandpa. Grandpa adds to that false guilt by telling Dylan that their confusing relationship was Dylan's fault because he sat on Grandpa's lap and gave him affectionate hugs. His grandfather also said that sexual expression is good. Some of it did give Dylan physical pleasure, but he knew it was wrong, so Dylan is haunted by guilt. He feels insecure, awkward, and alienated. Dylan is painfully shy and silently continues to isolate himself in the darkness that persists in his life.

Dispelling the Darkness

His grandfather has convinced Dylan that he is at fault, so he hides, hoping never to expose his shame. Dylan is silenced and paralyzed by the darkness that surrounds him.

Fear of being exposed may cause us to hide, but the shame of being sexually abused is not ours to bear. Jesus calls to us in our darkness and invites us to embrace him and to find in him the healing light we so desperately need. Being exposed can make us feel vulnerable, but as we learn how the gospel of Jesus impacts our lives, we will begin to see our stories in light of his beautiful and redeeming purposes. (See Hebrews 12:1-3.)

"Walk as children of light … [and] have no fellowship with the unfruitful works of darkness, but rather expose them" (Ephesians 5:8,11).

Embracing the Light

The heart and soul of *Treasure in the Ashes* is Jesus Christ. In the dark and stormy trials of life, he is our lighthouse and our anchor. As we learn to fix our eyes on him, his Spirit works in us to dispel our darkness with the light of his love, joy, peace, longsuffering, gentleness, goodness, faith and self-control (Galatians 5:22-23). But if we want to experience this amazing grace of God, we must be willing to receive and embrace Jesus.

"I have come as a light into the world, that whoever believes in Me should not abide in darkness" (John 12:46).

"God is light and in Him is no darkness at all" (1 John 1:5).

Growing in the Light

Have you grown up in church hearing pat answers about Scripture and prayer? Please let us challenge you to throw away the emptiness of that approach, and instead embrace the truth: Scripture is God's love letter to us and prayer is our lifeline. They both connect us to God. Their significance is essential and life changing.

Read Your Bible, Pray Every Day

All healthy relationships, human or divine, are built upon good two-way communication. Our walk with Jesus is nourished and fortified when we sit to listen to Scripture and talk with him. Having a childlike hunger to know God is essential for our growth as we journey in the light. Our deepest spiritual hunger can be satisfied by drawing near to God through consistent Bible reading and prayer.

Bible Reading

- Get a reliable translation (such as: NKJV, ESV, NASB) [21]

- Set a regular time to read

- Plan your study [22]

Some good questions to ask while reading Scripture:

1. What does this passage teach about God?

2. What is he like? How will I respond?"

"Your word is a lamp to my feet and a light to my path" (Psalm 119:105).

Prayer

Sometimes it can feel pointless to pray, especially if it seems that God isn't listening or answering, but prayer is so much more than seeking God's help or getting answers. We need him in every way, but not like a genie in a bottle. He is the almighty God, our heavenly Father, Savior, and Friend, and prayer is our connection to him. When we express ourselves to God, we acknowledge that he, above all else, is worthy of our dependence, adoration, and obedience. When we approach him with humility and respect, we can be sure he will receive us with grace and mercy (Hebrews 4:16)—no matter what we have done or what has happened in our lives.

Because we can't see or hear God, it may seem as if he isn't there. But his Word promises that he will never leave us. Jesus is near and he hears even if we don't perceive him. [23]

"Dear Jesus, I know that you are here, even though my heart may tell me that you aren't. I choose to believe what your Word

---

[21] New King James Version (NKJV); English Standard Version (ESV); New American Standard Version (NASB)

[22] If you have not been reading the Bible much, our book is a good start, because it is filled with Scripture references. Familiarize yourself with your Bible by looking up the verses you find most helpful.

[23] I John 5:14

says: that you love me and will never leave me."

C.A.T.S.

There isn't a perfect way to pray, but the acrostic CATS is a helpful place to start. Having a bigger view of prayer will help us to develop a broader and more robust relationship with Jesus.

Confession: *Admitting sin, weakness, and need*

"Lord Jesus, I am a sinner. I need you. Please show me the way. I read in the Bible that I can be forgiven and have eternal life if I believe in you. [24] But I really don't know what you mean by that. Is it really as easy as simply believing? I don't get it. Please teach me what it means to believe."

Adoration: *Recognizing God and praising him*

"God, you are good, beautiful, powerful, holy, merciful, and near. You are infinitely bigger and better than we are, yet you lavish love and kindness on us and call us your beloved. You are the Righteous Judge; you will make all things right in the end. We can trust your infinite truth, love, and power."

Thanksgiving: *Recognizing gifts and offering gratitude*

"Thank you, Jesus, for food to eat, for a beautiful spring day, for the phone call from my friend, for a rich time in your Word; thank you for good memories, for ten fingers, for eyes and ears, and for a local church that teaches your Word. I'm grateful that you are in the process of rescuing me. Thank you for helping me to be patient. You are faithful to help me in your good timing. Thank you for hearing me."

Supplication: *Asking for help*

- Spiritual concerns: "Lord Jesus, I'm not the person I think I should be, and I'm tortured by condemning thoughts. Please forgive me and help me. I need you."

---

[24] I John 5:12-13

115

- Emotional Stress: "I feel crazy! Please help me to center my thoughts in you, Lord. I am out of control; please teach me how to respond to my feelings so I can handle life."

- Practical needs: "Dear God, I can't pay the bills. Please help me! Give me wisdom to find work. Teach me how to wisely spend my money, and in the process strengthen my faith."

- Other people's needs: "Please comfort and heal my sister from her surgery. Help her to trust you."

Talking Points: Pray together and discuss the following with your leading friend.

1. Do you have a reliable version of the Bible? What are your current Bible reading habits? Why do you read?

2. Describe your prayer life. How often do you pray? What do you pray about? What is the purpose of your prayers?

3. God says he is near even if we don't feel that he is. Do you believe this? Why or why not?

Review and write down each aspect of prayer from the CATS acrostic. Practice praying CATS and write them in your journal. This discipline will guide and bless you in surprising ways!

Chapter 12

Jesus Is ...

Through our suffering, we are learning that the gospel is critical to our healing and growth. The fact is, we need Jesus at every point in our lives, and we are drawn to him when we see the wonderful dimensions of his beauty, grace, and care. Come with us to explore and discover how Jesus brings hope, healing, and redemption to our story. Meet the Savior who understands and provides for us.

Jesus Is ... the Light

We need a way out of the darkness

"I am the light of the world. He who follows Me shall not walk in darkness, but have the light of life" (John 8:12).

> Dylan sees God as a big, gray-bearded grandpa in the sky, mocking his pain and calling him stupid for feeling insecure. Dylan is fearful and doesn't trust God because he is certain that God is just like his abusive grandfather.

Our dark experiences may tempt us to think that God is cruel. Who wants to get close to a punitive, harsh, and unavailable god? We have already suffered enough abuse! But Jesus gently speaks into the darkness of those angry thoughts when he declares, "I am the light." He is not the aloof, mocking, cruel "old man in the sky." Instead, Jesus Christ is God's incredible expression of love. Jesus draws near to us because he cares. "[Jesus said] I have come that they may have life, and that they may have it more abundantly" (John 10:10).

- What is your current view of Jesus? (Who is he and what is he like?)

Jesus Is … Our Good Shepherd
We need care

"I am the Good Shepherd. The Good Shepherd gives His life for the sheep…. I know my sheep, and am known by My own" (John 10:11, 14).

Dylan feels betrayed by someone he trusted. Dylan can't remember a time when he felt respected and nurtured. He can't imagine gentleness, kindness, or pure love, so he doesn't recognize or accept expressions of care when people offer them. Instead, he pushes them away in fear. Having been treated as an outcast and mocked for his gullibility, he is suspicious of everyone.

Experience may tell us that nobody cares, but our understanding of God has been hijacked by lies. While it is true that life is full of suffering, in the midst of our confusion and pain Christ calls out in love:

"Come to Me, all you who labor and are heavy laden, and I will give you rest. Take My yoke upon you, and learn of Me, for I am gentle and lowly in heart, and you will find rest for your souls" (Matthew 11:28-29).

No matter what our experiences or emotions tell us, Jesus is our Good Shepherd, he cares, and he will always be with us. We can trust him.

- Do you believe that Jesus knows and cares for you always? Why or why not?

"I will never leave you nor forsake you …" (Hebrews 13:5b).

Jesus Is … Merciful
We need rescue and relief

Dylan feels damaged and beyond repair. He tries to get over

his past and get on with his life, but no matter what he does, he continues to feel dirty and disgusting. Does anyone care? Will he ever find relief?

Mercy is defined as *compassion for those in distress.* [25] Jesus, the Man of Sorrows and acquainted with grief, knows how deeply broken, weak, and needy we are, and responds with outstretched arms of mercy, no matter what the circumstances are.

"... not by works of righteousness which we have done, but according to His mercy He saved us, through the washing of regeneration and renewing of the Holy Spirit, whom He poured out on us abundantly through Jesus Christ our Savior" (Titus 3:5-6).

From this passage ...

Is there anything we can do to fix ourselves?

Can the good (righteous) things we do rescue us?

God saves us "according to His_____."

Dylan has tried hard, in his own strength, to move forward with his life, but God wants to show him a better way. When we receive Jesus, we are washed and renewed by the Holy Spirit, and our shame is exchanged for his beautiful righteousness and perfect love. We can't fix ourselves. Jesus, in his complete mercy, does it for us.

- In what ways have you tried to rescue yourself and move forward with your life?

- Which ways are healthy and helpful? Which are not?

Jesus Is ... Full of Grace

We need acceptance

"... to the praise of the glory of His grace, by which He made us accepted in the Beloved ..." (Ephesians 1:6).

---

[25] "Mercy," *Merriam-Webster's Collegiate Dictionary*, Tenth Edition.(Springfield, MO 1999), 727.

Dylan has never known grace before, only punishment and accusations, fear and pain, and rejection and hardship. But now Christ allows him to breathe freely—with the concept and Person of Grace.

As we learn more about the true and good character of God, we begin to see that he offers his grace to us fully and freely. Grace means that God accepts us because of who he is, because he wants to. There is nothing for us to do—in fact, nothing we can do—to earn it. We simply accept it.

The concept of grace can be difficult to grasp because it goes against our natural desire to prove ourselves worthy of acceptance, love, and forgiveness.

- Think about your life. What good things has God given you that you did not earn?

"By grace you are saved through faith, and that not of yourselves; it is the gift of God, not of works, lest anyone should boast" (Ephesians 2:8–9).

Jesus Is ... Our Defender

We need someone to stand up for us

Dylan has responded to God's mercy by placing his faith in Jesus, but he continues to wrestle with doubt and self-condemnation. He still thinks that God might be mad at him.

The Bible calls Jesus our Advocate (1 John 2:1). An advocate is an agent of goodwill who stands up for someone else. Because Jesus has fully paid the penalty for our sins, he alone can stand before God on our behalf. He is our defender. In other words, when we are accused, he says something like this to the Father, "I paid for that sin, so it can't be held against her"; and the Father agrees. His anger has been resolved and justice has been served. The Bible calls this propitiation. It means that because of what Christ has done for us, God is not angry with us.

"… if anyone sins, we have an Advocate with the Father, Jesus Christ the righteous. And He Himself is the propitiation [wrath-removing substitute] for our sins…. In this is love, not that we loved God, but that He loved us and sent His Son to be the propitiation for our sins" (1 John 2:1-2; 4:10).

From this passage …

Who is our advocate?

Is God mad at you? Why or why not?

As Dylan spends more time reading the Bible and praying, he is learning to choose to believe what the Word says: that God accepts and loves Dylan and will never leave him. When his heart tells him that God hates him, Dylan refuses that lie and turns to Jesus as his defender.

"There is therefore now no condemnation to those who are in Christ Jesus …" (Romans 8:1).

Jesus Is … For Us
We need help

From childhood, Dylan has believed that his suffering is a punishment from God. Loving-kindness and grace were not a part of Dylan's understanding of God. Now that he is a believer, he is learning that suffering is not punishment, nor is it a sign of God's disapproval. Christ himself suffered, even though he was perfect. Suffering is part of living in a fallen world; believers will have trouble.

But Dylan has always believed that only bad people suffer, and feels condemned because he frequently experiences a sense of being overwhelmed. His leading friend had him write a list of verses [26] to remind him of God's good purposes in suffering.

---

[26] Romans 5:3-6; I Peter 5:10; 2 Corinthians 1:3-7; and James 1:2-4

Let's review some of the ways that Jesus helps us as we tackle the difficulties of suffering:

Security

No one can take us away from Jesus. Ever! He promises that he will never leave us. His nearness is a great source of comfort, especially when suffering seems to have no reasonable explanation. "And I give them eternal life, and they shall never perish; neither shall anyone snatch them out of My hand. My Father, who has given them to Me, is greater than all; and no one is able to snatch them out of My Father's hand. I and my Father are one" (John 10:28-30). (See also Hebrews 13:5; Deuteronomy 31:6.)

- Do you struggle to believe that God loves you and will never let you go? If you do, why?

Meaning

We can have peace, even while we grieve, because we know that Jesus is our Redeemer. He will make beauty from our ashes. "Therefore, having been justified by faith, we have peace with God through our Lord Jesus Christ ... And not only that, but we also glory in tribulations, knowing that tribulation produces perseverance; and perseverance, character; and character, hope" (Romans 5:1–4).

- Can you see any redemptive or "good" reasons for your suffering? If so, list them.

Muscular faith

Like weight lifting, our faith is built up when it requires greater effort. During hardship, we need to exercise faith in new ways and as a result, God makes us stronger! "Be sober; be vigilant ... Be strong" (1 Peter 5:8; Ephesians 6:10).

Victory over evil

No matter how difficult life becomes, we don't have to be defeated. Instead, we can overcome evil with good (Romans 12:21). With Jesus our victory is secure! "Yet in all these things we are more than conquerors through Him who loved us" (Romans 8:37).

Guidance

Jesus shows us the way and cares for us as we journey through this life. He builds our patience, endurance, hope, character, and strength. "The LORD is my shepherd; He restores my soul ... He leads me ... Yea, though I walk through the valley of the shadow of death, I will fear no evil; for You are with me" (Psalm 23:1, 3–4).

> When his emotions reel out of control, Dylan works hard to change his thinking by praying for God's help, and reading and meditating on the verses he wrote down. Doing so helps him to gain God's perspective and find peace during his suffering.

Jesus Is ... Our Redeemer

We need to know that Jesus makes beauty from ashes

"In Him we have redemption through His blood, the forgiveness of sins, according to the riches of His grace which He made to abound toward us ..." (Ephesians 1:7–8a).

> Redemption is a new concept for Dylan. He is learning that Jesus is for him, not against him. He had always thought that his unchangeable past made him completely unacceptable and useless. But he is discovering that Jesus wants to reclaim and redeem his story. Dylan has hope because he belongs to the Redeemer—the One who loves to make beauty from our ashes.

Redemption means "bought back." We are not redeemed by corruptible things or by our good deeds, but by the precious blood of Jesus (1 Peter 1:18-19). Jesus redeems our darkness, and in its place, gives life and light to our souls, frees us from the prison of lies and despair, and brings purpose to everything we face.

- What parts of your suffering seem ignored and wasted?

- In what ways have you seen Jesus make beauty from your ashes?

He has sent Me [Jesus] to heal the brokenhearted, to proclaim liberty to the captives, and the opening of the prison to those who are bound ... to comfort all who mourn ... to give them beauty for ashes, the oil of joy for mourning, the garment of praise for the spirit of heaviness; that they may be called trees of righteousness, the planting of the LORD, that He may be glorified. — Isaiah 61:1-3

Jesus Is ... My Brother
God Is ... My Father
The Holy Spirit Is ... My Companion
We need a new home and a new family

"... you received the Spirit of adoption by whom we cry out, 'Abba, Father!' [Daddy!] ... Heirs of God and joint heirs with Christ" (Romans 8:15b, 17b).

Dylan has received Jesus and is part of God's family. But he finds this truth hard to grasp or accept, because he can't see or feel God. He tends to fall into doubt, with some long and intense times of struggle.

He chose us in Him before the foundation of the world, that we should be holy and without blame before Him in love, having predestined us to adoption as sons by Jesus Christ to Himself, according to the good pleasure of His will, to the praise of the glory of His grace, by which He made us accepted in the Beloved.... Now, therefore, you are no longer strangers and foreigners, but fellow citizens with the saints and members of

124

the household of God. —Ephesians 1:4–6; 2:19

From these passages …

Where is our citizenship?

What do we have to look forward to?

Why has God chosen, adopted, and accepted us "according to the good _____ of His will"?

As Dylan learns to inform his feelings with Scripture, he sees that even though his family rejects him, he has a new family and an amazing future. God has promised Dylan an eternal home with him and his other children forever. He reminds himself of this truth and fights to believe it. The Holy Spirit helps him to focus on eternity and gives him a growing sense of hope and peace.

"Let not your heart be troubled; you believe in God, believe also in Me. In My Father's house are many mansions … I go to prepare a place for you. And if I go and prepare a place for you, I will come again and receive you to Myself; that where I am, there you may be also" (John 14:1–3).

"But as many as received Him [Jesus], to them He gave the right to become children of God, to those who believe in His name" (John 1:12).

Jesus Is … Listening and Understanding
We need a voice

"Evening and morning and at noon I will pray, and cry aloud, and He shall hear my voice" (Psalm 55:17).

Prayer is surprisingly refreshing for Dylan. He expected God to answer his prayers with harshness and sarcasm, but instead he found a quietness that was new to him. At first, talking with God felt clumsy, but day by day he kept at it until he began to look forward to his time of rest with his Father. Dylan could be honest with God. He doesn't scold him or make him feel bad for asking questions, for expressing his thoughts and feelings, or for weeping with intensity.

Dylan has found the psalms to be beautiful expressions of God's care. After feeling alone for so long, he is beginning to realize that God has written Dylan's experiences into his Word in the Psalms. He has known Dylan all along. As he prays along with the psalmist, he finds great comfort in knowing that Jesus hears and loves him.

Talking to Jesus may seem a little weird or pointless at first, but God has given us a voice and wants to hear from us. We are important to him. When we pray, the Holy Spirit hears and understands our cries, calms our fears, and gives us hope.

- What is prayer like for you? Do you feel welcome to talk freely with God? Why or why not?

"I cried to Him with my mouth, and He was extolled with my tongue; if I regard iniquity in my heart, the Lord will not hear, but certainly God has heard me; He has attended to the voice of my prayer. Blessed be God, who has not turned away my prayer, nor His mercy from me!" (Psalm 66:17–20).

Jesus Is ... the Vine
We need nourishment

"I am the vine, you are the branches. He who abides in Me, and I in him, bears much fruit, for without Me you can do nothing" (John 15:5).

Dylan has never felt safe, so he hides and keeps people at arm's length. And when he feels highly emotional, he tends to push God away, too. He suspects God's motives and doubts his love. Dylan's fears keep him from understanding and embracing

God, yet God is the only stability Dylan will ever have. God will bring the nourishment and safety Dylan craves as he moves toward Jesus and develops a close relationship with him.

When we draw close to Jesus, we find nourishment for our souls. Jesus supplies wisdom, strength, provision, protection, acceptance, purpose, and comfort … everything we need! We are free to grow in beauty and grace. We can flourish.

- What passages from the Bible help you to understand God's love and care for you?

- In practical ways, how does it look for you to draw near to Jesus?

[Jesus said] "By this My Father is glorified, that you bear much fruit; so you will be My disciples. As the Father has loved Me, I also have loved you; abide in My love. If you keep My commandments, you will abide in My love, just as I have kept My Father's commandments and abide in His love. These things I have spoken to you, that My joy may remain in you and that your joy may be full." —John 15:8-12

Jesus Is … Our Freedom

We need to be set free from condemnation, guilt, and shame

"He has sent Me [Jesus] to heal the brokenhearted, to proclaim liberty to the captives, and the opening of the prison to those who are bound" (Isaiah 61:1).

Dylan feels broken in many ways, but he is gradually learning that he is not defined by his pain or sin. As he discovers what Jesus is like, he finds himself drawn to the Lord, wanting to be more like him. He learns from his mistakes, confesses his sins, and God helps him change the way he lives. Dylan finds freedom as he accepts his personal responsibility to follow Jesus, and refuses to blame other people for his failures. He had resisted admitting his faults in the past, but now he is surprised to find relief when he confesses his sin to God, works at following Christ, and turns away from his worthless strongholds. Dylan is breaking free of the condemnation, shame, and guilt that have kept him captive for years.

- In what ways do you feel chained or imprisoned?

"If you abide in My word, you are My disciples indeed. And you shall know the truth, and the truth shall make you free" (John 8:31–32).

According to this passage ...

What sets us free?

Where do we find truth? "If you abide in _____"

What are some ways that the words of Jesus have already made a difference in your life?

Because we live in a fallen world, we will not be free from hardship until we get to heaven (John 16:33). But as we fix our eyes on Jesus, and the beauty of his redeeming gospel, we will begin to experience his freedom in new and amazing ways. Shame and guilt will no longer rule our lives, and we will begin to have the inner strength to love and follow Jesus with all of our hearts, souls, and minds. This is freedom!

"For the law of the Spirit of life in Christ Jesus has made me free from the law of sin and death" (Romans 8:2).

Jesus Is ... LORD

We need a trustworthy leader

"... at the name of Jesus every knee should bow ... that every tongue should confess that Jesus Christ is Lord, to the glory of God the Father" (Philippians 2:10–11).

Dylan always thought running his life was all up to him. This seemed reasonable, based on his belief that no one could be trusted, no one cared, and no one loved him. Until he turned to Jesus, he was his own boss. But now he sees that Jesus wants him to submit to him and do things his way. He resists Jesus, because he is not sure where the Lord will take him. (Didn't Jesus allow Dylan to be abused?[27]) And he hasn't worked through his shame completely, so in weak moments he doubts that he really is forgiven and loved. His resistance to God's authority causes him to run to his old way of life, but it's just as empty and painful as before. He wants to be his own boss, but until he yields to Jesus, he will find no purpose and direction. Jesus is Lord—He alone. He loves Dylan too much to let him be in control.

Jesus is LORD. He alone is absolutely wise, purely loving, and completely in control. We can trust him to lead us in a good direction. But if we resist his leadership, we are likely to make more trouble in our lives because we can't see the future, we don't have all the information, and we tend to believe lies. Following Jesus in the face of the evil he allows is incredibly difficult, but he is good and we can trust him even if our heart screams against it. When we set aside our fears and opinions and follow Jesus instead, we will find him to be faithful and true. He never promised that life would be easy, but he did say that he came to give us abundant life (John 10:10) and we can trust him to do just that. Let's draw near to him.

Talking Points: Pray and discuss the following with your leading friend.

1. What makes trusting and following Jesus difficult?

2. In which areas of your life do you struggle to trust God?

3. When do you find yourself being controlling, and why?

"Whoever desires to come after Me, let him deny himself, and take up his cross, and follow Me" (Mark 8:34).

---

[27] See Chapter 8: Wrestling

Chapter 13

Jesus Understands Our Suffering

Jesus Is … the Man of Sorrows

We need His example to show us the way through suffering

> "For we do not have a High Priest who cannot sympathize with our weaknesses, but was in all points tempted as we are, yet without sin. Let us therefore come boldly to the throne of grace, that we may obtain mercy and find grace to help in time of need."
> —Hebrews 4:15–16

Dylan crawls into bed and cries for hours when his struggle becomes especially intense. The nightmares, the body memories, the family conflicts, and his ongoing insecurities seem too much to bear. He is ashamed of his emotions and he thinks God disapproves of his weakness.

But Scripture says that Jesus understands and sympathizes with us. He understands our struggle because he struggled, too. Instead of condemning Dylan, Jesus invites him to bring his sorrow to the throne of grace, to be comforted and strengthened by his mercy.

Rayna has never allowed herself to admit that she had been sexually abused. Instead, she distracts herself because she is ashamed and afraid of the emotional pain of grief. She doesn't recognize that her life is worse because she has bottled up her pain instead of expressing it as the psalmists did.

Sorrow is the vulnerable and deep expression of a soul that has been deeply wounded. Jesus' examples show us that it's more than okay to grieve over evil and the suffering it brings. Rayna's denial has magnified her pain. Dylan is easily overwhelmed by the emotional battle that resides secretly within him. Neither of them feels safe to grieve.

- Do you feel free to grieve over your losses and the suffering you have endured? Why or why not?

As the Man of Sorrows, Jesus is well acquainted with grief. While expressing his sorrow over suffering and pain, he keeps this truth in sight: God never wastes pain. In the following paragraphs we will see how Jesus' suffering and his response to it makes an amazing difference in our lives.

Jesus suffered because of other people's sin

Jesus was misunderstood, abused, disrespected, overlooked, falsely accused, betrayed, mocked, humiliated, tortured, put through a fierce trial, brutalized, and murdered. "So then Pilate took Jesus and scourged Him. And the soldiers twisted a crown of thorns and put it on His head, and they put on Him, a purple robe. Then they said, 'Hail, King of the Jews!' And they struck Him with their hands"(John 19:1–3).

Jesus suffered the punishment for our sin

Jesus knows what it's like to bear the crushing weight of sin. He never sinned, but he suffered under God's wrath as if he had. When we believe in Jesus, we bear no guilt, no shame, and no condemnation in his sight. We are righteous in spite of our failures because all of our sin is completely forgiven. He is our substitute, our Hero. "For He made Him who knew no sin to be sin for us, that we might become the righteousness of God in Him" (2 Corinthians 5:21).

Jesus shows us how to suffer well

The four Gospels (Matthew, Mark, Luke, and John) give us a biography of Christ's life on earth. Among many things, we learn that Jesus suffered from hunger, thirst, fatigue, dangerous weather, the corrupt government, evil philosophies, and cruelty. But in all of this,

Jesus never sinned. His perfect example shows us how to navigate and overcome our own suffering in this fallen world. "These things I have spoken to you, that in Me you may have peace. In the world you will have tribulation; but be of good cheer, I have overcome the world" (John 16:33).

When Dylan remembers that Jesus sympathizes with him in suffering and bore the weight of his sin, he finds great relief knowing that Someone finally understands. Now when he prays, he talks openly with God about his feelings of being overwhelmed and in despair. And as he reads Scripture, he is learning from Jesus' example how to handle the intensity of his suffering.

Jesus Endured Suffering with Truth

Here are a few ways we can learn from Jesus' responses to pain:

He focused on the joy that was coming (Hebrews 12:2).
Jesus endured knowing that God had a beautiful purpose in his pain: the redemption of mankind.

"… who for the joy that was set before Him endured the cross, despising the shame, and has sat down at the right hand of the throne of God" (Hebrews 12:2).

He overcame temptation with Scripture (Matthew 4:2-11).
When Satan tempted a very hungry Jesus to turn stones into bread, he said, "It is written, 'Man shall not live by bread alone, but by every word that proceeds from the mouth of God'" (Matthew 4:4).

He prayed, knowing his Father was listening (John 17).

"… in the days of His flesh when He had offered up prayers and supplications, with vehement cries and tears to Him who was able to save Him from death, and was heard because of His godly fear, though He was a Son, yet He learned obedience by the things which He suffered" (Hebrews 5:7–8).

As Rayna spends time in the psalms and learns to cry out to God honestly about her suffering, the Holy Spirit helps her to begin realizing how much she has held inside all these years. Her prayers become a conduit of strength as she finds God's Word to be trustworthy. She can feel tension draining away. She can breathe.

Jesus remembered God's purpose for suffering

Christ, in deep distress, cried out to his Father so intensely that blood dripped from his pores. He pleaded with God (Matthew 26:39). He wept in agony. (Matthew 26:26-37; Luke 22:44; Hebrews 5:8-9). But even through all that, he kept God's purpose in mind, giving him the ability to endure. Jesus remembered that his Father was with him and had hope that he was doing something eternally meaningful, valuable, and good. He understands our struggle because he's been there; he entered into grief on our behalf, to give us hope in something greater— redemption.

When Dylan focuses on his pain, he spirals into hopelessness identifying himself as a victim instead of a child of God. He retreats into shame and doesn't go to God with his grief, so he loses himself in despair.

Dylan is caught inside himself. All he sees is his own pain; he sees no purpose outside of himself. Jesus was tempted in the same way as Dylan (Hebrews 4:15-16). He could have focused on his pain, but he kept in mind that his purpose was larger than his suffering. He carried in his heart the most beautiful and redemptive reason to die: to demonstrate the Father's love for us and to win eternal life on our behalf. He died because doing so brought glory to his Father.

Talking Points: Pray and discuss the following with your leading friend.

1. What causes you to focus on your pain?

2. Do you, like Dylan, spiral into hopelessness? If so, what does it take to get out of that spiral? Is this healthy?

3. Do you believe that Jesus really understands your sorrow? Why or why not?

4. Is Jesus enough? Explain your answer.

Finding Hope

God says his purpose for all that comes into our lives is to make us like our beautiful Redeemer Jesus Christ (Romans 8:28-29). Everything, good or evil, will be crafted by God to promote love, joy, peace, long-suffering, kindness, goodness, faithfulness, gentleness, and self-control—the very character qualities of Jesus (Galatians 5:22-23).

The effects of being sexually abused can be disastrous, assaulting our heart, soul, and mind, affecting our sense of identity, purpose, and well-being. It feels like a walking death. But Jesus is in the business of raising dead people to life. When we reach for him, he lifts us out of the darkness and deadness of our suffering. When he rose from the grave, he reversed the destructiveness of sin so that we can be free to bloom and grow in a beautiful relationship with him. We live in a broken world, but suffering doesn't have to ruin us. Jesus, the Redeemer of our lives, gives us eternal life, makes us whole, changes our identity, gives us meaningful purpose, and redirects the trajectory of our story. When we fix our gaze on him, we will find in Jesus all that we seek.

"These things I have spoken to you, that in Me you may have peace. In the world you will have tribulation; but be of good cheer, I have overcome the world" (John 16:33).

"I have come that they may have life, and that they may have it more abundantly" (John 10:10b).

Chapter 14

Jesus Is Our Savior

"Jesus said to her, 'I am the resurrection and the life. He who believes in Me, though he may die, he shall live.'" —John 11:25

The horrors of the past may leave us feeling dead inside, confused, angry, ashamed, fearful, alone, and hopeless. But we do not have to suffer under the weight of this burden. Jesus, who is rich in mercy, laid down his own life so that we might have abundant and eternal life (John 10:15, 28). When we place our faith in Jesus, God raises us from death to life (Ephesians 2:1). Christ died to pay the penalty for our sin, so we can know for certain that we have life. New life. Eternal life. Forever (Romans 5:8–10; John 3:16).

Jesus Is ... the Way and the Truth, and the Life

We need a way to be free from guilt, torment, and shame. We need new life.

"I am the way, the truth, and the life. No one comes to the Father, except through Me" (John 14:6).

"Seeing the people, He felt compassion for them, because they were distressed and dispirited like sheep without a shepherd" (Matthew 9:36 NASB).

Dylan is wracked with shame on two levels. First, feelings of shame were provoked in him by his grandfather. Provoked shame arises from his grandfather's confusing claims that Dylan was at fault for Grandpa's advances and that there was nothing wrong with what he did to his grandson. Children like Dylan have no mental shelves for such experiences; young

Dylan accepted dark, cruel lies because he did not realize Grandpa was lying to protect himself. A little child has no understanding of adult insidiousness; he was prey. Now that Dylan is older and better able to sort truth from error, he needs to learn that God does not hold him responsible for his grandfather's lies or sexual sin. Because Jesus is truth, he will show Dylan the way to be free through his Word.

Dylan is also ashamed of the sinful ways that he has reacted to suffering. This feeling is sin-shame because it arises from personal guilt. As Romans 3:23 points out, everyone is guilty of sin, and Dylan is no exception. He hates his family for taking his Grandpa's side. While their responses were certainly wrong, Dylan's hatred is also wrong and contributes to his feelings of guilt and shame. He has also lied, committed self-injury, and cursed God repeatedly. Because Jesus is the way and the truth, he can go to Jesus for forgiveness and freedom from lies. The Lord removes Dylan's guilt by forgiving his sins.

We all carry a heavy burden of guilt for believing lies, participating in wrongdoing, and responding poorly. Our *sin-shame* is heavy and stands between us and God. But we also feel *provoked-shame* because of the deception and accusations of our abusers. God does not hold us responsible (*it's not your fault*) for what our abuser does or says, but we are responsible for our own sins and beliefs. Denying or running from our sin only offers compounded guilt, not relief.

"If we say that we have no sin, we deceive ourselves, and the truth is not in us. If we confess our sins, He is faithful and just to forgive us our sins and to cleanse us from all unrighteousness. If we say that we have not sinned, we make Him a liar, and His word is not in us" (1 John 1:8–10).

From this passage ...

What will God do when we confess our sin?

Christ gives us a lasting answer for guilt and shame: forgiveness and cleansing. When we receive Christ, he mercifully removes our guilt and replaces it with his righteousness—forever! "He who covers his sins will not prosper, but whoever confesses and forsakes them will have mercy" (Proverbs 28:13).

"… and be found in Him, not having my own righteousness, which is from the law, but that which is through faith in Christ, the righteousness which is from God by faith" (Philippians 3:9).

From this passage …

How do we get righteousness? "through _____ in Christ."

"For God so loved the world that he gave his only Son, that whoever believes in him should not perish but have eternal life" (John 3:16 ESV; see also Romans 10:9-13.

… if you confess with your mouth the Lord Jesus and believe in your heart that God has raised Him from the dead, you will be saved. For with the heart one believes unto righteousness, and with the mouth confession is made unto salvation. For the Scripture says, "Whoever believes on Him will not be put to shame" —Romans 10:9-11.

From this passage …

What must we do to be saved?

Has there ever been a time in your life when you confessed with your mouth and believed in you heart that Jesus died and rose again for you?

If so, when and where? If not, why not?

What does verse 11 say about a believer's shame?

"Whoever believes on Him will _____ be put to _____."

According to these verses, if you truly believe that Christ died for your sins and you have voiced that to him, God will never again bring up your sin to use against you. Not ever! The matter is settled.

And the testimony is this, that God has given us eternal life, and this life is in His Son. He who has the Son has the life; he who does not have the Son of God does not have the life. These things I have written to you who believe in the name of the Son of God, so that you may know that you have eternal life. —1 John 5:11-13 NASB

Jesus Is ... Our Assurance

We need rest

As believers, we can be sure that we will never lose our salvation. In Christ we are accepted; Jesus will never turn away from us, no matter what. We are in him, and he promises that he will never deny himself (Ephesians 1:4–10; 2 Timothy 2:13).

"Most assuredly, I say to you, he who hears My word and believes in Him who sent Me has everlasting life, and shall not come into judgment, but has passed from death into life" (John 5:24).

From this passage ...

If we hear Jesus words and believe in God what will we have?

How long is everlasting life?

Eternal life starts the moment we place our faith in Christ. We can rest in the fact that we are secure in Christ forever (Ephesians 1:13–14).

Choosing Well

When he first received Christ, Dylan thought the Lord would take over his life and do everything for him from that point on. But he soon discovered that this is not true. After some awkward (even frustrating) meetings, his leading friend explained that God does not remove Dylan's personal responsibility.

When we place our faith in Christ, nothing can separate us from him. He keeps us safe, leads us, and provides for us (John 10:29). Our salvation is by God's grace and we can't earn his favor by doing good works or being good enough, but Jesus does give us some responsibilities. He asks for a life of humility and dependence on him, for gratitude and worship, for wisdom rather than foolishness, and for us to be a reflection of his character. These things don't come automatically, but are deliberate expressions of the change that has occurred and continues to occur in our hearts.

As believers in Jesus, the suffering we endure is not punishment and never will be. God redeems our suffering by accomplishing his divine purposes. He makes beauty rise from our ashes! When we choose to accept and embrace our Redeemer in the midst of suffering, we learn to respond to the harshness of this life with grace and wisdom.

Let's look at two basic responses to our God-given responsibilities:

Choosing to Follow Jesus

> Blessed is the man who walks not in the counsel of the wicked, nor stands in the way of sinners, nor sits in the seat of scoffers; but his delight is in the law of the LORD, and on his law he meditates day and night. He is like a tree planted by streams of water that yields its fruit in its season, and its leaf does not wither. In all that he does, he prospers. —Psalm 1:1–3 ESV

Everyone then who hears these words of mine and does them will be like a wise man who built his house on the rock. And the rain fell, and the floods came, and the winds blew and beat on that house, but it did not fall, because it had been founded on the rock. —Matthew 7:24–25 ESV

From these passages ...

What words are used to describe the person who follows the Lord Jesus? "Everyone who hears these words of mine and does them will be like _____who built ..."

What does he do with the words?

What are the results?

Rejecting Jesus: Choosing to Go My Own Way

God has given us the choice to go our own way without regard for him, but he warns of the effects of such living.

And everyone who hears these words of Mine and does not do them will be like a foolish man who built his house on the sand. And the rain fell, and the floods came, and the winds blew and beat against that house, and it fell, and great was the fall of it.
—Matthew 7:26–27 ESV

> **From this passage …**
>
> What words are used to describe the person who does not follow the Lord?
>
> What does he or she do with Jesus' words?
>
> What are the results?

Talking Points: Discuss the following with your leading friend:

1. In what ways am I living wisely, as these verses describe?

2. In what ways do I contribute to my own problems?

My Response

How have you responded to Jesus? How will you respond? Take a few moments to consider each of these responses. Which choice have you made? Discuss your choice with your leading friend.

> ✓ **Yes, I choose Jesus, but I will need help.**
>
> You are right to admit you can't do this alone. Jesus knows we are imperfect and that we need to grow in our faith and knowledge. Rest assured that Christ justifies [declares righteous] those who believe, even when our faith in Christ is young, wobbly, and fragile. Consider the following verses:

But to him who does not [depend on] work but believes on Him who justifies the ungodly, his faith is accounted for righteousness…. Therefore, having been justified by faith, we

have peace with God through our Lord Jesus Christ…
—Romans 4:5; 5:1

But as many as received Him, to them He gave the right to become children of God, to those who believe in His name: who were born, not of blood, nor of the will of the flesh, nor of the will of man, but of God. And the Word became flesh and dwelt among us, and we beheld His glory, the glory as of the only begotten of the Father, full of grace and truth.
— John 1:12–14

… but grow in grace and knowledge of our Lord and Savior Jesus Christ. —2 Peter 3:18.

I can do all things through Christ, who strengthens me.
—Philippians 4:13

✓ **No, I don't want to receive and follow Jesus. I'll do just fine on my own.**

Discuss your answer with your leading friend and consider 2 Corinthians 3:5: "Not that we are sufficient of ourselves to think of anything as being from ourselves, but our sufficiency is from God …" and John 15:5b "[Jesus said] … without Me you can do nothing."

✓ **No, I'm not convinced that Jesus is the answer for me.**

Discuss your answer with your leading friend and keep searching for the truth, but be diligent because we are not promised another day of life or even another breath. Look at the warning in Hebrews 3:12-13; "Beware, brethren, lest there be in any of you an evil heart of unbelief in departing from the living God; but exhort one another daily, while it is called 'Today,' lest any of you be hardened through the deceitfulness of sin."

✓ **No, I don't know what to believe.**

Discuss your answer with your leading friend and continue to seek God. "Ask, and it will be given to you; seek, and you will find; knock, and it shall be opened to you" Matthew 7:7.

Consider the importance of pursuing truth:

> My son, if you receive my words [Scripture], and treasure my commands within you, so that you incline your ear to wisdom, and apply your heart to understanding; yes, if you cry out for discernment, and lift up your voice for understanding, if you seek her as silver, and search for her as for hidden treasures; then you will understand the fear of the LORD, and find the knowledge of God. For the LORD gives wisdom; from His mouth come knowledge and understanding. —Proverbs 2:1–6

Studying Scripture to get to know God will help you to overcome your doubts and fears. Consider how Jesus answered the man who is called "doubting Thomas": "Jesus said to him, 'Thomas, because you have seen Me, you have believed. Blessed are those who have not seen and yet have believed'" (John 20:29).

It's time for a scheduled break to read W. Phillip Keller's book, *A Shepherd Looks at Psalm 23* with your leading friend. **Appendix A** contains a worksheet that may be helpful to get more out of each chapter in the book.

Part VI

WHO AM I?

Chapter 15

What Do I Really Want?

Understanding Desire and Longing

We are created beings with an empty space for the Creator in our souls; we were made to long for him. Longing has been defined as "a strong desire, especially for something [or someone] unattainable" [28] All of humanity is driven by desires or longings.

When I (Maria) was a senior in high school, I learned that my dad had adopted me, and my biological father had no idea I even existed. I had been walking with God for a few years by this time and figured it was no big deal. I had a dad and knew in my heart that he loved me. But after high school, he and my mom divorced, and what I had known as a family quickly dissolved.

During college, I struggled academically, socially, and spiritually. I had no idea who I was. I tried hard to trust God with all the turmoil in my past, but I began to long for someone, almost anyone, to take away the oppressive pain in my heart. I continued to pursue God but, even as I submitted to him and sought to live for him, there remained a deep cavern in my soul.

Some of our longings are born from an innate desire for God, but others come from hearts shaped by disappointment, neglect, and abuse. When Maria began to process the truth of her adoption, she became unsettled and lonely. A longing for her family to be whole again and a desire to be accepted and wanted began to shape the way she saw everything.

---

[28] Merriam-Webster's Collegiate Dictionary, Tenth Edition (Springfield, MO 1999), 687.

Desperate soul-consuming longings are often created by loss and suffering, but they can also be fueled by our own sinful desires and poor responses. The purpose of this chapter is to help identify and prioritize our longings, so that we are better able to understand what is motivating us and whether or not our desires are healthy.

Longing for God: Top Priority

"I spread out my hands to You; my soul longs for You like a thirsty land" (Psalm 143:6).

God created us to fellowship with him and to find our deepest longings fulfilled in him. But because we struggle to see him through the chaos of our painful circumstances, we may be drawn away from God and long for something tangible. This is why we continue to wrestle with unhealthy expectations and big doses of disappointment, especially in our human relationships. People were never meant to satisfy the depths of our souls. That special privilege is reserved for God and God only.

The desire for companionship was placed within us by the Creator himself. But our greatest and most crucial longing, whether we realize it or not, is for God. Secondary to that is a longing for meaningful human relationships. Read the following passages and fill in the blanks.

- Psalm 63:1 "O God, You are my God, early will I seek You; my soul _____; my flesh _____ in a dry and thirsty land where there is no water."

- Psalm 84:2 "My soul _____, yes, even _____ for the courts of the LORD; my heart and my flesh _____ for the living God."

As believers in Jesus Christ, we have access to the almighty Creator of the universe. When we get a glimpse of how amazing this is, we will be drawn to our God and Father like never before. As we grow in relationship with him, we will begin to love what he loves and to long for what he longs for. What awesome truth!

Talking Points: Pray and discuss the following with your leading friend.

1. Have I dealt with my doubt and anger toward God?

2. Do I trust him? What unresolved questions may hold me back?

3. Do I long for him? Describe that longing.

4. What do I long for most?

Treasure: Appropriate longings are born from a heart that is regularly being satisfied in Christ and ultimately wants to love and be loved like he does.

"Whom have I in heaven but You? And there is none upon earth I desire besides You. My flesh and my heart fail, but God is the strength of my heart and my portion forever" (Psalm 73: 25–26).

Identifying Desires That Draw Us Away From God

"But each one is tempted when he is drawn away by his own desires and enticed" (James 1:14).

Rayna wants *acceptance*, so she busies herself with an endless list of projects that she hopes will make people admire her. Shanae can't *control* her past, so she turns to things she thinks she can control. She responds in rage over the disappointing results. Dylan seeks isolation to keep himself *safe*, but he lives with deep loneliness and hopelessness.

Rayna and Dylan realize that they are running after the wrong things. So they talk to God about their need for him, using frank and honest words to express their sorrow, grief, pain, and intense suffering. They humbly confess how they have contributed to their own problems by allowing their desires to control them.

But Shanae is just plain angry and continues to demand an explanation as to how and why a loving God would have allowed such horror in her life. She wants answers. She wants to feel safe and in control and will do whatever it takes to feel that way. Shanae is rude and pushes people away, but deep down she longs for someone to trust; someone who is safe. God is her safe place, but will she seek him, or will she be drawn away from God by her feelings and desires?

We are born wanting. Babies spend their existence learning how to make their desires known and fulfilled. Eating, drinking, and wanting to be loved are all natural and good desires. However, as a child grows, she may begin to throw tantrums to get what she wants. If these fits aren't handled wisely, she will most likely grow up to be whiney and demanding. But if she is taught to wait and learns to discern wants from needs, she will become better able to navigate the course of her life.

When self-serving desires rule us, as they do Shanae, our pursuits can consume and leave us empty, angry, and unsatisfied. Identifying our desires is a helpful way to discover what motivates and shapes the way we live. As you read through the list below, ask God to reveal the desires that motivate you the most.

- **I want control over my life.** I believe that freedom and happiness rest upon my ability to resist being used by anyone anymore. Weakness is bad; I must be strong. If I don't get control, I pursue something else to have power over (for example anorexia, promiscuity, substances). For God's perspective, see 2 Corinthians 12:9–10.

- **I want nice things.** I believe that beautiful things will dull my pain and make life meaningful. Denying myself is bad; I must have the best. I will go deeply into debt to get these things. For God's perspective, see Luke 9:23–25 and Luke 12:15.

- **I want to be accepted, appreciated, acknowledged, and considered.** I believe that being loved is the most important thing. Rejection and ridicule will destroy me. If I don't get approval, I will seek to win it or withdraw in shame. For God's perspective, see Proverbs 29:25.

- **I want to feel safe.** I am deeply hurt by betrayal. I believe that people should protect me. Trust is very difficult for me. I will hide fearfully or lash out when others threaten me. For God's perspective, see Proverbs 3:5–6 and Psalm 37:1–6.

- **I want life to be fun and easy.** I've had enough trouble for a lifetime; I deserve to enjoy myself. I will pursue whatever makes me happy, and won't worry about the future. When life gets hard, I will divert myself to pleasurable things. For God's perspective, see Ecclesiastes 2:1 and Philippians 4:8–9.

- **I want peace.** I will avoid anything that suggests danger, discomfort, or conflict. I will hide or run rather than facing problems and risking emotional turmoil. For God's perspective, see John 16:33.

Unnoticed and unrestrained desires can lead us to misunderstand our identity and God's purpose for our lives. But we can choose not to be drawn away and enticed by our own desires (James 1:14). As we begin to understand who Jesus is and who we are in him, we will find that he is the fulfillment of our deepest longings. Jesus loves to rescue, redeem, and free us as we consistently respond to pain and shame by seeking him and trusting his Word.

"Search me, O God, and know my heart; Try me, and know my anxieties; and see if there is any wicked way in me, and lead me in the way everlasting" (Psalm 139:23–24).

Talking Points: Pray and discuss the following with your leading friend.

1. With which desires in the list above do I most identify?

2. In the chart below, list some of your own wants and longings:

Wants and Desires	Longings
I want a shower.	I feel dirty and ashamed. I just want to hide. Will I ever be clean?
I'm bored. I want someone to come over.	I am alone. Will anyone ever understand?

3. Which of my longings might be motivated by events from my past?

4. What typically satisfies my desires? How long does that satisfaction last?

5. How do I feel when my desires are met?

6. How do I typically respond when I don't get what I want?

7. Read and Colossians 3:2–3, 15–17 and Philippians 4:4–10. How does God offer to rescue us from the tyranny of desires?

A Hard and Hopeful Truth

Suffering of any kind can make us tend to forget our own sinfulness and our desperate need of the hope of the gospel. Although difficult, confessing to God that we are selfish and sinful can be very liberating. No matter how much we have been sinned against, we too are sinners who answer to a Holy God.

Acknowledging our sinful desires gives us a great view of the mercy and kindness of Jesus. God doesn't leave us in shame over our sin. He loves to lift up his child in the arms of his grace. Because of the sacrificial death, burial, and resurrection of Jesus Christ, we can be forgiven and set free to find our home in God our Father. Our longings are meant to lead us to the Lover of our souls and drive us to our knees in awe and adoration.

"Humble yourselves in the sight of the Lord, and He will lift you up" (James 4:10).

Look up Psalm 37:3–4. Fill in the following blanks:

"Trust _____, and do good, dwell in the land and feed on His faithfulness.

Delight yourself also _____, and He shall give you the desires of your heart."

Talking Points: Pray and discuss the following with your leading friend.

1. On the chart below, list the longings you wrote on the previous chart, then look at Scripture to see how Jesus fulfills each of these longings. It may be helpful to review "Who Is Jesus," to find applicable verses.

Longings	Longing Fulfilled in Christ
Example: I long for someone to understand the depths of my pain. No one does.	Jesus bears my grief and carries the weight of my sorrow (Isaiah 53:3–6)

150

2. In what ways has God been good to me?

3. How might Jesus be satisfying my longing soul as I seek him and offer him worship?

"Oh, that men would give thanks to the LORD for His goodness, and for His wonderful works to the children of men! For He satisfies the longing soul, and fills the hungry soul with goodness" (Psalm 107:8–9).

A Softening Ache

It is critical for us to understand that our longings will not be entirely satisfied until we see Jesus face to face. We will continue to feel the ache because we live in a fallen and pain-filled world as we wait eagerly for our final redemption. But our yearning hearts will settle as we begin to see that Jesus Christ, our Rescuer and Redeemer, is always at work to raise beauty from our ashes (Isaiah 61:1–3).

This world is not our home. We are pilgrims on a journey with a beautiful and redemptive purpose: to know Jesus as Savior, Redeemer, and Friend, and to make him known to a broken and shattered world. Let's keep moving forward by faith.

> If we find ourselves with a desire that nothing in this world can satisfy, the most probable explanation is that we were made for another world. —C. S. Lewis

Treasure: It is good to give thanks to the Lord; he satisfies my longing soul with goodness!

Chapter 16

Self-Image

"Who am I, O Lord GOD? And what is my house, that You have brought me this far?" —2 Samuel 7:18

Fueled by a belief that she is at fault for the abuse she suffered, Rayna thinks the harder she works, the more acceptable she will be. She finds her identity in accomplishments, appearances, and her social agenda, not realizing that even as a believer she is living as though God has turned away from her. Productivity keeps her feeling better until she stops to rest. When heavy layers of guilt, shame, and consuming feelings of emptiness descend on her, she jumps into another project as an escape. The cycle is exhausting and bewildering. Rayna is ready to learn who she is in Christ so that she can embrace a new way of living.

Dylan's heart is torn between a desire to be close to someone and an urge to run away. He wants companionship, but hates the way he feels about himself. Because he can't find peace, Dylan sees himself as a failure. He has prayed for Christ's forgiveness and help, but constant feelings of shame, exhaustion, grief, and incompetence keep him from turning to God. Instead, he punishes and isolates himself. His self-condemnation, lack of confidence, and blatant sin trap him in a self-made prison, leaving him grasping for meaning and hope. Dylan is tired of living as though he is dead; he is ready to listen to a different voice—God's voice.

Shanae is enraged about the many injustices she has suffered. She feels helpless to change what has happened to her, so she strikes out, hoping for some justice and vindication. She craves power and freedom, but sees herself as irreparably damaged. She seeks to escape her grief by turning to sex, money, and substances. But Shanae feels empty and frustrated. Her life is a desperate and futile search for happiness, and she is drowning in the cruelties of her victim identity.

> But You, O GOD the Lord, deal with me for Your name's sake; because Your mercy is good, deliver me. For I am poor and needy, and my heart is wounded within me. I am gone like a shadow when it lengthens; I am shaken off like a locust. My knees are weak through fasting, and my flesh is feeble from lack of fatness. I also have become a reproach to them; when they look at me, they shake their heads. Help me, O LORD my God! Oh, save me according to Your mercy, that they may know that this is Your hand—that You, LORD, have done it!... For He shall stand at the right hand of the poor, to save him from those who condemn him. —Psalm 109:21-27, 31

Mistaken Identity

Why am I here? Am I meant to be hurt? Am I damaged forever? I am confused, angry, and ashamed. I am a mess. Am I always going to be like this?

Sexual abuse, especially in childhood, attacks our identity, saturating the very core of our soul with lies. God designed sex to be a beautiful expression of mind, body, and soul; but abuse distorts that good purpose, lacing it with disgust and horror, violating our sense of worth, safety, and well-being—our very identity.

For those of us who were children, we had no emotional or mental capacity to process the abuse we suffered. That's not our fault; the minds and souls of children are simply not equipped to handle adult themes. Some of us had no voice, no defenders, and were forced to grapple silently with unspeakable violence. Who wouldn't have trouble with that? We did the best we could, but our conclusions and interpretations may not have been based in reality. We may now believe that abuse is normal, that no one cares, that we are hopelessly bad, worthless, stupid, unlovable, and unworthy of sympathy. Unknowingly we have built our identity upon lies. Is there any hope? Yes. Oh, most definitely yes. But it means re-learning. Our typical responses must be re-informed with truth so that we view ourselves, God, and our experiences accurately. This process can evoke powerful emotions; take care then to follow the pace God sets. God does not find fault with human frailty. He's happy when we move toward him, because he knows how much we need him. He has given us a foundation of truth—alive with hope—to correct our broken self-image.

> "All flesh is as grass, and all the glory of man as the flower of the grass. The grass withers, and its flower falls away, but the word of the LORD endures forever." … Therefore, laying aside all malice, all deceit, hypocrisy, envy, and all evil speaking, as newborn babes, desire the pure milk of the word, that you may grow thereby, if indeed you have tasted that the Lord is gracious. Coming to Him as to a living stone, rejected indeed by men, but chosen by God and precious … —1 Peter 1:24–2:5

Looking in the Right Mirror

When feeling especially emotional, resistant, or doubtful, the best approach is to ask, "What does God say about this?" Scripture, the perfect mirror, is a trustworthy place to learn about our identity, our purpose, and the way to make good changes. Sometimes the Bible is used to manipulate people into submission. Such use of Scripture is detestable because it maligns the character of our good and loving Father. God's Word, when read and taught with the Holy Spirit's guidance, is powerful and effective because it leads us step-by-step toward the beauty of Christlikeness. We must receive and trust that mirror even when it's hard to accept what we see there.

Talking Points: Pray and discuss the following with your leading friend.

1. Considering your story, what conclusions have you made about God and yourself?

2. How might that logic be clouding your view of who you truly are?

3. In what ways has your view of God changed so that you now see him more accurately?

4. How might knowing God more for who he really is help us to answer the question "Who am I"?

Taking Off the Mask

Before we begin to unpack the question *Who am I?*, let's take a good look in the mirror. Who do you see? What does she look like? What does he feel? What does she say and do? Based on what you see, circle the words below that describe him or her best.

Ashamed, loathsome, chaotic, forever damaged, angry, anxious, desperate, confused, stupid, bitter, dirty, gay, useless, messed up, misunderstood, a fake, a non-person, a slut, lost, overlooked, ignored, unwanted, confused, unlovable, broken, wounded, lonely, depressed, faithless, afraid, dead inside, used up … Happy, gentle, funny, nice, outgoing, wise, forgiving, trusting, talented, a comfort to my friends, genuine, strong, helpful, thoughtful, brave, beautiful, alive …

Now, which mirror did you look into? How did you come to your conclusions? Who or what determined your view?

I (Maria) have four boys, which means I hear phrases like "Mom! He called me stupid!" My typical response to that brokenhearted little boy is to tell him firmly, "No one gets to tell you who you are! Only God can do that." We can't allow our circumstances, mistakes, or even how we feel to define us. Scripture tells us that as believers in Jesus, we are children of God, dearly loved and accepted. Nothing or no one can ever change that!

"… to the praise of the glory of His grace, by which He made us accepted in the Beloved" (Ephesians 1:6).

Misunderstanding our true identity (looking in the wrong mirror) can cause us to come to some destructive conclusions. Mark the statements below that best describe your responses:

- I deny the seriousness of what happened to me.

- I minimize my own sin.

- I cling to people.

- I avoid people.

- No one cares. They couldn't handle the truth anyway.

- I am a victim.

- It's my fault. God wouldn't allow something so terrible. I must have deserved it.

- I have to save myself.

- I have to prove myself.

- God is weak. I have to take matters into my own hands.

- I am damaged and irredeemable.

- I need relief. I am an addict.

The exercises above are designed to help you express how you truly feel about yourself. Our abuser's sins have harmed us, but we are not defined by our experiences. Jesus invites us to take off the mask and to embrace our true identity in him. Your past has shaped you, but it does not define you.

"Search me, O God, and know my heart; try me, and know my anxieties; and see if there is any wicked way in me, and lead me in the way everlasting" (Psalm 139:23–24).

I Am Angry

Anger is a common feeling that is fueled by judgments about God, us, and our circumstances. Two factors govern our emotion of anger: (1) head: thoughts and beliefs, and (2) heart: motives, desires, passions, and will.

> Shanae is angry that her abuser has never been sorry for hurting her; angry that he shows no remorse while she lives with continual inner torment and physical consequences; angry that nothing eases her anguish; angry that her relationships are so difficult; angry that she feels hopeless and dead inside; angry that her life has produced nothing but pain, while her tormentors mock her from their perch of safety and prosperity.

When Shanae *thinks* about the terrible abuse she endured, she is tempted to believe that God is cruel (head) because she *wants* him to change her circumstances, so she *feels* angry that she can't make God do her will (heart). [29] If our conclusions and beliefs are not based in truth, we will suffer in a vicious cycle of bad thinking, unhealthy emotions, and self-pity. So, how do we stop the cycle?

We must align our beliefs and thoughts with truth, not just rely on our past conclusions and personal feelings.

We make the choice daily: *Will I allow my feelings to determine my faith, or will my faith tell my feelings the truth?*

> Shanae begins to pay attention to what her anger is "saying." When she experiences or sees injustice, she asks God for help and wisdom. Shanae is beginning to see that her anger flows from false beliefs that God doesn't care about her, justice will never happen, and that her life will never improve.

Shanae's anger is righteous when it objects to sin's perversions and destruction, but that is seldom the reason we feel angry. We can usu-

---

[29] Review Chapter 15 for more about longings of the heart.

157

ally justify ourselves and even validate our anger, but in fact our anger points to what we believe about God. Indulging unrighteous anger can quench faith. It helps to consider what our anger is saying. Do we believe that God was not there to help us in our suffering and that he is lenient with those who have hurt us? That is simply not true and it needs to be counteracted every time we realize what is going on.

Jesus Christ is God's ultimate gift of justice. He was murdered on a cross and buried in the cold earth because God was righteously angry. Scripture assures us that "The LORD tests the righteous, but the wicked and the one who loves violence His soul hates. Upon the wicked He will rain coals; fire and brimstone and a burning wind shall be the portion of their cup. For the LORD is righteous, He loves righteousness; His countenance beholds the upright" (Psalm 11:5–7). As we fix our eyes on Jesus, his Spirit will begin to settle the angry waters in our souls.

I Am Sad

Grief is defined as "keen mental suffering or distress over affliction or loss; sharp sorrow; painful regret."[30] Sadness is the honest expression of a soul that is deeply wounded by suffering and loss. Some of us may be tempted or feel pressured to deny or hide our pain, but feeling sad about evil and the suffering it brings is more than okay—even Christ himself grieved.

In Matthew 26:38 Jesus cries, "My soul is exceedingly sorrowful, even to death. Stay here and watch with Me."

From this verse ...

Did Jesus hide his sorrow? How sorrowful was he?

"O My Father, if this cup cannot pass away from Me unless I drink it, Your will be done" (Matthew 26:42).

---

[30] www.dictionary.com/browse/grief. Accessed May 30, 2018.

From this verse …

What did Jesus want God to do with his cup (sorrow, suffering and death)?

If the cup couldn't pass away, what was Jesus' attitude toward God?

God allowed Jesus to be sorrowful and to suffer knowing "… that He might redeem us from every lawless deed and purify for Himself His own special people" (Titus 2:14).

According to this verse …

Why did God allow Jesus to suffer and to be exceedingly sorrowful?

Jesus expressed his sorrow freely and with hope knowing that God creates treasure from ashes. Do you believe God can redeem your sorrow too? In what ways might God be transforming your sadness into a story for his glory and your peace?

> Rayna never allows herself to admit that she is sad. Instead, she distracts herself because she is ashamed and afraid of the emotional pain of grief. She doesn't recognize that life is worse because she bottles up her pain instead of expressing it as the psalmists did.

Rayna's pain has been magnified by her unwillingness to admit her sorrow. Take a few moments to look back at chapter 2 and refresh your memory about lamenting as the psalmists did. Although their grief was deep, they cried out to God, disciplined their thoughts, and believed that he would comfort, guide, and strengthen them.

Talking Points: Pray and discuss the following with your leading friend.

1. When you looked in the mirror, what and who did you see? By what standard did you assess yourself?

2. When does your anger flare up the most?

3. What is your anger saying? Identify your thoughts, beliefs, emotions, and actions.

4. When are you most sad?

5. Trace your sadness back to your beliefs and desires. Which of those thoughts contradicts what God says about himself and his involvement in your life?

6. What do you want that you are not getting right now?

7. Do you believe that God is faithful to care for you and that he will bring perfect justice in his time (Psalm 10:14-18)? If not, why?

Accepting Our True Identity

We are learning that we are not defined by our pain or our past, but we still haven't answered the question "Who am I?" Let's look more closely at God's view of self-image.

Regardless of our beliefs, God says all people have some things in common. Here are just a few:

1. We all have good qualities. "So God created man in His own image" (Genesis 1:27). All of humanity was designed to bless and glorify God by reflecting and magnifying his character. Every person worships, thinks, believes, feels, and has the capacity to love and do good things.

2. We all have bad qualities. "For all have sinned and fall short of the glory of God" (Romans 3:23). Everyone sins and contributes to the pain of this fallen world. To varying degrees, we all think poorly, worship the wrong things, believe lies, have twisted emotional responses, make unwise decisions, and love selfishly.

3. We all respond. Our experiences do not define us, but we do respond to them. Circumstances draw out what's already in our hearts, revealing what we believe, how we think and feel, and what we long for. God uses those thoughts, feelings, and desires to drive us to a place of decision. Will we turn to God, or to something else? Will we let pain destroy our spirit? Or will we exercise our faith to overcome evil with good? Responding to our circumstances is one thing we have freedom to control.

Every human being is a walking contradiction! We are made in God's perfect image, but in our freedom, we sin and mar that beautiful reflection. We live with the tension of that reality. Is it any wonder that we find ourselves confused about our identity?

> As a father pities his children, so the LORD pities those who fear Him. For He knows our frame; He remembers that we are dust. As for man, his days are like grass; as a flower of the field, so he flourishes. For the wind passes over it, and it is gone, and its place remembers it no more. But the mercy of the LORD is from everlasting to everlasting on those who fear Him.
> —Psalm 103:13–17

I Am a Child of God

God recognizes the magnitude of our self-image problems and has provided a beautiful solution. When we believe and receive Jesus, we are accepted as God's children, dearly loved, with eternal purpose and value. We are no longer defined by our experiences or emotions.

"But as many as received [Jesus], to them He gave the right to become children of God, to those who believe in His name" (John 1:12).

From this passage ...

When we receive Jesus, what right does he give us?

"And you, who once were alienated and enemies in your mind by wicked works, yet now He has reconciled in the body of His flesh through death, to present you holy, and blameless, and above reproach in His sight" (Colossians 1:21–22).

From this passage …

Jesus died to reconcile us to God. He did this … " to present you _____ and above reproach in his sight."

Holy and blameless in God's sight; this is who we are! "… He who has begun a good work in you will complete it" (Philippians 1:6).

The Spirit Himself bears witness with our spirit that we are children of God, and if children, then heirs—heirs of God and joint heirs with Christ, if indeed we suffer with Him, that we may also be glorified together. For I consider that the sufferings of this present time are not worthy to be compared with the glory which shall be revealed in us. —Romans 8:16–18

Choosing Well

"Fight the good fight of faith …" (1 Timothy 6:12).
Our longings and responses are deeply impacted by what we desire, think, and believe. We can't directly change how we feel, but we can begin to think differently. We must be ready to reject lies and to stop blaming others for what we have chosen to believe about ourselves. Our responses are our choice now.

So, what will you believe; the opinions and actions of people, or the truth of God's Word? Sometimes it's hard to know the difference, but the more time we spend with God, the clearer the choice becomes. Regardless of the logic we might have relied upon in the past, we can choose now to accept our true identity. We are children of God. We are his kids! Fighting to believe the truth is an exercise of faith. God doesn't condemn us for struggling; he commends us for coming to him and promises to give us everything we need (Psalm 69). "For a righteous person may fall seven times and rise again" (Proverbs 24:16.)

Talking Points: Pray and discuss the following with your leading friend.

1. Shanae responds to emotional pain angrily, Dylan by withdrawing, and Rayna by distracting herself with activity. How do you respond?

2. Look up Proverbs 4:23 and Romans 12:21 and write these verses in your journal:

Trust in the LORD, and do good; dwell in the land, and feed on His faithfulness. Delight yourself also in the LORD, and He shall give you the desires of your heart. Commit your way to the LORD, trust also in Him, and He shall bring it to pass. He shall bring forth your righteousness as the light, and your justice as the noonday. Rest in the LORD, and wait patiently for Him; do not fret because of him who prospers in his way, because of the man who brings wicked schemes to pass. Cease from anger, and forsake wrath; do not fret—it only causes harm. —Psalm 37:3–8

The Egg, The Carrot, and The Coffee Bean

A young woman went to her mother and told her about her life and how things were so hard for her. She did not know how she was going to make it and wanted to give up. She was tired of fighting and struggling.

Her mother took her to the kitchen. She filled three pots with water. In the first she placed carrots, in the second she placed eggs, and in the last she placed ground coffee beans. She let them sit and boil, without saying a word.

In about twenty minutes she turned off the burners. She fished the carrots out and placed them in a bowl. She pulled the eggs out and placed them in a bowl. Then she ladled the coffee out and placed it in a bowl.

Turning to her daughter, she asked, "Tell me; what do you see?"

"Carrots, eggs, and coffee," she replied. Her mother brought her closer and asked her to feel the carrots. She did and noted that they were soft and mushy. The mother then asked the daughter to take an egg and break it. After pulling off the shell, she observed the hard-boiled egg. Finally, the mother asked the daughter to sip the coffee.

The daughter smiled as she tasted its rich aroma. The daughter then asked, "What's the point, mother?"

Her mother explained that each of these objects had faced the same adversity—boiling water—but each reacted differently. The carrot went in strong, hard, and unrelenting. However, after being subjected to the boiling water, it softened and became weak. The egg had been fragile. Its thin outer shell had protected its liquid interior, but after sitting through the boiling water, its inside had become hardened. The ground coffee beans were different, however. After they were in the boiling water, they had changed the water.

"Which are you?" she asked her daughter.

"When adversity knocks on your door, how do you respond? Are you a carrot, an egg, or a coffee bean?"

Think of this: Which am I? Am I the carrot that seems strong, but with pain and adversity do I wilt and become soft and lose my strength?

Am I the egg that starts with a malleable heart, but changes with the heat? Did I have a teachable spirit, but after a death, a breakup, a financial hardship or some other trial, have I become hard and inflexible? Does my shell look the same, but on the inside am I bitter and tough with a bitter spirit and hardened heart?

Or am I like the coffee bean? The bean changes the hot water, the difficult condition that brings the pain, into coffee! When the water gets hot, it releases the fragrance and flavor. If you are like the bean, when things are at their worst, you get better and change the situation around you. When the hour is darkest and trials are the greatest, do you improve the situation?

How do you handle adversity? Are you a carrot, an egg, or a coffee bean? [31]

---

[31] Author unknown. http://heavensinspirations.com/carrots-eggs-coffee.html. Accessed 5/1/2017.

Chapter 17

Embracing Our True Identity

"Let us cast off the works of darkness, and let us put on the armor
of light … put on the Lord Jesus Christ." —Romans 13:12,14

As true believers in Christ, we are clothed in his righteousness and
protected by the armor of his light. Now we are ready to embrace
and "put on" our new identity (Ephesians 4:24). If we have come to
Jesus by faith, we are redefined. We need only to believe that we are
a new creation in him.

What Does God Think of Me?

Read Ephesians 1:3–14 below. Notice how God describes us and what
he has given us according to the riches of his grace. God is good and
merciful to us because he loves us, not because we deserve it. We can't
earn his grace; it is his gift to us.

> Blessed be the God and Father of our Lord Jesus Christ, who
> *has blessed us* with every spiritual blessing in the heavenly places
> in Christ, just as *He chose* us in Him before the foundation of
> the world, that we should be holy and *without blame* before
> Him in *love*, having predestined us to *adoption* as sons by Jesus
> Christ to Himself, according to the good pleasure of His will,
> to the praise of the glory of His grace, by which He made us
> accepted in the Beloved. In Him we have redemption through
> His blood, the forgiveness of sins, according to the riches of His
> grace which He made to abound toward us in all wisdom and
> prudence, having made known to us the mystery of His will,
> according to His good pleasure which He purposed in Himself,
> that in the dispensation of the fullness of the times He might
> gather together in one all things in Christ, both which are in
> heaven and which are on earth—in Him. In Him also we have

obtained an inheritance, being predestined according to the purpose of Him who works all things according to the counsel of His will, that we who first trusted in Christ should be to the praise of His glory. In Him you also trusted, after you heard the word of truth, the gospel of your salvation; in whom also, having believed, you were sealed with the Holy Spirit of promise, who is the guarantee of our inheritance until the redemption of the purchased possession, to the praise of His glory.
—Ephesians 1:3–14

In Christ I Am ...

As redeemed children of God, we are forever changed! Believers in Jesus have a divine and eternal inheritance, a new family, and a new purpose. Ephesians chapter 1 is a great description of our new identity. Fill in the following blanks using Ephesians 1:3–14 above (the first few are done for you):

- In Christ, I am **blessed**.

- In Christ, I am **chosen**.

- In Christ, I am **holy** (set apart for him).

- In Christ, I am **blameless**. (He does not hold my sin against me.)

- In Christ, I am **loved**.

- In Christ, I am **adopted**.

- In Christ, I am _____.

- In Christ, I am _____.

- In Christ, I am _____.

- In Christ, I have _____.

- In Christ, I have _____.

- In Christ, I have _____.

Write Ephesians 1:3–14 on paper and read it often, remembering that this is God's image of a believer, so we can embrace it as our self-image, too. When insecurity comes, read the verses again. They are true regardless of how we feel. Doubt begins to fade when it is diligently and consistently replaced with truth.

> When Rayna realizes that she is trying to earn God's acceptance, she reminds herself that God identifies her as holy and without blame in his love. She is accepted because she is in Christ, not because of her productivity. Her acceptance doesn't depend upon other people's treatment and she doesn't have to work to be loved or forgiven. When she feels unworthy, she tells herself, "I am blameless, accepted, and loved by God."

> Dylan sees himself as a failure, but he is actually set apart with every spiritual blessing in Christ. He fights negative feelings by reminding himself that his flaws are not his identity. God graciously sees him as redeemed, loved, forgiven, and accepted in the Beloved. When Dylan feels like withdrawing in despair, he tells himself, "I am blessed, redeemed, loved, forgiven, and accepted in Christ. I have hope in him."

> Shanae's love of control frustrates her. She can't see that the sovereign, all-powerful God has given her an eternal purpose. She has been chosen and set apart to follow Jesus, but she can't see where God is taking her, so she resists because he won't give her the explanation she demands. Jesus invites Shanae to give up her need for control and to trust him. If she turns to him, he will infuse her with hope and new insights into his plan for her life. But she must choose to follow him.

"For you did not receive the spirit of bondage again to fear, but you received the Spirit of adoption by whom we cry out, 'Abba, Father.' The Spirit Himself bears witness with our spirit that we are children of God" (Romans 8:15–16).

From these verses ...

Do you believe that God chose and adopted you, and sees you as holy and blameless, even if it doesn't feel that way right now?

If not, review chapters 3–4 to be reminded of God's good character.

"The LORD has appeared of old to me, saying: Yes, I have loved you with an everlasting love; therefore with loving kindness I have drawn you" (Jeremiah 31:3).

From this verse ...

How long will God's love last?

How does he draw us?

[The LORD] has not dealt with us according to our sins, nor punished us according to our iniquities. For as the heavens are high above the earth, so great is His mercy toward those who fear Him ... As a father pities his children, so the LORD pities those who fear Him. For He knows our frame; He remembers that we are dust. —Psalm 103:10–14

... for He who touches you touches the apple of His eye. —Zechariah 2:8

According to these verses ...

What is God like?

What does God think of me, and of you?

From the verses above we see that he loves us with an everlasting love, is full of mercy toward us, doesn't punish us according to our sin, knows our frame, remembers that we are dust, is full of compassion, and has pity on us. He is our good and kind Father. No matter what we have done or what has been done to us, we are God's precious, beloved, and accepted children. That's what he thinks of you and me.

In Christ ... I Am Forgiven

"There is therefore now no condemnation to those who are in Christ Jesus" (Romans 8:1).

> Dylan condemns himself for his faults and failures. He is imperfect and he knows it. He believes that Jesus forgives him enough to get him to heaven when he dies, but he struggles to believe that his forgiveness really extends to him now. He hates himself for falling short. But as Dylan grows in the knowledge of Christ's forgiveness and acceptance, he learns to believe that Jesus cleanses him when he tells Jesus about his sin. Dylan realizes more and more that Jesus doesn't want him to punish himself, because Jesus already took all Dylan's punishment. Jesus will never bring up his sin again to use it against him. He is forgiven forever. He is safe in him. Dylan realizes that no one can take away what Jesus has given him. Dylan begins to feel relief—he can breathe.

Through faith in Christ, we are completely forgiven. Clean! Jesus took away the guilt and penalty we deserve. God will never use our sins and faults to accuse, shame, or condemn us. Instead, he will teach us about himself, remind us of our identity in Christ, and how to live in this fallen world.

"If we say that we have no sin, we deceive ourselves, and the truth is not in us. If we confess our sins, He is faithful and just to forgive us our sins and to cleanse us from all unrighteousness" (1 John 1:8–9).

According to this verse ...

How much of our sin and unrighteousness does God promise to forgive and cleanse?

But I don't feel forgiven because ...

God wants us to confess the sin that comes to mind and to believe that he forgives and cleanses us from all of our sin. Once sin is confessed, any further feelings of guilt or condemnation can be rejected. They are not true.

"Most assuredly, I say to you, he who hears My word and believes in Him who sent Me has everlasting life, and shall not come into judgment [condemnation], but has passed from death into life" (John 5:24).

In Christ … I Am Fully Known and Accepted

"… to the praise of the glory of His grace, by which He made us accepted in the Beloved" (Ephesians 1:6).

Shanae attempts to drown her shame in anger and wild behavior. With every fiber of her spirit, she cries out for an explanation for the injustice and evil she has suffered. "Why, God? Why?" She's angry and afraid to be known by God or anyone else because she feels so ashamed. Nothing erases the taunting, cruel voices that tell her it's all her fault and that she'll never measure up. Shanae feels dirty and damaged, but she can't bring herself to talk to God about it. She doesn't trust God.

The voices Shanae hears are from her accusers, not from Jesus. Christ's voice calls to her in her wilderness of misery. Jesus tells her she is already fully known and accepted, and he invites her to come to him. She doesn't know what that means, and she is afraid. In her experience, to be known is to be mocked and condemned. She has been betrayed before; she steels herself against anyone who would use enticing lies to lure her into another trap. She will never let anyone hurt her again.

But she is already being hurt. Shanae doesn't see that her attempts to cover her shame have locked her in a prison of her own making. Her life has been marked with unspeakable suffering at the hands of her abuser, but her efforts to cover shame and escape oppression have led her to a miserable refuge of loneliness, destructiveness, and futility. Jesus offers her the key: removal of shame through forgiveness and acceptance into his family. He doesn't promise to answer all her questions, but he does promise to unlock her prison and make something beautiful of her life.

> For you were once darkness, but now you are light in the
> Lord. Walk as children of light (for the fruit of the Spirit is
> in all goodness, righteousness, and truth), finding out what
> is acceptable to the Lord. And have no fellowship with the
> unfruitful works of darkness, but rather expose them. For it is
> shameful even to speak of those things which are done by them
> in secret. But all things that are exposed are made manifest by
> the light, for whatever makes manifest is light. Therefore he
> says: "Awake, you who sleep, Arise from the dead, and Christ
> will give you light." —Ephesians 5: 8–14

The passage above can be used inappropriately to say that we shouldn't talk about sexual abuse. However, the context reveals that it is shameful to talk about sin in an approving way, out of a desire to participate in evil or to delight in the sins of others. These verses actually encourage us to expose abuse so that Jesus can shed his light in that dark and lonely place. His light exposes evil for what it is: not something desirable, but something destructive and wicked.

God knows every detail and even with all the shameful and painful things in our lives, he still loves and accepts us. This is grace. Embrace the freedom to expose the darkness of your story to the light of Jesus Christ by talking with Him and someone you trust about your experiences and emotions.

> When Shanae found the courage to talk about her abuse, she
> began to wrestle with powerful emotions—as though years of
> bottled-up poison broke loose. But as she cries out to God and
> reads Scripture, the Spirit is leading her to a place of relief and
> freedom. But it's going to take hard and honest work.

> I sought the LORD, and He heard me, and delivered me
> from all my fears. They looked to Him and were radiant,
> and their faces were not ashamed. This poor man cried
> out, and the LORD heard him, and saved him out of all
> his troubles … The LORD is near to those who have a

broken heart, and saves such as have a contrite spirit.

—Psalm 34:4–6, 18

According to these verses ...

What did the psalmist do?

What was God's response?

How does God treat imperfect and brokenhearted people?

Talking Point: Pray and discuss the following with your leading friend.

1. What parts of your story trigger feelings of rejection and abandonment?

Take some time to read Luke 6:17–19; 8:43-48, and 1 Peter 2:9–10. These are beautiful accounts of Jesus' kindness. Choose a few verses that are especially meaningful for you, write them out, and read them often. God will use the light of Scripture to assure you of his everlasting love and acceptance.

Shanae is learning to identify the negative statements she makes when she is angry, including "I deserve better!" "I shouldn't have to go through this!" "No one loves me." She struggles to stay focused on Scripture, so she writes verses on her inner forearm and on note cards. Her learning friend encouraged her to write out the "I am" statements from Ephesians 1:3–14 and is helping her apply truth when she feels angry and wants to take control. She programmed her phone to remind her to read Scripture every morning and is also learning how to journal. Before bed, she reads her verses again and thanks God for specific ways he has seen her through another day. At first, these things seem impossible to remember. She feels awkward and even resentful, but she pushes through her feelings. She fights the urge to quit by reminding herself that her own way has led only to heartache. As she yearns for control, she tells God how she feels and seeks to do what she knows God wants. As she struggles to trust God, she is beginning to recognize how actively he is helping her: her anger is decreasing as her desire to pursue Christ is increasing.

Treasure: I still sin and make mistakes, my past is still painful, and I may feel insecure; but in Christ I am no longer shameful, dirty, damaged, bad, rejected, or alone. I am fully known and accepted.

In Christ ... I Am Free

"Therefore if the Son makes you free, you shall be free indeed" (John 8:36).

What does freedom in Christ look like?

- **Freedom is not** license to do whatever we want. **Freedom is** having the choice to get to know God and to follow him well, confident and trusting that he is for us (Matthew 6:33; Romans 6; 8:30–39).

- **Freedom is not** the end of pain. **Freedom is** hope in the midst of pain, because we are accepted and loved. We are on our journey home and we will reach our destination. Christ, who suffered immeasurable pain to rescue us, is the way (1 Peter 2:20–25).

- **Freedom does not mean** everything works as we think it should (after all, we still live in a fallen world). **Freedom means** there is no condemnation for us, even though we continue to be imperfect beings in need of change and growth. God frees us from all spiritual condemnation and gradually transforms us into Christ's image (2 Corinthians 3:18). An ongoing tension exists between the reality of who we are in Christ and how we see ourselves. We have perfect standing in Christ, yet we live in a fallen world as sinners among sinners longing for home, knowing we will get there, and knowing he walks with us to show us the way (Luke 9:23–24; Hebrews 12:5–11).

- **Freedom is not** an escape from the consequences of bad behavior or attitudes. **Freedom is** choosing to trust that God will work all things together for good. Our past includes inexpressible abuses we cannot forget, and our responses (past and present) may bring more pain in addition to that suffering. Freedom recognizes that God's goodness is never hindered by our suffering or failures, but God is teaching us as he leads us to a better way of living (Matthew 7:27–29; Romans 8:28–38).

"Then Jesus said to those Jews who believed Him, 'If you abide in My word, you are My disciples indeed. And you shall know the truth, and the truth shall make you free"… Therefore if the Son makes you free, you shall be free indeed'" (John 8:31–32; 36).

According to these verses …

Where and with whom do we find freedom?

In what ways has Jesus already set you free? In what ways would you still like him to?

The Spirit of the Lord God is upon Me [Christ], because the LORD has anointed Me to preach good tidings to the poor; He has sent Me to heal the brokenhearted, to proclaim liberty to the captives, and the opening of the prison to those who are bound; to proclaim the acceptable year of the LORD, and the day of vengeance of our God; to comfort all who mourn, to console those who mourn in Zion, to give them beauty for ashes, the oil of joy for mourning, the garment of praise for the spirit of heaviness; that they may be called trees of righteousness, the planting of the LORD, that He may be glorified.
—Isaiah 61:1–3

In Christ … I Am Loved

"As the Father loved Me, I also have loved you; abide in My love" (The words of Jesus from John 15:9).

Jesus loves me, this I know
For the Bible tells me so.
Little ones to Him belong,
They are weak but He is strong.
Yes, Jesus loves me,
Yes, Jesus loves me.
Yes, Jesus loves me.
The Bible tells me so. [32]

Dylan struggles to believe that God loves him or that *anyone* loves him, for that matter. He believes that he is utterly and completely unlovable. His family ridicules and rejects him. He has no friends and people at work are distant. He keeps himself isolated most of the time. Dismally he wonders, "Why would anyone want to know and love a loser like me?"

Dylan thinks that God's love is extended only to worthy people, and that being abused has disqualified him. But after hearing a sermon at church, he realized that God's love was demonstrated in mankind's darkest hour, while we were all at our worst. Everyone turned away from Christ, yet he still sacrificed himself for us. Dylan is beginning to recognize that he doesn't have to earn God's love. The warm light of Christ's acceptance is beginning to dawn on Dylan's soul, and he hungers to know God more. Because he is in Christ, he is forgiven and accepted (Ephesians 1:6–8; 2:1–9). Armed with truth, he wrestles with his feelings of condemnation and rejection by declaring: Jesus loves me. The Bible tells me so!

"For I am persuaded that neither death nor life, nor angels nor principalities nor powers, nor things present nor things to come, nor height nor depth, nor any other created thing, shall be able to separate us from the love of God which is in Christ Jesus our Lord" (Romans 8:38–39).

---

[32] "Jesus Loves Me," a hymn by William Bradbury, as published in *The Celebration Hymnal* (Word/Integrity Music, 1997) 185.

From this passage ...

What can separate us from the love of God?

Write your responses to the following statements:

* *God has lavished his love on me because he is good.*

* *God is not mad at me.*

God's love toward his children is everlasting, unchanging, and complete. Although we remain unworthy, he lavishes his love upon us out of his goodness. Our failures, sins, and faults will never diminish his love toward us.

In Christ ... I Am Cared For and Cherished

I am not abandoned, orphaned, or despised.

Really? God cares? Then why did he let my abuser do that to me?
This truth can be awfully hard to believe. The question "Why?" is universal and urgent. Everyone wants to know why God does what he does. We have touched on this question already (see chapter 3), but ultimately we can't completely answer why. In the Bible, we read of Job who experienced enormous losses and suffering. He cried out and begged God to explain. Instead, God asked him questions, reminding Job that he doesn't owe anyone an explanation. Even though we have suffered grievously, faith accepts God for who he is and asks questions reverently without demanding answers (James 4:1–10).

When our questions remain unanswered, we can exercise our faith by trusting in the truths that God has already revealed. For example, we know:

- Scripture is completely true and sufficient. No matter what! (Hebrews 4:12, Psalm 12:6)

- God is always good, loving, and caring (1 Corinthians 10:13; Romans 8:28–29).

- God's agenda is different than ours: He is impacting people's souls with truth, and because souls are eternal everything else is temporary (John 6:40; 2 Corinthians 4:15–18).

- God is right and just—no matter what! (Psalm 72:4)

God promises to meet our needs, not to keep us from evil or to give us everything we want. We may not understand his ways, but we can choose to dwell on his goodness rather than fixating on evil. As finite beings, we don't know what's best and our desires are tainted by deceitful hearts. Sadly, we can be so preoccupied and fearful that we overlook the many ways God provides for us each day. We must fight to believe that he is active on our behalf in the midst of this harsh world, even if we don't understand him. God is perfectly wise, completely loving, and working out a redemptive story far beyond our ability to perceive. He knows that we struggle and offers unending grace and mercy. God is good; we can trust him.

"… casting all your care upon Him, for He cares for you"(1 Peter 5:7).

Talking Points: Pray and discuss the following with your leading friend.

1. How might life be different if we choose to turn our thoughts to God's grace and goodness instead of indulging our feelings?

2. Think about your favorite psalm (e.g., Psalm 11 or 143). What qualities of God are mentioned in that psalm? Write down how God helps us in this fallen world.

3. Expressing gratitude helps us to recognize the provisions God is constantly making for us. How is he taking care of you? Make a list and add to it often, thanking God for his goodness to faithfully provide for you.

In Christ ... I Am Clean

To those who receive him, Jesus says, "*You are already clean* because of the word which I have spoken to you. Abide in Me, and I in you. As the branch cannot bear fruit of itself, unless it abides in the vine, neither can you, unless you abide in Me" (John 15:3–4).

From this passage ...

If you have put your faith in Jesus, how does He describe you? "*already* _____"

How does He ask us to respond to that truth? "_____ *in Me*"

What do you think it means to "*abide in Him*"?

"But if we walk in the light as He is in the light, we have fellowship with one another, and the blood of Jesus Christ His Son cleanses us from all sin.... If we confess our sins, He is faithful and just to forgive us our sins and to cleanse us from all unrighteousness" (1 John 1:7–9).

According to this passage ...

What or who cleanses us?

What is our responsibility?

When we receive Jesus, he washes away all of our shame and guilt. He makes us clean. Notice that he doesn't tell us to clean up. However, he does ask us to walk in his beautiful light, to have fellowship with other believers, and to confess our own sin. So, no matter what our past may contain, God clothes us with a new identity and begins to retell our story in light of his beautiful and redeeming grace.

In Christ ... I Am Sexually Pure

"So God created man in His own image; in the image of God He created him; male and female He created them" (Genesis 1:27).

Because childhood sexual abuse left her with intense loathing about sex, Rayna struggles with intimacy in her marriage. She hates her body for feeling good when she was being abused. She detests the constant reminders of this ultra-personal betrayal and violation. Even though she loves her husband, she hasn't been able to overcome her negative feelings about sex. She feels defiled. If not for her husband's patience and kindness, she wonders if they would still be married.

Being sexually abused can cause profound damage to our understanding of sex. God created us male and female and his design for sex is good, but our dark experiences challenge and taint this beautiful truth. Rayna's dad exposed her to sexual intimacy at a very young age; it's no wonder she's confused and hates her own body. But she is not defined or defiled by what her dad did to her or by what she thinks about it.

In Mark 7:15, Jesus offers us great hope. He said, "There is nothing which enters a man from outside which can defile him; but the things which come out of [his heart], those are the things that defile a man."

From this verse …

Can anyone else defile us?

Where does defilement come from?

We are not responsible for what has happened to us, but we are exhorted to guard and guide our own hearts. Proverbs 4:23 reads, "Keep your heart with all diligence, for out of it spring the issues of life." What freedom! No one can defile another; no matter how impure the offense. As we seek Jesus and allow him to transform our own hearts, he will change our thinking and we will begin to see sex as the beautiful and pure act that God intends it to be.

A thorough discussion of this subject goes beyond the scope of this book, so our purpose in this section is to heighten awareness of God's magnificent design and encourage further biblical study. [33] Here are some basic truths about sex from Scripture:

---

[33] Recommended books on human sexuality include the following: Robert Smith, M.D., *Biblical Principles of Sex* (Hackettstown, NJ: Timeless Texts, 2003); Ed & Gayle Wheat, *Intended for Pleasure* (Fleming H. Revell, 1977); *Biblical Principles of Love, Sex, and Dating* (Lafayette, IN: Faith Resources); David Powlison, *Sexual Assault: Healing Steps for Victims* (Greensboro,

God's Design for Sex:

- God designed sex to be very good (Genesis 1:31).

- God designed sex to be an expression of a believer's devotion and purity in Christ (2 Corinthians 11:2–3).

- Sex was created to be holy and exclusively within the union of one man and one woman in marriage (Genesis 1:27–28; 1 Corinthians 7:1–4).

- Sex within a biblical marriage fulfills the plan of the Creator and is, therefore, as holy as any other expression of devotion to God, including prayer and Scripture reading (Genesis 2:25).

God's Purpose for Sex:

- Procreation (bearing children), not self-gratification (Malachi 2:14–15).

- Unity and relationship-building (affection) in marriage (1 Corinthians 7:3).

- Picturing the relationship of Christ and the church (Ephesians 5:23–24).

- Protection from temptation (1 Corinthians 7:5, 9).

- Pleasure for both husband and wife, when a couple is biblically married and actively seeking one another's well-being (Proverbs 5:18–19; 1 Corinthians 13:1–8).

Sexual Confusion

Experiencing sex in an abusive and manipulative way can evoke deep and gripping confusion. Our culture's acceptance of fornication, pornography, gender neutrality or fluidity, and homosexuality makes addressing our own sexual confusion very difficult.

NC: New Growth Press, 2010); Brad & Cheryl Tuggle, *A Healing Marriage* (NavPress, 2004); Paul David Tripp, *Sex in a Broken World* (New Growth Press, 2018).

Being sexually abused, especially by someone we love, can distort our God-given desire for relationships. Having an intimate connection with anyone outside of marriage awakens sexual and emotional desires, creating bonds that were meant only for the permanent relationship of marriage. Promiscuity and same-sex attraction are natural expressions of this confusion. An innocent desire for meaningful relationships can easily turn sexual, causing deep shame and guilt.

Learning to identify the thoughts that provoke sexual feelings will help us to understand what is motivating our behavior. When an otherwise healthy relationship begins to stir sexual desire, we can ask, "What do I want and why?" Then tell ourselves these truths: "I don't have to give in; God wants sex to be pure and beautiful within a loving marriage, and I don't need to have these desires fulfilled. I have all that I need in Christ. If God wants to bless me with a sexually satisfying relationship, I'll wait for him to do that. I am sexually pure. How beautiful! How freeing."

Body Memories

Body memories have been defined as "a sensory recollection of traumatic experiences related to pain, discomfort, tension, and arousal."[34] These memories can be unexpected and very powerful. Our bodies respond physically as if the abuse is occurring again. They are usually triggered by a stimulus, such as a picture, a smell, a sound, a certain food, a touch, a memory, or a nightmare, but the cause is not always easily identified.

When experiencing body memories:

1. Dwell on truth

As real as it may seem, the abuse is not happening again. It may be frightening and feel horrible, but we must tell ourselves, "This is not real. My body is responding to something awful that happened in the past. I am not crazy. God is with me and he will get me through this." It will be help-

---

[34] Pam Nugent, "Body Memory" (April 7, 2013, https://psychologydictionary.org/body-memory), Accessed June 23, 2018.

ful to pray and to recall Scripture that assures us of God's care, such as Romans 5:1–2 and 1 Peter 5:7.

2. *Patiently endure*

The body memory will go away eventually. While remaining as calm as possible, we are overcoming not only the present body memory, but also the fear of future body memories.

3. *Tell someone you trust*

Telling someone you trust can limit the intensity of the experience and may resolve it entirely. Ask for prayer from your leading friend or another believer you trust.

Be assured that Jesus accepts us right where we are and receives us with an everlasting love. He is gently healing and changing us, even in this sensitive way. We can walk patiently with him through the process, knowing that he will lead us with wisdom and love on our journey home.

From the lists above, circle concepts that are new or unfamiliar to you. Write out any questions or concerns and discuss them with your leading friend or someone you trust.

He will gather the lambs with His arm, and carry them in His bosom, and gently lead those who are with young.... Lift up your eyes on high, and see who has created these things, who brings out their host by number; He calls them all by name, by the greatness of His might, and the strength of His power; not one is missing.... The everlasting God, the LORD, the Creator of the ends of the earth, neither faints nor is weary. His understanding is unsearchable. He gives power to the weak, and to those who have no might He increases strength. Even the youths shall faint and be weary, and the young men shall utterly fall. But those who wait on the LORD shall renew their strength; they shall mount up with wings like eagles, they shall run and not be weary, they shall walk and not faint.

—Isaiah 40:11, 26, 28–31

In Christ … I Am an Overcomer

"You are of God, little children, and have overcome them, because He who is in you is greater than he who is in the world" (1 John 4:4).

Rayna's young daughter runs flushed with excitement into the kitchen where Rayna is washing the dishes. "Mommy, come and look at the pretty butterflies!" Engrossed in her task, Rayna absently responds, "In a minute. I'm busy." Several minutes later, she remembers that her daughter wanted her to come outside. "Oh, I missed the moment," Rayna thinks as she starts the vacuum cleaner.

When Rayna's days are not filled with activities and projects, she feels restless and anxious, unable to measure up. Her busyness is her shield to keep her "safe." She invests herself in tasks because she feels more acceptable with measurable accomplishments. But when she can't finish something, when people interrupt her, or when something goes wrong, anxiety and hopelessness quickly consume her.

Although Rayna has received Christ, she fails to understand the depth and beauty of his forgiveness and love. Her self-reliance blinds her to Christ's full payment for her sins and shortcomings. She could have comfort, peace, and an abundant life in him, but she turns to productivity instead. She doesn't realize that she is deeply loved and accepted.

Rayna fears telling her story because she thinks she won't be believed and that she'll hurt her family. She is afraid to trust, she fears reliving the memories and expects the worst to happen. Fear is a huge reason we hide behind masks or lose ourselves in activities. All our lives we will be tempted to fear, and we may not even recognize that fear can be a primary motivator—our functional god.

Instead, we can turn to the true and living God who has promised to redeem everything that touches his children, in his perfect timing (Romans 8:28–29). God is with us and he is for us (Psalm 139:7–12; Romans 8:31). Jesus gives us hope and power to overcome fear, despair, hopelessness, and anxiety. As we grow in love and learn to put our hope in God, he will show us how his "perfect love casts out fear" (1 John 4:18). The next time Rayna's daughter asks her to enjoy the butterflies, Rayna can think, "What does Jesus want me to do right now? Does he want me to be frantically cleaning my house or showing love to my daughter?" Those simple questions define our priorities and push fear aside in favor of love.

Choosing to trust God rather than our own efforts is challenging. But as we exercise faith, doubt and fear will no longer paralyze us, and gratitude will become the expression of our hearts. This is when fear is replaced by love.

Each day, read one or two of the verses below. As you read, briefly summarize what you learn about trust and hope. Write out the verses you find most helpful and put them where you will read them every day.

Psalm 42:8; 63:3; 86:13; 100:5; 103:4; 145:8–9;
Isaiah 43:1–3
Jeremiah 31:3; 31:14
Hosea 2:19–20; Zephaniah 3:17; Malachi 1:2
John 3:16; 15:13; 17:23, 26
Romans 5:8; 8:38–39
Galatians 2:20; 2 Thessalonians 2:16; Titus 3:1–4
Hebrews 12:5–6
1 John 3:1; 4:7–10; 4:16; 4:18–19

In Christ ... I Am Grateful

"In everything give thanks; for this is the will of God in Christ Jesus for you" (1 Thessalonians 5:17).

Suffering and pain can cause "gratitude amnesia." When we grieve, fear, despair, or rage, we tend to get caught up in emotion and forget about God or doubt him. But there is always something good happening in and around us. Scripture has lots of good things to say about God's good character and his activity in our lives and in our world. We can look through our pain and give thanks for what we see God has done, even when our situation remains difficult. Gratitude does more for us than we may realize.

Take a moment to write fifteen things for which you are thankful today. We will share a few of our own: ten fingers, the ability to read and pray, friends, a place to live, and a good rain.

Sing a hymn of praise to God. If you don't know one, make one up by singing a favorite Bible verse (or Psalm 150).

Treasure:

"... your life is hidden with Christ in God. When Christ who is our life appears, then you also will appear with Him in glory."
—Colossians 3:3b–4

Part VII

WHO ARE YOU?

Chapter 18

Laying the Groundwork

What is a relationship? The intersection of the stories of two people; the problem is that an awful lot of carnage takes place at this intersection. [35]

Maintaining healthy relationships is challenging, no matter who you are, but when lies, deception, and manipulation have been the theme of your life, relating well to anyone can feel impossible. This part of our study will help us discover God's purpose for relationships, how to navigate the ever present challenges, and to begin our walk through the valley of forgiveness and redemption.

Longing for Happily Ever After

In Disney's *An American Tail*, a desperate little mouse sings, "Somewhere out there ... someone's thinking of me, and loving me tonight." Can you hear the sweet music and feel his longing as if it were your own? We sing along with that little mouse because we too long to be thought of and loved.

God has created us, in his image, as community, to need and desire meaningful relationships, but when they prove to be difficult and disappointing, we can begin to lose hope. Maybe that's why Disney does not produce reality TV. If Cinderella didn't have some issues to deal with after living with that wicked woman and her nasty daughters, then she must be—a cartoon! Hmmm.

Why is relating to others so challenging? Our own pain, pride, and selfish ambition tempt us to expect and demand things from people

---

[35] Tim Lane and Paul David Tripp, *Relationships: A Mess Worth Making* (Greensboro, NC: New Growth Press, 2006), 63.

rather than relying on God, but the basic fact is that we live as sinners among sinners in a fallen world, and that causes a lot of trouble. [36] Our culture can also influence our perspective. From the day we began to watch television our dreams, self-image, and view of other people has been manipulated. As a result, we build towers toward unattainable dreams, have an inflated sense of self, and we use people to maintain it all. It is part of our sinful nature to think more highly of ourselves than we ought, and we hurt each other deeply in the process. We simply have a wrong view of our purpose for being on this planet.

Relationships come in all shapes and sizes. Some of them began when we were born and others have just begun. But whatever the case, they all prove to be more challenging than we ever expected them to be. For those of us who are survivors of sexual abuse, our God-given longings can become confused and distorted. A history of disapproval, harsh treatment, and feelings of emptiness can distort our view of God's beautiful purpose for relationships, causing confusion and deep anguish.

Over time, the abuse we suffer may begin to seem tragically normal. Something is dreadfully wrong. We continue to long for Disney's happily ever after view of life, but find ourselves in a cycle of delusional hope and disappointment. There must be a greater purpose, a better way, but we feel hopelessly lost and have no idea where to go.

But wait! Disney didn't write our story. Psalm 139 tells us that the very Author of life wove and knit us together in our mother's womb. We are his children. The Father of the heavenly lights knew us even before he created the earth, and he has the power to transform our dashed hopes and dreams into a tangible and redemptive reality.

Because God is marvelously faithful, he will not allow his children to wander without guidance and correction. The journey may be hard, but that does not mean we have failed. Jesus knows the depths of our pain and how gut-wrenching and confusing it is to suffer a lifetime of shame because of someone else's sin. *He* knows just how risky it is to love and be loved.

---

[36] Paul David Tripp, *War of Words* (Phillipsburg, NJ: P&R Publishing, 2000), 46.

When we look to Jesus, he shows us that love never gives up, that love is never conditional, and that love is always pure (1 Corinthians 13:1-8). God's love overcomes our fears and gives us the courage to love people more than we need them. [37]

"My soul, wait silently for God alone, for my expectation is from Him" (Psalm 62:5).

Jesus and Me and You

We have an eternal soul that longs endlessly for its Creator. This longing cannot be filled by temporary or physical things, but can only be satisfied by the very presence of God. We have been asked to walk with him by faith, not by sight (2 Corinthians 5:7), and it can be difficult to understand and even appreciate his presence. Because God is merciful and knows that we long to see, hear, and touch him, he will often demonstrate his love to us through human relationships.

As we pursue relationships with believers who love Jesus and radiate his love, we are drawn to *him* in them. This is not shameful, but natural and good because it teaches us about love in new and refreshing ways.

"We love, because He first loved us" (1 John 4:19 NASB).

"Hope does not disappoint" (Romans 5:5).

As a young girl, Rayna was molested by her father and rejected by her mother. She learned by experience that no one could be trusted. Not even God, it seemed.

Rayna appears to have overcome her past. She has grown up to be an outwardly successful wife and mom who is active in her church and who even manages a side business, but Rayna is painfully lonely. Her heart aches for honest and vulnerable companionship, but fear and shame keep her so busy and "in control" that no one can ever get close enough to hurt her again. She is dying inside.

---

[37] Ed Welch, *When People Are Big and God Is Small* (P&R Publishing, 1997), 183, 193.

Dylan was his grandfather's favorite. His grandfather manipulated him by his "kindness" and attention, and Dylan hates himself for falling for his grandpa's lies. He resists feeling vulnerable, so he hides in his little apartment and is quiet when he is around others.

Shanae was a child victim of a neighborhood pedophile. A man and his two children invited her to spend Saturday nights at their house and to attend church with them on Sunday morning. These visits began as innocent playdates but slowly and deceptively transformed into sexual adventures and experiments. The man had already been abusing his own children and had manipulated all of them to believe that what they were doing was normal.

Shanae felt dirty, and knew that a lot of what was happening was wrong, but she felt a strange and powerful attraction to the man and his children and found herself looking forward to the illicit visits. Shame and confusion kept her silent for six dreadful years.

Today Shanae's relationships are shattered as she drifts from one man to another. She struggles to keep a job for more than a month and is always behind in paying her bills. She is in and out of the women's shelter or crashes with her sister or her mom, who tolerate her at best. She desperately tries to dull the deep ache in her soul with drugs, sex, and alcohol. Her friendships revolve around her addictions.

Rayna, Dylan and Shanae are terribly affected by their experiences, and their relationships are suffering as a result. Rayna struggles to trust anyone, so she stays busy to keep herself "safe." Dylan's anger and insecurity cause him to hide, and Shanae's shameful secrets imprison her in destructive relationship patterns. As we move through this chapter, we will keep Rayna, Dylan, and Shanae in mind while we consider our own relational tendencies.

Talking Points: Pray and discuss the following with your leading friend.

1. Which of my relationships are most significant and why? Identify powerful emotions.

2. What do I want or hope for from these relationships (e.g., happiness, respect, love, fun, peace, security, kindness)? What do I offer each relationship?

3. Am I willing to consider changing my expectations?

4. In what ways might I identify with Rayna, Dylan, or Shanae?

5. What relationships do I find most difficult? Why?

6. Do I believe that God has a good plan for me and that Jesus can truly meet my needs?

Treasure: "When I live out of a biblical sense of who I am and rest in who God is, I will be able to build a healthy relationship with [others]." —Tim Lane and Paul David Tripp, *Relationships: A Mess Worth Making*, 57.

Purpose for Relationships

Picture yourself sitting in ninth grade math; not algebra or geometry or advanced calculus, but remedial "I'm-not-very-good-at-this" math. You struggle to figure out what is going on and finally give up and stare out the window in a daze of the "why-does-this-even-matter" blues. When something does not seem to have a purpose, it can be really hard to apply ourselves, especially if it doesn't make any sense or come easily to us.

As victims of sexual abuse, we were expected to figure out some very complicated situations. As a result, strong and negative emotions can dominate our thinking and make relating to anyone feel daunting. We may begin to lose hope and wonder if it's worth the effort to try.

Shame and confusion can distort and complicate the way we see everything, but there is hope! In Jesus, we find purposes for our relationships that are both refreshing and redemptive.

We Are Created for Love

"Beloved, let us love one another, for love is of God; and everyone who loves is born of God and knows God. He who does not love does not know God, for God is love" (1 John 4:7–8).

In order to love and be loved, we need to receive God's love and grow in our understanding of him. Read the following verses from your own Bible and fill in the blanks.

Be loved

John 3:16: "For God so _____ the world that He gave His only begotten Son, that whoever believes in Him should not perish, but have everlasting life."

Ephesians 3:19: "… to know the _____ of Christ which passes knowledge; that you may be filled with all the fullness of God."

Love God

1 John 4:19: "We _____ Him because He first loved us."

John 14:15: "If you _____ me, keep my commandments."

Matthew 22:37–38: "Jesus said to him, 'You shall _____ the LORD your God with all your heart, with all your soul, and with all your mind. This is the first and greatest commandment.'"

Love people

Matthew 22:39: "And the second [great commandment] … You shall _____ your neighbor as yourself."

John 15:12: "This is My commandment, that you _____ one another as I have loved you."

Ephesians 5:1–2: "Therefore be imitators of God as dear children. And walk in _____ as Christ also has _____ us and given Himself for us."

Because we are completely loved and accepted by our heavenly Father, and our brother Jesus, we are empowered by the Holy Spirit to love one another just as he loves us (1 John 4:10–11). Notice that these verses do not require us to change *other* people. That's God's job. We love as we have been loved to bring Jesus glory, which is what we were designed to do (Isaiah 43:7). This is why we are alive! Purpose, sweet purpose.

Talking Points: Pray and discuss the following with your leading friend.

Think back to the beginning of this study. Our view of God has everything to do with how we function in life.

7. In what ways has your view of God changed?

8. Are there any unspoken questions or concerns in your mind about the character of God?

9. Do you trust him as you move forward?

Guarding Our Hearts

Relationships are messy, and thinking about connecting with other people can be scary, but we are not alone on this journey. Our Good Shepherd already knows the depths of our struggle and bears the weight of it with us. The answers for this journey are not found in a list of do's and don'ts, but in a Person who is completely and amazingly "able to do exceedingly abundantly above all that we ask or think" (Ephesians 3:20). Jesus Christ is the Rock upon which the foundation stones of healthy and meaningful relationships are built.

Considering a foundation may seem strange when we have been talking about taking a journey. Ultimately, a believer's home is in Christ with God. However, we live here on earth right now. Home is more than a place—it's a Person; and a journey is more than movement—it's belonging and becoming. Therefore, in Christ we have a foundation that keeps us anchored as we become the people God wants us to be, with Someone and with someplace in which to dwell while we journey toward our ultimate home.

Rayna moans, "Do I really have to go to church today? I am so tired of feeling anxious. Will I ever handle this life or will I always struggle? I feel so weird around all those people who 'have it together.' I feel so broken, so needy, so ashamed. Jesus, please help me." Rayna has always seemed fine. She wears the right clothes, sings the right songs, and even manages to be social and invite people from her church over for fellowship, but she is weary and desperately lonely. No one, not even her husband, can see the depths of the pain in her heart.

Shanae is sick and tired of her boyfriend. He is demanding and insists on knowing what she is doing all the time. She loves him, she thinks, but is confused by his ever-changing mood. She feels trapped and has no idea what is wrong or how to fix it. She is painfully burdened by her lack of any kind of relationship with her family. She has been angry for a long time but isn't sure why, and her natural response to heartache is to lash out in anger at anyone who seems to be a threat.

Dylan is afraid, so he remains in his apartment as much as possible. When he has to go out, he targets quiet places during less busy times of the day. He avoids eye contact with others, and when he must speak, he keeps his head and his voice low.

Understanding Our Hearts

A longing for companionship is part of God's beautiful plan for us, but our desire for it will only be healthy if it is secondary to and born out of our relationship with him. Most of us long to be loved by someone we can see. We battle with the temptation to look for security and fulfillment in people, instead of waiting for God to redirect and satisfy the longings we feel.

We are frail, imperfect creatures with a great capacity to wander away and oftentimes our longings get misdirected. Unbelief and disappointment can cause us to look away from God and look instead to his creation, specifically people, for satisfaction.

From Maria's Journal

"Oh Jesus, I am angry! Why do I continue to struggle so much in my perception and understanding of what relationships are for? Does it even matter why? I'm tired of needing anything from anyone. I'm tired of my screwed up past and I'm tired of not having enough faith or not being surrendered enough. I'm sorry for my sinful responses to everything I have experienced. I want to submit to you. I know that you are good and kind, but I can't figure out how to muster up that type of faith; the kind that produces a resting heart when I feel used and stepped on by someone I love, and when I feel anger for my unruly affections. I'm sorry for loving others in your place. I know that you know I am incapable to obey and trust, and that even as I write this, you are gently listening. You do love me. I don't want to be needy! Please, Lord, without your intervention I will ruin everything. Change my thinking; change my heart. I am desperate for you."

Destructive Tendencies

God wants us to love one another, but when we find human relationships to be difficult and disappointing, we may react in one of two extremes:

- **Dependent** (a longing to be close or immersed). If we seek comfort in relationships, we may feel desperately drawn to the other person and only feel safe when we are in that person's presence. Like Shanae, we can demand or expect that people meet our needs to the point that they feel pressured, used, and overwhelmed. Relating in this way causes tension, resistance, and frequently leads to the end of the relationship.

- **Independent** (a self-sufficient tendency toward isolation). If our experiences have led us to believe that people aren't trustworthy, we may isolate ourselves and struggle with deep feelings of loneliness. Like Dylan, we may even feel a strange sense of safety in being alone. When we choose to build walls and isolate ourselves, we usually don't remember to build a door for mercy. Like Rayna, we can become so accustomed to living life on our own that we have no idea how to relate to anyone, even those closest to us. Then it is common to feel misunderstood and to find little or no relief from the suffering we experience.

Identifying Our Desires

Both dependence and independence can leave us floundering in a raging storm of pain and confusion. Powerful emotions like shame, fear, and anger can make finding relief a desperate pursuit. After being sexually abused, it may seem logical to think that God isn't trustworthy, but doubting him fuels unhealthy desires. We may begin to manipulate people and circumstances hoping to fulfill our longings by finding someone to take away the pain. But those desires can smother, damage, and starve our relationships.

"Each one is tempted when he is drawn away by his own desires and enticed. Then, when desire has conceived, it gives birth to sin; and sin, when it is full-grown, brings forth death" (James 1:14–15).

The following chart illustrates some of those desires and their unintended consequences.

Distorted Desires or Longings (Seeking Fulfillment Without Christ)	Results
To be parented: "Maybe *they* will love and care for me."	A blending and confusion of roles …
To be comforted: "Maybe *they* will understand my pain."	Unbalanced human dependency (fear of man) …
To escape: "I want to get lost in the other person. I feel safe there."	Rejection or an overly controlling relationship, feeling trapped …
For satisfying sexual experiences: "I always feel used."	Shame, loss, disappointment, adultery…
For control: "I'll make sure no one will ever take advantage of me again."	Conflict and frustration, fear, hatred…
For justice: "I'll take revenge. They will pay for what they did."	Anger, anxiety, bitterness …
To be wanted and loved: "Sex will bring intimacy."	Emptiness, a feeling of being used, shame …
To be safe: "I will escape danger if I hide from everyone."	Isolation, loneliness, same-sex attraction…
To escape: "I will avoid anything that makes me feel anxious or out of control."	Self-centeredness, confusion, hopelessness, isolation …

Consider the dangers of emotional dependency:

I know a number of individuals … who struggle with unhealthy emotional dependency on others. It can be agonizing when an otherwise great friendship starts to become the object of intense and unwanted longing. One friend described the experience as like taking "friendship heroin": finding yourself suddenly "high" when being affirmed by a particular friend, and then feeling a crushing sense of absence when apart from them. Needless to say at such times, it is vital to have others who will help, support and talk it through.[38]

---

[38] Sam Allberry, *Is God Anti-Gay?* (UK: The Good Book Company, 2013), 56.

If we allow our desires (affections, expectations, longings) to be primarily in people, we will become frustrated and disappointed. People will never completely satisfy us. If we look to anyone other than Jesus to quench our thirst (John 4:14), we will continue to thirst without satisfaction. Asking God to search our hearts (Psalm 139:23-24) and to reveal any unhealthy or wicked desires will free us to discover and work through some of the root issues that continue to hold us captive in a lifestyle of depressing and destructive behavior (Psalm 32:5; James 5:16).

Ephesians 5:8-13 teaches us that it is good to expose the secret things that bind us to shame and defeat. As we learn to identify unhealthy desires, confess known sin, and replace lies with truth, we will see that God is faithful to cleanse us and to give us a way of escape through his love (1 John 1:9; 1 Corinthians 10:13).

Considering that our desires lead to temptation, what temptations do you see in yourself? Maria will list a few of hers to give you some courage.

> I am tempted: to hide from people who don't understand me; to give up on the church; to find security in my friendship with my leading friend; to despair and unbelief; to withdraw sexually and emotionally from my husband; with same-sex attraction and or confusion; and to be angry and run from everything and everyone.

Are you feeling brave? List yours.

"If we confess our sins, He is faithful and just to forgive us our sins and to cleanse us from all unrighteousness" (1 John 1:9).

Scripture says that cleansing comes as a direct result of confession. Asking you to identify your desires and temptations isn't an attempt to cause you embarrassment or pain but to expose the darkness and bring you to the forgiving, cleansing, and healing light of Jesus.

Interdependence

We have discussed our tendency to swing between dependence and independence in our relationships, but it is refreshingly possible to find a solid and healthy third way. God has designed his church to reflect and experience his love in a beautiful way. Because Jesus created us as social beings, he will often nourish his children with the living waters that flow from the heart of another believer who is regularly being satisfied in him (1 John 4:7–11; John 7:37–38). Because God's kind of love is a gift, we must not extract or demand this love from one another or we will end up in grief and disappointment. Many of our relationships may be suffering because one or both parties are full of demands rather than love.

As we seek first the kingdom of God, he will fill us with his Spirit so that we can share with others the nourishment that God gives. Then we will find our relationships growing in healthy ways (Matthew 6:33).

"Jesus stood and cried out, saying, 'If anyone thirsts, let him come to Me and drink. He who believes in Me … out of his heart will flow rivers of living water'" (John 7:37–38).

Establishing Appropriate Boundaries

Because of the changing nature of our longings and affections, it can be difficult to know where someone belongs in our hearts. A coach may provide a father's encouragement, a teacher might share a mother's patience, and a mentor might be the friend we've never had, but none of these people can replace a lost or damaged relationship. If we allow these relationships to substitute for God, we will add pain to our already troubled hearts.

Healthy relationships exist because they are established and nourished with good understanding and wise boundaries. When I (Maria) was in high school, I felt a strong connection with my choir teacher. Our interactions were limited to the classroom, but I remember wishing she could be a bigger part of my life. These desires aren't bad; they just need to be carefully controlled. It wouldn't have been healthy for us to have more time together because she had a family and I was a busy student. It was wise and appropriate for this relationship to be limited.

But there are people that God wants to weave into our hearts. Paul speaks of believers as being "knit together in love" (Colossians 2:2).

So there is a place for close relationships, but we need wisdom. That is why we will continue to draw near to our Good Shepherd. He promises to give us all the wisdom we need (James 1:5).

Talking Points: Pray and discuss the following with your leading friend.

1. Am I trying to find satisfaction in other people? In what ways? How long does this satisfaction last?

2. In what ways do I want people to fix me or fulfill me?

3. In what ways have I seen my relationships suffer because of my demands or desires?

4. What are some of the critical events in my past that may be influencing what I want from my relationships?

5. Which extreme do I tend toward most often—dependence or independence? Have I experienced both extremes? Explain.

6. Discuss the following statement: "I have been searching my whole life for someone to love me as much as I love myself."

Treasure: When our longings are satisfied in Christ, we are free to love others without expectation.

A good relationship has a pattern like a dance and is built on some of the same rules. The partners do not need to hold on tightly, because they move confidently in the same pattern, intricate but [merry] and swift and free, like a country dance of Mozart's. To touch heavily would be to arrest the pattern and freeze the movement, to check the endlessly changing beauty of its unfolding. There is no place here for the possessive clutch, the clinging arm, the heavy hand; only the barest touch in passing. Now arm in arm, now face to face, now back to back-it does not matter which. Because they know they are partners moving to the same rhythm, creating a pattern together, and being invisibly nourished by it. The joy of such a pattern is not only the joy of creation or the joy of participation; it is also the joy of living in the moment. Lightness of touch and living in the moment are intertwined …

… But why is it so difficult? What makes us hesitate and stumble? It is fear, I think, that makes one cling nostalgically to the last moment or clutch greedily toward the next … But when the heart is flooded with love there is no room in it for fear … [39]

---

[39] Anne Morrow Lindbergh, *Gift from the Sea* (New York: Pantheon Books, 2003), 96.

Chapter 19

Building Healthy Relationships

Imagine yourself relaxing in your dream home with a steaming cup of coffee in your hand. Are you sitting in a little cottage by a river, or in a mansion on a mountaintop? Does your cozy cabin in the woods have a loft? How many levels does your mountaintop mansion have? What kind of floor plan does it have?

We have already acknowledged how critical it is to have Jesus Christ as our foundation, and now we will begin to unpack the blueprints and discuss the fundamental truths that are needed to build and maintain healthy relationships.

Approaches to Relating

Let's allow the approaches to a house to represent relational boundaries in our lives. The depths of our relationships can be compared to how closely one may move about the house. For example, a stranger cannot enter your house, although you may wave casually to them as they stroll by on the sidewalk. An acquaintance may sit with you on the porch, but they rarely come inside. A significant person may enter into the main part of your house, but not go everywhere. A close friend may move freely throughout your house. Let's look more closely at each of these relationships:

Stranger	These are people we randomly encounter while shopping, attending sporting events, etc. They are outside. They do not even know where we live, nor do they care to know.
Acquaintance	These are people we see only occasionally, who we know by name but little more. They may rarely, if ever, visit our house, even if they know where we live.

Significant	These are people who share our activities, values, and/or interests, and may share our genes. They spend time at our house, and we exert effort to make them feel comfortable there.
Close	These are people who share our secrets, burdens, trust, desires of the heart, mutual understanding, etc. They are an integral part of our house; it would not feel like home without them.

Strangers are people we encounter randomly and do not know at all. Our appropriate role with them is minimal, although in a crisis we may seek them out. Normally, we may choose to smile and nod, say hello, or to do nothing at all. Their responses are relatively meaningless to our well-being.

> Dylan chooses to avoid any relationship. He is afraid of everyone—even strangers. He hides in his apartment because he isn't willing to let anyone near his heart, and as a result finds himself isolated and lonely.

Acquaintances are people whose names we know, but little else. Acquaintances may include our bank teller, our doctor, churchgoers, teachers, online friends, neighbors, and even some distant relatives. Typically, our role is limited to casual conversation in the environment where we usually see them.

> Shanae tends to seek out acquaintances after church and talk about her life story for a half hour or more. She thinks her openness will gain their sympathy and affirmation, but instead she feels them pull back from her. She wonders why people turn away when she walks by. Their responses anger her.

> Shanae needs to recognize that her role with strangers and acquaintances is limited and fragile. A healthy relationship is never one-sided, but mutually caring and respectful of the other person's time, emotions, and willingness to be involved. Socially, she must nurture an acquaintance-level relationship appropriately until it becomes significant or close before her role will allow for burden-sharing.

Significant relationships are people who share our activities, employment, interests, values, and may share our genes. Things become more complex as our role requires more interaction. These people are an important part of our lives. We have some relationships based upon necessity. Our boss, coworkers, and immediate family are significant no matter how we get along with them or how we feel about them. Other significant relationships include friendships at various stages of development. These relationships take work. We must be willing to learn to interact according to our role in each one.

Rayna finds relationships to be exhausting and risky, so she hides in a busy maze of productivity to keep her distance. She is afraid to be known, so her social interactions exist only to accomplish her goals. Her husband and children feel the weight of her fear as they struggle under her lofty and endless expectations. She, too, feels lonely and isolated, even in a crowd.

Close relationships are people who share our trust, burdens, and secrets. Close relationships grow out of significant relationships with friends or family when we trust the other person and choose to share our thoughts, hopes, and interests with them over time. Close relationships are mutually giving and rare, requiring wisdom, time, and careful investment of emotional energy and effort. Most of us have only a few close relationships in our lifetime, and it may take a long time to find the right person with whom to develop a close relationship. When we do, our role is to support, pray, humbly care, share, and walk alongside such a person selflessly.

Maria used to fear close relationships because she felt needy and thought she'd smother anyone who seemed interested in her, but she is learning to place her hope and expectations in God, and he is teaching her how to love people more than she *needs* people. Jesus is giving her freedom to invest in and benefit from close relationships without the heavy chains of unhealthy expectations.

Primary Impact Relationships

In this chapter we refer to biological and adoptive parents, siblings, spouses, children, and certain close friends as primary because they have (or had) the greatest influence upon us, even in their absence. For example, a child adopted at birth has an emotional attachment to her birth mother, even if she never sees or meets her. That relationship has a primary impact, and its effects can't be ignored. Other primary impact relationships may include teachers, mentors, ministry leaders, and possibly our abuser, depending on his or her role in our life.

Two Basic Relationships

Our discussion so far may be making some of us feel a little confused. We do need to discipline ourselves to do the hard work of learning, but let's break this down to something a bit simpler.

From a Christian worldview—that is, from a biblical perspective—we relate to people in one of two basic ways:

1. As fellow believers in Christ or

2. As a believer to an unbeliever.

Regardless of a person's place in our lives (spouse, parent, child, friend, stranger, etc.), these two perspectives will help us to determine our purpose as we pursue and maintain a relationship with each individual.

Relating to Believers

God has fashioned our hearts individually (Psalm 33:15) and has given believers special roles to play in one another's lives (1 Corinthians 12:1-27). When considering our relationships to other believers, we will find a renewed sense of purpose and hope when we keep these few truths in mind:

- Each believer in Jesus is in process; we are all imperfect, sinfully broken, and in need of grace. Our hope and expectation has to be in God, not in the performance of the other person. We have come to the Savior to receive forgiveness and healing. As we grow in the fear and knowledge of God, we will walk together with other believers in love; ready to forgive and be forgiven, just as Christ has forgiven us.

- Each believer lives as a temple for the Spirit of God, designed to reveal his glory (1 Corinthians 6:19-20). As we seek to know and love God, we are less enamored by our own desires and make room in our hearts for him to shine. We are drawn to other people because we see Jesus reflected in them; he makes our relationships beautiful and pure, in spite of our flaws.

Relating to Unbelievers

An unbeliever's greatest need is to hear and see the gospel lived out. It is crucial for us to understand that unbelievers are completely incapable of loving others with pure motives. Apart from Christ, an unbeliever's best attempts to serve and love others are drawn out of a heart that seeks its own good. Consider these truths:

- Each unbeliever needs to know that there is a marvelously kind, merciful, and good God, and that he is the almighty Creator who is worthy to be feared and trusted.

- Each unbeliever is a slave to sin. Without Christ, we are all enticed by our own desires. Even "nice" people need to be rescued and redeemed.

- Unbelievers, regardless of their belief system, are accountable to God. Jesus Christ offers the only way to God and eternal life, and the unbeliever needs to receive him (John 1:12).

Are you sighing with relief right now? We hope so, but if you find yourself not convinced and even argumentative, pray and ask God to show you how these truths might begin to look in your life. He will amaze you.

Talking Points: Pray and discuss the following with your leading friend.

1. What are some challenges you encounter in relating to other believers? To unbelievers?

2. Identify and list the people in your life who fit into each of the following relationships:

   * *Strangers*

   * *Acquaintances*

   * *Significant relationships*

   * *Close relationships*

   * *Primary relationship*

3. What are some of the ways you would like to improve your relationships with each of these people in your life, both believers and unbelievers?

   * *Strangers*

   * *Acquaintances*

   * *Significant relationships*

   * *Close relationships*

   * *Primary relationships*

Father, you are gloriously beautiful, but oh how we fight to see and believe you when our world is clouded with pain, anger, doubt, and what seems like constant struggle. Please comfort, strengthen, and assure our readers of your faithfulness and love as they pour themselves out to you for hope and healing. You are good and always do what is good. We trust you; please help us. Amen.

Treasure: Understanding the boundaries of relationships will help us to prioritize our affections, time, and energy so that we can better fulfill God's purposes.

Chapter 20

Relationship Foundations

So far, we have acknowledged Jesus Christ as the Rock upon which the life of the believer is built. He is the One who defines relationships, and he teaches us how to build sustainable ones. We have also discussed several approaches to relating (types of relationships). Now we will start setting the foundation stones. We will define and unpack each stone and then look at some examples to see how this biblical structure actually works.

Foundation Stones

1. **Love**: Expressing the character of God for the well-being of the one loved (1 John 4:7-12).

2. **Roles**: Acting with biblical purpose and character. Reflecting the character of Christ in desire, thought and action.

3. **Communication**: Using words God's way; speak the truth in love; keep current; attack problems, not people; act, don't react; (Ephesians 4:25-32).

4. **Forgiveness**: Promising to handle offenses as Jesus does.

Stone 1: Love

Love expresses the character of God for the well-being of the one loved.

The word "love" can be overused and is often misunderstood. When we say things like, "I love my new shoes," or, "I love a good thunderstorm," we really mean that we enjoy them. We have defined love by how we feel, but our feelings change quickly and cannot be trusted

(Jeremiah 17:9). If we want to develop and maintain healthy relationships, we have to know what it really means to love and be loved.

Discovering Love

Look up 1 John 4:16 and fill in the following blanks. "God is_____, and he who abides in_____ abides in_____, and God in him".

From this passage ...

Who or what is love and how do we find it?

Look up I John 4:10-11. "In this is love, not that we loved God, but that_____".

"We love Him because He first loved us" (1 John 4:19).

From this passage ...

Why are we able to love God and others?

In the framework above, we have defined love as "the expression of the character of God for the well-being of the one loved." How does this definition of love differ from the way most people think of love?

Observing Love

In the following chart, fill in the blanks to see what love looks like. We have given you a few examples.

Verses	What is God/Jesus like?	What does love look like?
Psalm 1:6 "For the LORD knows the way of the righteous."	He knows. He is aware.	Love knows and pays attention.
Psalm 3:3 "But You, O LORD, are a shield for me, my glory, and the One who lifts up my head."		

Verses	What is God/Jesus like?	What does love look like?
Psalm 3:4 "I cried to the LORD with my voice, and He heard me ..."		
1 John 3:16 "By this we know love, because He laid down His life for us."	Jesus gave his life for me. He gives until it hurts; even unto death.	Love gives.
Romans 5:8 "God demonstrates His own love toward us, in that while we were still sinners, Christ died for us."		
1 Corinthians 13:4-8 " Love suffers long and is kind; love does not envy; love does not parade itself, is not puffed up; does not behave rudely, does not seek its own, is not provoked, thinks no evil; does not rejoice in iniquity, but rejoices in the truth; bears all things, believes all things, hopes all things, endures all things. Love never fails."		

Demonstrating Love

Looking in the Bible to learn what God is like and how he shows his love gives us all we need to begin to love others well. Abiding in his love and learning to walk in his Spirit will produce in us a beautiful expression of his character.

"...the fruit of the Spirit is love, joy, peace, longsuffering, kindness, goodness, faithfulness, gentleness, self-control" (Gal. 5:22-23).

Caution: Love Is Never Abusive!

Since God is love, true love must always honor the noble, holy, and good character of God. Abuse of any kind violates love because it dishonors and mocks God's good character, endangers our family, keeps our abuser from facing God, mangles the principles of biblical submission, damages marriages, distorts the picture of Christ and the church, enables and promotes evil, and elicits society's contempt. Abuse is dark and destructive, completely unlike our gracious Lord of light. Love is never mean or manipulative: it always seeks the well-being of the one loved. Anything else is sin. If you are currently in an abusive relationship, we strongly recommend that you seek help from a wise and trusted person who will take your concerns seriously. Protecting an abuser by keeping quiet is not love; it allows them to continue to hurt people and consequently themselves.

Sometimes love is just hard. Self-sacrifice and biblical confrontation can be scary, but like skillful surgery, the pain is necessary so that we can heal and function better. Love always seeks the other person's good—even when it initially hurts.

Love suffers long and is kind; love does not envy; love does not parade itself, is not puffed up; does not behave rudely, does not seek its own, is not provoked, thinks no evil; does not rejoice in iniquity but rejoices in the truth; bears all things, believes all things [thinks the best until proven otherwise], hopes all things [wants what is best], endures all things. Love never fails. —1 Corinthians 13:4–8

From this passage ...

Underline what God says love is not:

"The wisdom that is from above is first pure, then peaceable, gentle, willing to yield, full of mercy and good fruits, without partiality and without hypocrisy" (James 3:17).

Treasure: Love gives for the well-being of another whether or not it is deserved.

Stone 2: Communication

Speak truth in love, keep current, attack problems rather than people, act—don't react (Ephesians 4:25–32).

Using Words God's Way:

Some relationships are just hard no matter what we do, but God has given some foundational truths to equip us to communicate with wisdom, grace, and love. Let's start with the principle from Ephesians 4:22–24 of put off, renew, and put on:

> … put off, concerning your former conduct, the old man which grows corrupt according to the deceitful lusts, and be renewed in the spirit of your mind, and that you put on the new man which was created according to God, in true righteousness and holiness.

Simply stated, we must stop living for ourselves, get a new perspective from Scripture, and start living according to God's desires. The result? True righteousness and holiness.

Four Principles of Communication:

Dr. Bob Smith offers four principles for communicating from Ephesians 4. [40]

1. Speak truth in love. "But, speaking the truth in love…Therefore, putting away lying, 'Let each one of you speak truth with his neighbor,' for we are members of one another" (verses 15, 25).

2. Keep current. "Be angry, and do not sin': do not let the sun go down on your wrath, nor give place to the devil" (verses 26–27).

---

[40] Dr. Robert (Bob) Smith, "*Communication,*" Track 1 of the Biblical Counseling Training Conference, Faith Church, Lafayette, Indiana. From unpublished notes taken February 1998.

3. Attack problems, not people. Speak to build up rather than tear down. "Let no corrupt word proceed out of your mouth, but what is good for necessary edification, that it may impart grace to the hearers" (verse 29).

4. Act, don't react. "And do not grieve the Holy Spirit of God, by whom you were sealed for the day of redemption. Let all bitterness, wrath, anger, clamor, and evil speaking be put away from you, with all malice. And be kind to one another, tenderhearted, forgiving one another, even as God in Christ forgave you" (verses 30–32).

The following chart summarizes how these principles apply.

What to Stop Doing	Renewing My Mind	What to Start Doing
Put away lying.	We are members of one another. Think of others as highly as we think of ourselves.	*Speak truth in love;* don't avoid talking about the hard stuff, but do so honestly and in love.
Stop avoiding confrontation. Stop verbally or physically attacking people.	Beware of letting evil prevail. Overcome evil with good.	*Keep current;* communicate truth in love as soon as possible to get the reconciliation process going.
Let no corrupt (sinful, hurtful, destructive) communication come out of your mouth.	Impart grace to hearers, to build others up rather than tearing them down.	*Attack problems, not people;* speak what is good that it may build up and offer grace to the hearers. Think bigger than me; let my actions accomplish a greater good.
Do not grieve the Holy Spirit.	I am redeemed, and my life needs to reflect that.	*Act, don't react;* Be sensitive, teachable, humble … like Christ.
Put away bitterness, wrath, anger, clamor (obnoxiousness), and evil speaking with all malice.	Remember the gospel and be grateful that I am forgiven and tenderly loved in Christ.	*Act, don't react;* Be kind, tenderhearted, and forgiving—just like Jesus.

Christ motivates good communication. For someone like Dylan who chooses to avoid people, using words God's way means deliberately hearing what others have to say, and then speaking wisely when it would be easier to hide or be silent. For Rayna, godly communication means stopping her tasks to think, ask good questions, and listen for the interests and concerns of others—especially those closest to her. Shanae must lay aside anger and bitterness, allowing Christ to renew her mind, and live with consideration for others.

All true growth is a result of a mind that is being renewed through daily submission to Jesus, and this takes work! "… and be renewed in the spirit of your mind" (Ephesians 4:23).

Stone 3: Roles

Acting with biblical purpose and character; reflecting the character of Christ in desire, thought and action, while living out our biblical purpose

By the term role we mean the way we function according to our purpose. Our roles differ according to the nature and development of each relationship. We must recognize the differing social roles we hold as daughters, neighbors, wives, mothers, friends, professionals, and churchgoers. To have healthy connections with other people, we need to understand our roles. We must not reveal our burdens, secrets, and feelings to strangers; an acquaintance will feel crowded by expectations that are normal in a significant relationship; and a close friend would be offended if we treated her like a stranger when we meet her on the street.

God designed us to be social, so close and significant relationships are good for us. However, we cannot be close with everyone; we do not have the emotional capacity for that. Most of us have many contacts every day, but we relate differently, according to our level of relationship. Our responses in a given relationship will largely determine its depth, but the other person's efforts either hinder or contribute to that depth. The better we get to know others and function according to our social roles, the stronger the relationship can become.

The following outline will simplify our most basic roles and the purpose for which we relate:

Two Basic Roles (in this order):

Love God (James 4:8)

- Seek to know God; read Scripture

- Submit to God as first priority (Acts 5:29; James 4:8; Matthew 22:37)

- Glorify and reflect God through the fruit of the Spirit (Galatians 5:22–23)

- Act with wisdom; use knowledge well (Proverbs 1:1–7; 2:6)

Love People (Matthew 22:39)

- Look for the higher good; reflect God's love

- Be humble; consider others above myself, submit to other believers in the Lord (Philippians 2:3–5)

- Be teachable; consult wise resources [41]

We have tried to make understanding our roles simple, but that doesn't mean that fulfilling our roles is easy. We need God's grace and lots of practice in order to function well. Our hope has to be in Jesus because our roles are easily misunderstood and people are complicated. The church can also be part of the problem when tradition or comfort become of greater importance than love. Still, our roles can be carried out (admittedly imperfectly) when we follow the principles of Scripture, which means loving God first.

---

[41] Talk to your pastor or your biblical counselor. Other suggested resources: (1) the bibliography at the end of this book; (2) recommended resources at www.biblicalcounselingcoalition.org.

All healthy and growing relationships have some things in common: we acknowledge the person's importance to us, seek their well-being, support them, resolve conflicts, show concern, share interests, interact positively with them, and treat them well. Relationships can be fragile, especially at the acquaintance and early-significant levels. Be mindful that harmful responses or self-absorption can damage or destroy the relationship, especially if problems are not resolved in a biblical and timely way. Always seek to give rather than to get, and "be part of the solution, not part of the problem." [42]

> Like all of us, Dylan and Rayna are social beings, designed for companionship. Even though they have been hurt in the past, they can learn to function in their roles according to God's purpose. Learning to identify trustworthy people, reaching out with gentleness and sincere interest in the other person, and trusting God to guide them will give Dylan and Rayna the confidence needed to develop and nurture healthy relationships.

Stone 4: Forgiveness

Promising to handle offenses as Jesus does

Ironically, the word forgiveness can incite harsh arguments and cause boiling fires of anger and bitterness. Because forgiveness is so often misunderstood and mishandled, we may rage at its demands and insensitivity. How could anyone forgive a man who has forced his way with a tender, precious, helpless child? Where is the justice in forgiving? When someone has been mercilessly abused and tossed aside as trash, the idea of forgiveness can become awfully hard to grasp.

The Merriam-Webster Dictionary defines the word forgive in this way: "to stop feeling anger toward (someone who has done something wrong): to stop blaming (someone)." That definition would be fine if we could stop ourselves from feeling angry, but we can't, so it offers no hope.

---

[42] Familiar proverb, source unknown.

Vertical Surrender

Through the gospel, however, forgiveness gives us welcome relief. Are you seeing glimmers of hope? The forgiveness that Jesus offers acknowledges the wrong that has been done, never minimizing it or saying we shouldn't feel angry. Because Christ paid for every sin, we can approach God humbly, as the rightful Avenger and Judge, releasing the offense and our anger into his capable hands. We call this kind of forgiveness vertical surrender. Vertical surrender occurs between the offended person and God. It is unconditional and does not depend in any way upon the offender's response.

When Rayna's dad died without ever acknowledging his sin against her, she began to suffer debilitating panic attacks, anxiety, and depression. She felt betrayed by God, abandoned by her parents, and unable to reconcile why all of this had happened.

Rayna won't be able to confront her dad, but she can find peace. Jesus is graciously aware of her dad's sin against her because he already bore the weight of her sorrow. As the Holy Spirit helps her, she will be able to lift up her hands and heart in vertical surrender, offering her desire for justice and the anger she feels into God's gentle and just hands.

Horizontal Forgiveness

On the other hand, reconciliation with another person (which we will call horizontal forgiveness) is possible only if our offender is repentant (that is, to admit with godly sorrow that the offense was hurtful and sinful). [43] Repentance is sincere when an offender makes changes consistent with his verbal regrets (2 Corinthians 7:10-11). Horizontal forgiveness is possible only when an offender is truly repentant (Luke 17:3-4). [44]

---

[43] See 2 Corinthians 7:10-11 for a description of godly sorrow.
[44] For more on horizontal and vertical forgiveness: Wendell Miller: *Forgiveness: The Power and the Puzzles* (Warsaw, IN: Clear Brook Publishing, 1994).

To *repent* means to turn around and go in the opposite direction. In a spiritual context, repentance means to turn away from evil desires, thoughts, and actions, and turn to God wholeheartedly. Second Corinthians 7:9-11 describes repentance as godly sorrow; diligence to pursue repentance; clearing our testimony; indignant at our own sin; fear of God; intense longing to be reconciled; demonstrations of godly passion and compassion; taking God's side against our sin; and restoration to fellowship and ministry. If we see these qualities at work, we know the person has repented.

According to the gospel, forgiveness is a promise to handle my offender's sin as Jesus does. Many questions and objections arise from this definition. Let's clear up some common misconceptions about forgiveness.

Forgiveness does not mean excusing what happened. God never minimizes sin; he treats it seriously. Sexual abuse provokes his wrath because it hurts us and mocks his justice, goodness, love, and decency. He was and is angry about evil and our suffering; so much so that Jesus was pierced, crushed, and killed to redeem us (Isaiah 53:5-7; 2 Corinthians 5:21). Jesus' sacrifice makes it possible for us to have peace in spite of what has happened. Even if our offender never repents or asks for our forgiveness, we can rest knowing that God doesn't overlook our suffering. That is amazing grace.

Forgiveness does not mean immediate justice. Forgiveness and justice are different. Forgiveness is an attitude. Justice is the impartial act of punishing wrong and rewarding right in accordance with the law. We all want justice, but it is beyond our power to make it happen perfectly. We must wait upon our just God for that. Forgiveness grows out of a heart that stops demanding "my justice in my timing," but instead leaves justice to God and the governing system he set in place. Forgiveness is possible when we believe God's promise to bring perfect justice according to his absolute wisdom and goodness in his time. "He will bring justice to the poor of the people; He will save the children of the needy, and will break in pieces the oppressor" (Psalm 72:4).

Forgiveness does not mean "once and done." Contrary to common belief, forgiveness must be renewed, perhaps many times. Each time an offense comes to mind, or whenever an offender fails, we have an occasion to renew that promise just as Jesus does every time we offend him (1 John 1:9–2:2). But that doesn't mean we didn't really forgive the first time. Think of forgiveness as a series of promise renewals.

Forgiveness does not mean trusting my offender. Forgiveness is a gift we offer, but trust is earned. Trusting someone who continues to offend is not wise; God warns us not to do so (Proverbs 26:24–25). Even when the offender's sorrow is sincere, accountability is necessary to prove sincerity and restore trust. [45] We recommend seeking wise counsel to help determine whether or not to extend trust.

Forgiveness does not mean feeling better immediately. Some form of grief and sorrow may remain as long as we live in this fallen world. Still, Christ's example calls us to forgive (vertical surrender) no matter how we feel. Easy? No. But we grieve with hope because we are not alone. Our burden is cast on the finished work of Christ, and we are free (Matthew 11:28–30).

Forgiveness is a promise to handle offenses as Jesus does. Christ's forgiveness went to the heart of the problem by dealing directly and effectively with the horrors of sin. Forgiveness is possible only because God took pity on our desperate souls and stepped in to redeem us through the sacrificial death and resurrection of Jesus Christ. Because of his forgiveness, we are now able and commanded to forgive those who sin against us (Matthew 18:21–34).

Forgiveness is the path to peace for the offended person, even if the abuser never repents. See the section on Vertical Surrender.

---

[45] For more on forgiveness: Robert Jeffrey, *When Forgiveness Doesn't Make Sense* (Colorado Spring, CO: Waterbrook Press, 2000).

How Is Forgiveness Offered and Received?

How Jesus Christ offer forgiveness ...

- **Humility**: Jesus did not defend his own well-being; Jesus died so that we can be forgiven.

- **Communication**: Christ made our needs and our offenses clear in his spoken and written Word.

- **Invitation**: Jesus seeks restoration by offering forgiveness to those who confess sin and receive him by faith.

How we offer forgiveness

- **Humility**: Acknowledge my own sin, repent, and ask for forgiveness for my part of the problem, if any.

- **Communication**: Tell my offender what he has done to hurt me and how it is affecting our relationship.

- **Invitation**: Ask my offender to respond and be ready to forgive if genuine repentance is expressed.

Dylan reaches out to his grandfather by writing a letter. He realizes that he can't go to his grandpa with a self-righteous attitude, even though he is not responsible for his grandfather's sin. Dylan writes about how he came to believe in Jesus and how he is learning to look at his past with new perspective. He goes on, "I can see now that years of resentment and fear have isolated me. I thought I was keeping myself safe, but now I know I was hurting everyone including myself. I was punishing myself, but I now know that Jesus took the punishment for me and gave me forgiveness. So based on his forgiveness, I am asking you to forgive me for hating you, and for letting that hate define my life."

The gospel points to reconciliation in Christ alone. Jesus always offers hope for those in sin, without minimizing or excusing it. In that same spirit, we speak to our offender by pointing out his need for Christ, not by excusing him or giving in to his sinful responses and demands. Wisdom and truth must guard us at this point. We need biblical guidance and the work of the Holy Spirit to navigate this path. [46]

> Dylan goes on, "I have to tell you that using me like you did has caused a lot of pain." He describes his pain as he refers to his story, [47] and then asks for his grandfather's response. "I will not easily get over this; I have been working toward this moment for many years, and now because of the relationship I have with Jesus, I want to forgive you. But it will depend on how you respond to this letter."

Asking for forgiveness and sharing our faith in Jesus opens the door for an abuser to repent. This is an objective that pleases God, but it doesn't guarantee a good response. [48] God may use our faithfulness to move our abuser to repentance and faith, or he may not. Whatever the result, we can rest assured that we have done our part in reconciliation.

Is there ever a time to withhold forgiveness? When someone has sinned against us, vertical surrender to God's authority and care is always possible. [49] As we release our anger and the need for immediate justice, we will find peace in Jesus, and wait patiently for the biblical process of reconciliation, however long it may take. However, because God is just, we can courageously pursue earthly justice by contacting the governmental authorities (Romans 13:1–5), as well as the leadership of the local church to call the offender to repentance and faith (Matthew 18:15–17; Galatians 6:1–3). If the offender genuinely

---

[46] Patrick H. Morison, *Forgive! As the Lord Forgave You* (Phillipsburg, NJ: P&R Publishing, 1987) Jim Wilson, *How to Be Free from Bitterness* (Moscow, ID: Canon Press, 1999)
[47] See chapter 2: "My Story"
[48] We may need help to differentiate our responsibilities and sins from those of our offenders.
[49] See page 219.

repents, then horizontal forgiveness can be offered (Luke 17:3–4; 2 Corinthians 7:10–11). If he doesn't repent, then we withhold horizontal forgiveness.

Our Father in heaven, hallowed be Your name. Your kingdom come; Your will be done on earth as it is in heaven. Give us this day our daily bread. And forgive us our debts, as we forgive our debtors. And do not lead us into temptation, but deliver us from the evil one. For Yours is the kingdom and the power and the glory forever. Amen. —Matthew 6:9–13

Treasure: Abiding in Christ's love and walking in the Spirit will produce in us a beautiful expression of his character.

Chapter 21

Building on the Foundation Stones in Primary Impact Relationships

Our Abuser

We have taken care to lay the groundwork, establishing a good foundation, and now we will begin to apply what we have learned to our relationships. As believers in Jesus, we have everything we need to build and maintain healthy interactions. He has provided us with his faithful written and living Word; the Spirit as our strength, comforter, and guide; and a promise that our labor is never in vain.

Choosing to follow God's blueprint for relationships isn't easy. Our environment, personality, and body chemistry can influence what we believe and how we act. But we don't have to give in to our difficult circumstances. In Christ, we have a new family, a home where we belong now and for all eternity, and a position of great significance as a child of the one true and living God. We will do well if we continue to follow him no matter how difficult and scary the journey may be.

> I bow my knees to the Father of our Lord Jesus Christ, from whom the whole family in heaven and earth is named, that He would grant you, according to the riches of His glory, to be strengthened with might through His Spirit in the inner man, that Christ may dwell in your hearts through faith; that you, being rooted and grounded in love, may be able to comprehend with all the saints what is the width and length and depth and height—to know the love of Christ which passes knowledge; that you may be filled with all the fullness of God.
> —Ephesians 3:14–19

Primary Impact Relationships

Christ gives us power in our relationships, not to change other people, but to change how we live with and respond to others. Now that we've defined and unpacked the four foundation stones (**love, roles, communication, and forgiveness**), we will examine some ways to apply them in each of our primary impact relationships. The charts included are not exhaustive but rather provide a springboard for discussions with our leading friends and biblical counselors.

My Abuser and His Allies

We will start with our abuser and those who side with him. What is our role? How can we appropriately communicate with our abuser, without excusing or condoning what he did? What does forgiveness look like?

> Dylan feels paralyzed when he thinks of his grandfather. Grandpa used to tell him that their sexual exploration was an expression of love. This confusion has confined him to a lonely cell of anger, shame, and fear, but Dylan is slowly learning that God is nothing like his grandfather. God's love is pure and holy, and never provokes shame. As Dylan seeks after God, he is beginning to desire healthy and pure relationships.

If Dylan decides to communicate with his grandfather, he will need lots of wisdom and grace. Loving an abuser requires learning how to identify and resist evil as Jesus did—never enabling or excusing abusive behavior. Jesus did not participate in evil by enabling his abusers, nor was he a helpless victim. Jesus said, "No one takes [my life] from Me, but I lay it down ... I have power to lay it down, and I have power to take it up again" (John 10:18). Jesus knew when to remove himself from an abusive situation (Mark 1:45; Luke 4:28–30). Learning from his example will equip us to love our abuser.

Ultimately, by enduring abuse, Jesus accomplished a specific and divine purpose: the salvation of men for the glory of God (Matthew 26:47–56). As we seek God for wisdom and allow him to teach us to love from our own place of suffering, we, like Christ, can bring him glory by displaying his beautiful love and redemption.

What If My Abuser Is Still Hurting Me?

Jesus teaches us not to approve of or overlook evil. To allow an abuser and his allies to continue to sin is not good for anyone. Love doesn't do that. We do not have to submit or contribute to abuse and should remove ourselves and other victims, if possible, and seek to stop its continuance.

Abusers can be so subtle and deceitful that we may not even realize we are being abused, especially if the offenses are not sexual. Because of individual factors, a complete treatment of domestic abuse goes beyond the content of this book. Leading friends can be helpful, but it would be wise to seek a good, experienced biblical counselor, one who has training in this area. This counselor must be able to recognize what has happened to us, and whether or not our present relationships are healthy. If you are currently in an abusive or unhealthy relationship, sexual or not, we strongly advise that you get immediate help. You may also want to consult books like Debi Pryde's *A Biblical View of What to Do When Your Husband Abuses You* or Lundy Bancroft's *Why Does He Do That? Inside the Minds of Angry and Controlling Men.*

No matter what we have experienced or how we have responded, *we are not at fault for being abused*, nor are we condemned for our wrong responses. In Christ, we are forgiven and bear no guilt (but we are to follow him rather than continue in sinful ways). Therefore, we can humbly cast away shame, knowing God nailed it all to the cross to set us free.

We can't fix the past. However, we can learn from it and stand with hope, confidence, and determination. We can help our abuser and other victims by stopping the cycle of abuse to the best of our ability. In so doing, we demonstrate Christlike love that seeks the well-being of others for the glory of God.

"Thus says the LORD: 'Execute judgment and righteousness, and deliver the plundered out of the hand of the oppressor. Do no wrong and do no violence to the stranger, the fatherless, or the widow, nor shed innocent blood in this place"(Jeremiah 22:3; see also Zechariah 7:9–10).

From this passage ...

How does God want people to be treated?

"But may the God of all grace, who called us to His eternal glory by Christ Jesus, after you have suffered a while, perfect [mature], establish [stabilize], strengthen, and settle you" (1 Peter 5:10).

From this passage ...

What is God like?

What four things does God eventually bring to those who suffer?

How might these four things bring hope and change in my life?

Therefore, having been *justified* by faith, we have *peace* with God through our Lord Jesus Christ, through whom also we have *access* by faith into this *grace* in which we stand, and *rejoice* with *hope* of the glory of God. And not only that, but we also glory in tribulations, knowing that tribulation produces *perseverance*, and perseverance *character*, and character, *hope*. Now hope does not disappoint, because the *love of God* has been *poured out* in our hearts by the *Holy Spirit* who was given to us.
— Romans 5:1–5

From this passage ...

List the good things God does for those who have been justified by faith (see the italicized words above).

How do those promises help us to cling to God and learn to love as he does?

"The LORD executes righteousness and justice for all who are oppressed.... The LORD is merciful and gracious, slow to anger, and abounding in mercy. He will not always strive with us, nor will He keep His anger forever" (Psalm 103:6, 8–9).

"I know that the LORD will maintain the cause of the afflicted, and justice for the poor" (Psalm 140:12).

"Repay no one evil for evil.... Do not be overcome by evil, but overcome evil with good" (Romans 12:17, 21).

The following Challenges apply the four foundation stones to the difficulties of relating to my abuser.

Relating to My Abuser

Challenge 1

Should I trust my abuser if he seems to be sorry?

Love

Love expresses the character of God for the well-being of the one loved. Love is just and true; therefore, I will trust only the trustworthy.

Communication

Communication uses words in God's way: Speak the truth in love; keep current; act wisely, don't react emotionally; and attack problems rather than people. I will ask my abuser about the source of his sorrow. Does he admit to his sin? I will resist accusations and caustic speech. My words will honor God and I will speak truth with respect, share the gospel, and solve specific problems that arise from the hurtful actions of my abuser.

Roles and Responsibilities

My role is to become part of the solution rather than contributing to the problems in our relationship. I will trust my abuser only if he has truly repented according to 2 Corinthians 7:10–11. Then I will seek counsel to know how to carefully extend appropriate trust to someone who has been untrustworthy.

Forgiveness

Forgiveness and trust are different. I will exercise vertical surrender by refusing to dwell on the hurt and choosing to allow God to open the door for horizontal forgiveness, but will offer horizontal forgiveness only if my abuser truly repents according to 2 Corinthians 7:10-11. I will trust only to the degree that is wise.

Challenge 2
Should our relationship be restored?

Love

Good relationships are built upon biblical love, which seeks the other person's well-being based on gospel truth. Restoration of the relationship is possible only when biblical love is extended by both parties.

Love does not enable sin. If I restore the relationship too soon, I am not loving my abuser as Christ would.

Often, a relationship with an abuser cannot be rightly restored. In that case, I can extend godly love when my abuser does not, but those expressions of love are more complicated and difficult to express. Wisdom is essential, so godly counsel should be sought.

Communication

Communication with my abuser may be extremely difficult. It requires wisdom regarding whether or not to be in contact, what can and should be said, and how and when attempts to communicate should be made. Writing a letter and doing role-plays with a leading friend may be helpful. I need to stay in close communication with God in prayer and in his Word. Christ's example through the gospel will give me wisdom.

Roles and Responsibilities

My abuser is responsible to change. His willingness to be accountable to authority is part of that. My role is to be aware of that process and be cautiously hopeful in Christ while guarding myself against evil. I am to overcome evil with good, but if I am too quick to restore this relationship, I may enable further abuse.

Forgiveness

Remember God's way of forgiveness (Luke 17:3–4; 2 Corinthians 7:9-11). I will not consider restoring the relationship until horizontal forgiveness can be extended, but I will maintain personal willingness to forgive biblically, and I will seek to reflect Christlikeness at all times.

Challenge 3

I continue to struggle with strong feelings of anger, fear, shame, and horror when I remember my abuser.

Love

God says, "Love your enemies, do good to those who hate you, bless those who curse you, and pray for those who spitefully use you. . . . Love your enemies, do good, and lend, hoping for nothing in return; and your reward will be great, and you will be sons of the Most High. For He is kind to the unthankful and evil. Therefore be merciful, just as your Father also is merciful" (Luke 6:27-28, 35-36). Loving my enemy means acting wisely and mercifully to overcome evil with good.

Communication

I will admit my struggle and talk to God about my feelings and experiences in light of psalms and other Scriptures that address fear, anger, and suffering. I will tell myself the truth about God's love, wisdom, and power. Rather than tearing down those who have hurt me, I will seek out godly counsel, first from God and then from believers who will tell me the truth and encourage me to respond in healthy ways. I will be honest with my leading friend and others I can trust. I will ask them to pray for me and keep me accountable.

Roles and Responsibilities

My role is to respond with faith that God is doing something good with this pain. I will treat my mind and body well, as a good steward of God's creation. I will resist the urge to respond with destructive actions, sinful speech, vengeance, or withdrawal into isolation. I will seek ways to encourage others who are suffering as I have (2 Corinthians 1:3-6).

Forgiveness

When I feel the pain of my abuse, I will renew my promise to forgive my abuser (vertical surrender) and will pray that eventually horizontal forgiveness can be offered.

Challenge 4

What if my abuser never changes?

Love

God does not promise that our abuser will change, but he does give us the ability to love our enemy. Love embraces the truth even when the truth is difficult to accept. Truth does not internalize or take responsibility for my offender's sin, but accepts my offender's right to choose not to repent of his sin. Love recognizes that my abuser's failure does not mean that God has failed or that I am at fault.

Communication

Communication will be very limited with an unrepentant abuser, and it should be offered only with godly counsel, in order to avoid manipulation, danger, and further abuse.

Roles and Responsibilities

My role is to act wisely, according to truth. I must accept that it is my offender's decision to be unrepentant without believing that it is my fault. Allowing him to manipulate me, or make me or others vulnerable to danger, would not reflect the wisdom and goodness of God, and is therefore not good for anyone.

Forgiveness

With an unrepentant abuser, I can offer vertical surrender to God but not horizontal forgiveness to the abuser. I continue to be willing to forgive only when repentance is present. While awaiting confession and repentance from my abuser, I will nail to the Cross the injury of the offense in order to make horizontal forgiveness possible. The relationship must be very limited unless the abuser repents.

Talking Points: Pray and discuss the following questions with your leading friend.

1. In what ways have I responded to my abuser and his allies?

2. Which of my responses could be characterized as "good" (prayer, kindness, patience, grace, etc.)?

3. Which of my responses could be characterized as "sinful" (rage, unbelief, lack of faith, hatred)?

4. Where does God place the responsibility for my responses?

5. How does the gospel give me hope?

6. How might hope help me to change my responses?

Discuss the following scenarios. What might the foundation stones of love, roles, communication, and forgiveness look like in each of these situations? Remember that forgiveness isn't an event; it's a process.

- As adults, a sister and her much older brother have to deal with her memories of incest in their childhood. A conversation about the memories leads to his admission of guilt. He repents and asks for her forgiveness. Discuss this situation in this light: *God takes evil so seriously that he sacrificed himself to make forgiveness possible* (John 3:16).

- A thirteen-year-old girl finally gathers the courage to tell the counselor at school that her softball coach has been molesting her. He has been arrested and she is awaiting court hearings. Discuss the situation in this light: *God put governmental authorities in place to protect and reward good and to restrain and punish evil* (Romans 13:1–5).

- A twenty-five-year-old wife and mom reels in grief over the sexual abuse she suffered as a child when she begins to fear that her own children may be abused. She is angry with her mom and dad for their inattentiveness and inability to protect her. She suffers from fear and panic attacks. Discuss the situation in this light: *To forgive is not the same as to trust. To forgive does not mean putting myself or anyone else in danger* (Luke 17:3–4; 2 Corinthians 7:10–11; Proverbs 2:3–14).

- Close friends and family blame a woman for the abuse she suffered as a child. They tell her she should have run away. She feels hurt, but wants to continue the relationships. Discuss the situation in this light: *Jesus knows what it's like to be misunderstood and falsely accused* (Isaiah 53:3).

- "Let all bitterness, wrath, anger, clamor, and evil speaking be put away from you, with all malice [wishing bad things to happen to someone else]. And be kind to one another, tenderhearted, forgiving one another, even as God in Christ forgave you" (Ephesians 4:31–32). Based on this passage, *discuss how kindness, tenderheartedness and forgiveness might look in each of the following relationships after abuse has occurred.* Who probably needs to be forgiven, and why?

* *Family, including parents, children, spouse, and other relatives*

* *Friends*

* *Church or community group*

Treasure: My shame landed squarely upon Jesus Christ who bears it for me, and no one can make it mine anymore. Grace and forgiveness are fully available because Christ loved me and gave himself for me.

Chapter 22

Building on the Foundation Stones in Primary Impact Relationships

Family

Marriage and Parenting

Being married and having kids can seem like the perfect salve for a broken heart. Most of the time, however, God uses these very relationships to show us how desperately we need him.[50] For a survivor of sexual abuse, the complexity of marriage and parenting relationships can seem overwhelming.

From Maria's Journal: **When It's Really Difficult**

Sometimes, there are no perfect Bible verses ... no answers. Sometimes, we just fall on our faces before our almighty God and beg him to help us love like he does. Sometimes, he brings us into valleys of testing. When my heart screams to be understood and have its way, will I make demands or will I tell my heart to submit to truth? The truth is that, in Christ, I am completely safe. He knows exactly what I am enduring and instead of changing my circumstances, he wants to change me. He wants me to believe that he is enough. I don't need anyone to be or to do anything in order for me to love them. I can love them because, in Christ, I am loved. When I know in my head and my heart that Jesus bears my pain, I can love with wisdom and grace, even if I'm not loved in return.

---

[50] For further study on marriage: Dave Harvey, *When Sinners Say "I Do"* (Wapwallopen, PA: Shepherd Press, 2007).

236

When we pour our hearts out to Jesus, and find rest and hope in him, he motivates and empowers us to love even when it's hard. As we begin to understand the amazing and unconditional love of our Father, we will want to respond in kind. When marriage gets tough and parenting overwhelms,[51] we can faithfully seek Jesus and trust him to help us.

Relating to My Husband and Children [52]

> ### Challenge 1
>
> I feel sexually used by my husband. Sex is not enjoyable. It feels like performing a duty for someone who can never be satisfied.

Love

Love expresses the character of God for the well-being of the one loved. God created sex for a loving marriage relationship, to accomplish good purposes. Sin has distorted sex, but in God's context it is still good. As a wife, I will consider what my husband wants and needs. Love is wise and kind, but it does not condone or enable sin.

Communication

Use words in God's way. Speak the truth in love, keep current, act wisely, don't react emotionally, and attack problems rather than people. I will tell myself the truth about God's purposes and expressions for sexual intimacy. I will speak patiently and clearly with my husband about my sexual concerns, likes, and dislikes, with a desire to solve problems and build our relationship rather than to assign blame or attack his character.

---

[51] Resources: Ginger Hubbard, "*Don't Make Me Count to Three!*" (Wapwallopen, PA: Shepherd Press, 2003) and John A. Younts, *Everyday Talk* (Wapwallopen, PA: Shepherd Press, 2004).
[52] These examples apply only to a marriage that is not abusive.

Roles and Responsibilities

In Christ, I am completely cared for, so I will not demand that my wants and needs be met by my husband. I will trust God to show me how to communicate well and to seek unity with my husband.

Forgiveness

Forgiveness is a promise to handle offenses in light of the gospel, as Christ did. Is my response part of the problem? Do I act out of bitterness? Or do I act out of grace and forgiveness? Do I need some help to sort out all of this?

Challenge 2

I'm afraid to be close to my husband because of recurring memories, body memories, and nightmares.

Love

In love, I will choose to draw near to God through searching the Scripture and praying. Then I will reach out to my husband as my leader and partner in order to build up our marriage.

Communication

I will tell God and my husband my fears and explain the memories that are fueling those fears. I will tell him what God is teaching me about applying God's Word when I am afraid (e.g., Psalm 56), and I will seek other appropriate help, if needed.

Roles and Responsibilities

I will refuse to blame my fears on my husband, or to take out my emotions on him. Instead of distancing myself, I will draw closer to him through good communication and seek to do helpful things that I know he likes.

Forgiveness

I will tell myself the truth: my memories are not reality now. The past is not happening again. Then I will pray for God to reveal what he wants me to learn. Do I need to renew my vertical surrender? Will I take steps to pursue horizontal forgiveness? Will I trust God more? Should I stop trying to hide or control everything?

Challenge 3

What does love look like when I'm tired of fighting and I want to run away?

Love

Love suffers long and is kind; love does not envy; love is not obnoxious or proud or rude or self-seeking. Love is not provoked to anger and keeps no record of wrongs. Love does not rejoice in evil of any kind, but rejoices in truth. Love endures all things, believes the best, hopes always, and keeps going.

Communication

Love shouldn't drag up the past to use against my husband. Yes, he has failed, but instead of blaming and accusing, I will talk to him about how to solve the problems that have come between us.

Roles and Responsibilities

Love doesn't give up. I am called to be my husband's helper (Genesis 2:18–23), so I will accept that role and its responsibilities to respect and submit to his authority in Christ. If our problems are too big for us to handle without help, I will suggest biblical ways for us to seek that help. I can get help even when my husband doesn't want it.

Forgiveness

It takes two people to start a problem, so I must accept my part in instigating it—running away instead of working to restore and build our marriage. After confessing this sin to God, I will ask my husband to forgive me.

Challenge 4

My husband doesn't listen to me when I try to express my thoughts and feelings. He wants me to get over this.

Love

Although my husband doesn't always listen to me, Jesus does. I am loved, even if my husband fails me. Am I listening to my husband, or am I responding in self-love more than love for God and my husband? How may I express myself in a more truthful, faith-filled, positive way without being demanding?

Communication

How may I seek my husband's input more effectively? Is there some distraction that we need to address? Is there anger? Am I attacking his character when I express myself? If so, how might I express myself to build him up rather than tear him down. How can I solve problems rather than complain?

Roles and Responsibilities

In what ways can I seek to understand my husband's point of view and help my husband understand me better—to build unity, rather than discord. How can I be patient with my husband when he needs more time to think?

Forgiveness

Do I need to ask his forgiveness for being selfish and demanding? I need to pray rather than nag. I also need to forgive him rather than holding his faults against him.

Challenge 5

I'm paralyzed by fear that my children will be abused.

Love

I will look out for my children's well-being, no matter how I feel. I will protect them wisely but also give them appropriate freedom. When I don't know what to do, I will talk to my husband and get godly counsel from Christians who parent well.

Communication

My speech will be full of grace and truth, expressing trust in God but also wisdom for living in this fallen world.

Roles and Responsibilities

I will teach my children about appropriate forms of touch and promote careful behavior in our home. Christ is pure and good, and I want them to learn about his behavior as they grow up. I will teach my children to wisely trust God more than they trust people; to recognize and reject evil in worldly philosophies, in media and books, and in their own hearts.

Forgiveness

In the context of Christ's forgiveness, I will surrender my fear to God's good and sovereign control. He is my children's redeemer and savior, not me.

Challenge 6

My children won't behave.

Love

A child needs to be diligently taught to obey because "foolishness is bound up in the heart of a child." (Proverbs 22:15). To love my children is to teach them to follow wisdom, because that's what is best for them (Ephesians 6:1-4).

Communication

I need to talk to my children daily about the importance of honoring God and obeying their parents. When I get overwhelmed as a parent, I need to talk to my husband and other godly Christian parents for advice.

Roles and Responsibilities

I am the parent, instructed by God to teach my children his way (Deuteronomy 6:4-12 and Ephesians 6:1-4). Children are not to run our household; God made parents the authorities in the home.

Forgiveness

When my children sin, I must teach them how to ask for forgiveness and how to forgive one another.

Cultural Distortion

In chapter 17, of Part VI entitled, *"Who am I?"* we discussed sex as a pure and good part of God's image in us. But our culture influences our definition and expectations for "good" sex. Visual images, sexual innuendo, careless conversations, and inappropriate public displays distort our desires and understanding of sex. Cultural stimuli saturate the marriage bedroom in an attempt to define sexual experience, crowding out the beauty of God's plan for unity between a husband and wife. This intimacy is unlike any other, reserved for one another and expressed privately and uniquely within marriage. We have to take great care to let God define good sex. As we seek to understand his heart for our marriage, especially sexual intimacy, he will begin to show us the way to a healthy and fulfilling sex life.

Marriage and parenting challenges can be very complex. We have given you a small sample of how to respond biblically, but we cannot cover each issue fully. Therefore, discuss further questions or concerns with your leading friend and your counselor.

"Trust in Him at all times, you people; pour out your heart before Him; God is a refuge for us" (Psalm 62:8).

Talking Points: Pray and discuss the following questions with your leading friend.

1. In what ways is my marriage flourishing?

2. In what ways do I see my marriage suffering:

   * *In communication (example: dishonesty, and verbal attack)?*

   * *In sexual intimacy (example: withholding affection, lack of desire, fear, shame, disgust,and bad memories)?*

   * *In finances (example: hoarding, or overspending)?*

   * *In social involvement (example: isolation, or being overcommitted)?*

3. How is my husband handling the stress of this journey? Does he need help, too?

4. In what ways do I or we need help with parenting? (Examples: hovering or excessive controlling, fear, isolation, lack of affection and touching, fear of how and when to discipline)

Use the chart below to apply the four foundation stones to one challenge you face.

Challenges:	Love	Communi-cation	Roles & Responsi-bilities	Forgiveness
Marriage and Parenting	Expresses the character of God for the wellbeing of the one loved.	Use words God's way: Speak truth in love; keep current; act wisely, don't react emotionally; attack problems rather than people	Biblical purpose and character	A promise to handle offenses in light of the gospel, as Christ did

A Call to Persevere

Marriage and parenting were not created to give us relief from the pain and difficulty we face in this life, but to reflect Christ's relationship with us. Our struggles are intensified when we misunderstand God's purposes for family life, thinking that fulfillment is wrapped up in human connections. We may have entered into marriage and parenting hoping to find answers, only to experience challenges that cause us pain.

Sometimes God gives amazing and merciful relief, but oftentimes he asks us to wait and trust him during difficult times. "Take up your cross" sanctification is definitely not a day at the spa! But when we turn to Jesus, he meets us in our suffering, uniting us with him in fellowship that is intimate, maddening, beautiful, hard, and awesome all at the same time. It's a bit like childbirth, but even more divine.

And, in Christ, it is definitely worth the bewilderment, complexity, and pain.

Suggested Resources: *Your Family God's Way* by Wayne Mack; *Shepherding A Child's Heart* by Tedd Tripp; *What Did You Expect?* by Paul David Tripp.

Please see Additional Resources, pages 270–271, for help to strengthen your marriage.

Immediate Family

"The same Jesus who turned water into wine can transform your home, your life, your family, and your future. He is still in the miracle-working business, and His business is the business of transformation."—Adrian Rogers [53]

> Shanae is disrespectful toward her mother and can't seem to get along with her older sister. She is destructively unstable and drinks so heavily it affects every area of her life. She wears her family out by her constant need to be rescued from her obsessive and abusive boyfriend. Deep down Shanae is angry with her mom for being inattentive during her childhood and blames her for the abuse she suffered. Her sister is a successful business owner and has three beautiful kids. Every time Shanae sees her sister she is bombarded with triggers and memories of her childhood. Envy, bitterness, and insecurity fuel her rebellion and continue to dominate her heart and mind.

Sometimes relationships with non-offending members of our families can be disheartening. Maybe Mom didn't protect you from Dad, or no one believed you when you said that your big brother came into your bedroom after the lights were out. The pain from not being believed or protected can be as bad as, or even worse than, the abuse we suffered. Even if someone believed us, and the offender was confronted and

---

[53] https://www.lwf.org/articles/posts/the-transforming-power-of-christ-10479. Accessed January 3, 2017.

removed, feelings of fear, bitterness, resentment, and loss can darken the nature of all of these relationships.

Complications

No matter how wonderful or terrible our childhood family dynamic was, serious complications result from being sexually abused by someone who we should have been able to trust. Dishonesty and mistrust can become controlling attitudes in families where abuse has occurred. Manipulation and fear can also dominate and poison the family atmosphere. These effects can blind us to what is actually healthy.

Talking with our leading friends about the nature of our families can help us to recognize distortions and can relieve us of the weighty burdens that come from simply not knowing what is good and acceptable.

Relating to My Family

Challenge 1
I'm angry with Mom for not protecting me.

Love

Love expresses the character of God for the well-being of the one loved. Mom has failed, but I can still love her. God made her my mom, and I need to respond by honoring her (Ephesians 6:2–3). When I have failed God, he continues to love me. My heavenly Father is my true protector even when my mom fails me.

Communication

Use words in God's way. Speak the truth in love, keep current, act wisely, don't react emotionally, and attack problems rather than people. Mom and I can talk about our experiences and the hope that is found in Christ. She has suffered, too. How might I share my faith with her as we discuss the anger and pain of our lives?

Roles and Responsibilities

No matter what Mom has done or failed to do, my role is to love and honor her the way Christ loves me (Matthew 22:37–39; Ephesians 6:2–3). I am not my mom's righteous judge; I am her daughter and will treat her as I'd like her to treat me.

Forgiveness

Forgiveness is a promise to handle offenses in light of the gospel, as Christ did. Everyone sins and needs forgiveness. Because Christ has forgiven me, I will not hold my mom's failure against her. When I feel angry, I will not take it out on my mom (James 1:19–20; Ephesians 4:30–32).

Challenge 2

My family doesn't believe me. They tell me I'm crazy. They say I'm lying and blame me for hurting the family. They cover up my abuse rather than dealing with it.

Love

My family is shocked by the thought of abuse, and they don't want to have to deal with it. Their response hurts me, but it doesn't change the truth. I can continue to love my family, no matter how they react, because God enables me.

Communication

I will not participate in my family's accusations because they are built upon lies and denial. Instead, I will speak truth in love whenever possible, and build up my family rather than tearing them down (no matter how they treat me).

Roles and Responsibilities

I am not a scapegoat; I am a member of my family, put there by God to represent him well. I am not responsible for what my family says about me or how they treat me; I am responsible for responding honorably. That may mean seeking safety and avoiding danger or further abuse.

Forgiveness

I will forgive by releasing the pain of these offenses to God's control (vertical surrender), but I can only offer horizontal forgiveness if my family repents. Meanwhile, I will be gracious and kind no matter how I am treated, and I will ask God to forgive me for my poor responses.

Challenge 3

How should I handle my suspicions about a family member?

Love

I must cling to truth, not suspicions, and believe the best until the truth is made known, taking care to be motivated by love rather than fear (I John 4:18).

Communication

If my suspicions seem reasonable, I will seek a way to find out the truth. I may have to consult godly counsel for an appropriate way.

Roles and Responsibilities

I will seek to act and speak respectfully as Christ would, in my biblical role as daughter, sister, etc. If necessary, I will appropriately seek wisdom and safety for myself and those in my family.

Forgiveness

Forgiveness is granted according to truth, not suspicions. If I have held suspicions against my family and they are proven to be unfounded, I will ask for their forgiveness. But if my suspicions are proven to be correct, I will seek reconciliation with them.

> **Challenge 4**
> **I can't trust my family with my kids.**

Love

Love means accepting the truth and acting accordingly. It is not loving to subject my children to possible abuse.

Communication

I will communicate my concerns with my family in a loving way. I may need to role-play this conversation with a counselor first.

Roles and Responsibilities

I am my children's parent, and have been called by God to protect and nurture them. My role as a parent supersedes my other family roles, and my responsibility to protect my children supersedes my family's feelings.

Forgiveness

My family's opinion of me must not be the motivation for my actions. I do not have to regret or need forgiveness for doing what is right, unless I am hateful about it. I must offer vertical surrender regarding my family's sin and be ready to forgive them when they repent.

Learning to relate well to family members requires supernatural wisdom and love. Abiding closely with Christ in the family of God is helpful too. His local church body gives us a new family in which to live and learn how to develop healthy relationships (Psalm 27:8–10; Romans 12). God's love is pure and safe. He will never manipulate or confuse us.

If you are currently living in an unhealthy and possibly dangerous family environment, please seek out help from a godly person you believe will take you seriously. They will not allow you to continue living in an abusive situation. Your circumstances may be serious enough to involve the police. God has established our government to serve and protect us (Romans 13:1–5). Don't hesitate to involve the authorities. It may be necessary to set boundaries (e.g., restraining orders) and make a plan for your safety in the event of a crisis. Seek God for wisdom and trust him to lead you. Please be safe. You are loved.

Talking Points: Pray and discuss the following questions with your leading friend.

1. Name each member of my family and describe the past or present condition of the relationship. Take note of any reoccurring themes.

2. Which relationships, specifically family relationships, seem to be the most difficult? Why?

Breathing Grace

Relationships are messy. As we consider in detail the depths of our pain and the catastrophic effects of sexual abuse, specifically within a family, we must stay close to Jesus and hide with him in the shelter of our heavenly Father's wings; we are always safe there. If this part of our journey is too painful, take some time to rest and pray. Our good and gentle Shepherd is beautiful, strong, and wise. He will always lead us well. Gaze upon Jesus and find rest for your weary heart. He loves you. He really does.

"The LORD is my shepherd; I shall not want. He makes me to lie down in green pastures; He leads me beside the still waters. He restores my soul" (Psalm 23:1–3).

Let's spend some time being nourished from these quiet waters. Read Galatians 5:22–23. It is common to think of the list of the fruit of the Spirit as evidence of what God is doing in and through us, but let's consider this list to be a character description of Jesus. Fill in the following blanks with the way Jesus demonstrates this fruit. The first few have been done for you to get you thinking.

- Jesus is love.

- Jesus knows joy.

- Jesus is my peace.

- Jesus _____.

- Jesus _____.

- Jesus _____.

- Jesus _____.

- Jesus _____.

- Jesus _____.

As believers in Jesus, we are given an amazing gift, the Holy Spirit. He will never leave or forsake us because he *lives* within us. When we depend on and submit to Christ, the fruit of the Spirit living in us can transform every area of our lives. Let's let these amazing truths build our hope and wash over and satisfy our dry and thirsty souls.

Treasure: Christ gives us the ability to address hard things in good ways.

> "Wait on the LORD; be of good courage, and He shall strengthen your heart; wait, I say, on the LORD!"
> —Psalm 27:14

Chapter 23

Building on the Foundation Stones in Primary Impact Relationships

Friends

"So Jonathan said to David, 'Whatever you yourself desire, I will do it for you.'" —1 Samuel 20:4

Rayna is lonely, but you would never know it. She is a busy bee. She has two young daughters, a faithful and gentle husband, and a great job. Most people like Rayna. She is thoughtful and kind, putting others always before herself. But making friends has never been easy for her. She fears rejection, she is too needy, and she hates conflict. These fears keep her painfully isolated. Failed friendships and the pain of gossip have taught her not to risk being known.

Nicole Braddock Bromley gives us some great insight concerning why we may have trouble navigating friendships when she writes:

Abuse produces a haze that obscures our view of relationships. We not only can't breathe, but we also can't see clearly anymore. Our pain clouds our vision, and we see everyone in light of our fear of being hurt and our need to feel safe. When we're not able to talk through our past and process our emotions, we look at ourselves and others through a distorted lens. We see every relationship in light of the impact that sexual abuse has had on us. This is why healthy relationships are crucial. They provide a true mirror that reflects us back to ourselves.

If we don't run, we go to the opposite extreme and cling to try to ensure that the one person we've been able to relate to won't leave just as everyone else has. In the end, the result is the same. Feeling suffocated, the person leaves, and the relationship ends. [54]

Uncertainty and Fear

Friendships are especially risky because there are no binding contracts or family reunions to define them. The shifting and shaky nature of these relationships can create some scary and complicated situations.

I (Maria) write to you from the chair of a thirty-something woman who is just beginning to find freedom and safety in my friendships. For a very long time, shame and fear confused my desires for deep and meaningful relationships. Like Shanae, I felt dirty and ashamed for being drawn to another woman; even if my desires were purely motivated. Lies and distortions of the truth bound me and kept me guarded for years. But now I am learning that God delights in friendships that center on him. Friendship can be one of the most sacred and holy expressions of our faith.

Friendships can be beautiful and healthy. Lets keep our eyes on hope and our hearts open to the Holy Spirit's teaching. Our chart for this section will center on relationships with leading friends, but these principles can be used with other friendships as well.

---

[54] Nicole Braddock Bromley, *Hush* (Chicago: Moody Publishers, 2007), 46.

Relating to My Friends

> **Challenge 1**
>
> **My friend doesn't respond to my phone calls or texts.**

Love

Love expresses the character of God for the well-being of the one loved. God knows that my heart aches. He loves me and is closer to me than any phone call or text (Psalm 139). I can talk to him any time. He will care for me. I don't have to make demands of my friend. I also don't have to be afraid that she is rejecting me, because perfect love casts out fear (1 John 4:18). Love is kind and thinks the best (1 Cor. 13:4, 7), and love is more concerned about the other person than about myself (Philippians 2:3-4). Love gives my learning friend some space without punishing her or making her feel guilty.

Communication

Use words in God's way. Speak the truth in love, keep current, act wisely, don't react emotionally, and attack problems rather than people. How much have I asked of my leading friend lately? How much have I demanded of her time? Am I respecting her time and energies, or am I acting selfishly? I will ask her if she feels crowded or smothered, and I will ask her to set appropriate boundaries for calling or texting.

Roles and Responsibilities

My role is to be a friend. I need to be careful to respect and even embrace the fact that my leading friend has roles to fill that do not include me: she is a wife, mother, grandmother, etc. I will be thankful for the time she has already given me, and I will accept the limits of our friendship roles without fearing rejection when we aren't able to get together as often as I would like. I will develop other appropriate friendships in my local church.

Forgiveness

Forgiveness is a promise to handle offenses in light of the gospel, as Christ did. There is probably nothing to forgive my friend for. My friend is not sinning when she doesn't answer her phone or texts. I should consider whether I am becoming sinfully demanding, and, if so, ask her to forgive me. Then together we will work out a plan to decide when calls and texts are most appropriate.

Challenge 2

My friend doesn't seem to need this relationship as much as I do.

Love

My impressions are not necessarily truth. I must not make assumptions and get caught up in self-pity. Love thinks about what is best for the other person. What is best for my leading friend?

Communication

I will talk about our relationship and my fears with honesty, giving my friend the benefit of the doubt, and communicating concern for her well-being.

Roles and Responsibilities

My responsibility is to be the best friend I can be, treating my friend as Christ would treat me. I am not responsible for my friend's responses, and I will resist the urge to sin by clinging too tightly or lashing out in anger.

Forgiveness

My friend not needing me as much as I need her is not a matter requiring forgiveness unless one of us sins. I will consider my friend's perspective and will communicate with grace, knowing we both need room to grow in love.

Challenge 3

I never know what to say to my friend.

Love

Love thinks about what interests or concerns my friend. Love cares about the things my friend cares about, and seeks to know more about those things.

Communication

When we are together I will listen for the subjects that interest my friend and ask questions about those things. I will ask my friend for prayer requests and pray with her frequently. I will discuss our assignment topics honestly and ask risky or scary questions that I am tempted to keep to myself. I will frequently express gratitude.

Roles and Responsibilities

My role is to participate in this friendship by giving of myself for the well-being of my friend. My discomfort is less important than my expression of kindness, grace, love, and honesty.

Forgiveness

Not knowing what to say to my friend is not a matter requiring forgiveness unless one of us sins in speech or knowingly withholds good from the other.

Challenge 4

I talk too much.

Love

Love cares more about knowing and reaching out to the other person than about me being known. If people try to get away from me when I speak, I am probably not expressing biblical love.

Communication

Is my speech expressing love to my friend, or am I self-focused? Do I allow my friend to speak, or do I dominate the conversation? Do I ask good questions and listen to the answers? Are my responses thoughtful and biblical?

Roles and Responsibilities

The development of a strong friendship is a two-way street, with attention and activity going in both directions. Does one of you always give and the other receive? If that is the case then work at balancing your friendship by deliberately focusing on the other person more often.

Forgiveness

Proverbs 17:27 says, "He who has knowledge spares his words." Overtalking can be self-focused and thoughtless. Consider whether forgiveness should be sought.

> **Challenge 5**
>
> Why do I feel like a fraud? Please help me tear down my walls; get past my fears of what people think of me and of being known. What does a healthy friendship look like?

Love

Love overcomes fear because it looks out for the well-being of others more than self. I John 4:18 says that Christlike love overcomes fear. A healthy Christian friendship grows between two believers who patiently exercise biblical love: showing interest and concern for one another, with a mutually growing respect and commitment to the friendship.

Communication

Communication is built upon trust; therefore, friendships can't be rushed or forced. They take time to develop as people learn about one another's character and gradually open up. Honest, caring communication is shared, but self-revelation should be shared only with trustworthy people. Like every other human being, I am flawed and fall short of perfection. But that doesn't make me a fraud. It just makes me human and in need of Christ.

Roles and Responsibilities

Abuse distorts roles, so it may take some time to figure out how to function in a given relationship. But my friendships do not define me: Christ does. I have a lot of freedom because of God's acceptance. I don't have to fear people's rejection because I know I am beloved and accepted in Christ. I am free to love others instead of needing them.

Forgiveness

I must avoid unnecessary regret. I cannot change the opinions or faults of other people, but I can respond in love because God has forgiven and received me into his family.

> **Challenge 6**
>
> **I fear entering into friendship and being known, because I have been betrayed in the past.**

Love

Love is wise about giving appropriate weight and trust to a friendship. All levels of friendship are legitimate, and God's wisdom will guide us in what to trust people with. Fear is good when love tempers it, because fear can keep us from too much inappropriate self-revelation. Love shows compassion and keeps a godly kind of fear, rather than a fear that dominates and overcomes us. Ask your counselor and your leading friend for help to learn about godly fear and love.

Communication

The extent of our communication will be different with each person we know, but should always begin cautiously. Some people will be trustworthy; to them, I can let my story unfold. Others should be told very little. Wisdom will guide me when I pray for it, follow Scripture, and rightly discern truth.

Roles and Responsibilities

My role will differ with each friendship depending on the availability, interests, and values of the other person. I need to discern the person's godliness and trustworthiness (will our companionship build up my faith?), my time and resources, the wisdom of getting closer to them, and the needs and demands of the relationship.

Forgiveness

Conflict is a part of every human relationship, so I should not consider a friendship to be over just because we may struggle. Instead, I should see conflict as a potential to deepen our friendship as we solve problems and forgive one another biblically.

When Friendship Hurts

"For it is not an enemy who reproaches me; then I could bear it. Nor is it one who hates me who has exalted himself against me; then I could hide from him. But it was you, a man my equal, my companion and my acquaintance" (Psalm 55:12–13).

Conflict is part of every relationship because we live as sinners among sinners. We may feel like hiding or quitting because trusting people often leads to hurt, but isolation leads to a deeper loneliness. We may need some help to work through our questions and concerns such as the following:

- Did I do something wrong?

- Is my friend struggling with something, or was she struggling with me?

- What makes being my friend so difficult? Am I hard to be around?

- When I feel hurt, used, or overlooked, how do I handle that?

- Is my hurt perceived or is it real?

When we are angry, it's helpful to ask ourselves this simple question: What do I really want? Asking God to show us what we want will help us to know what to do with the longings we feel. (See chapter 5 on the six categories of heart desires.) Oftentimes, we are simply lonely, uncertain, and scared. The presence of our friend seems to calm the ache in our soul, but she cannot remove it. If she is a friend of godly character, she will walk with us to Jesus, not replace him. If we want people to be our savior, we will turn to friends instead of Jesus. That will not work.

Christlike Friends

When someone is kind, thoughtful, and loving it is only natural to be drawn to that person. James 1:17 tells us that "every good and perfect gift is from above, and comes down from the Father ..." God is gracious to give us friends. And oftentimes he reaches deep into our hearts through a gentle word or touch from human hands.

It can be hard to navigate these kinds of relationships and the emotions that come to the surface as we grow closer to one another. It may be very tempting to cling to someone who looks and acts a lot like Jesus. But as we seek diligently to know Christ, we will discover that Jesus is who we long for. It is his presence in that person that we are drawn to. This is not shameful, but we need wisdom and strength to know when and how to reach out to another person. If we keep this important truth fresh in our minds, we will find freedom to love and be loved without the heavy chains of demanding and suffocating expectations. We can take a deep breath of hope as we fix our eyes on our truest and most faithful friend. Learning to gaze upon the glory of God in the person of Jesus will help us to love people more than we need them.

Three Types of Friends

We are social beings who were created to interact meaningfully with one another. God created us with different gifts and characteristics that help us to grow and function well, especially when we follow Christ together. Ideally, three types of friends will help keep us balanced. We recommend seeking each type of friend in a Christian setting such as your local church.

1. *A teacher* to explain how things work—someone who instructs us well as we learn how to do life. Teachers share knowledge in lots of practical and philosophical ways, but especially concerning the things we have covered in this book. A godly teaching friend shows us how and why things work as they do, according to a scriptural worldview in various settings.

2. *An advisor* to guide in wisdom—someone who helps us to apply what we are learning. This kind of friend helps us to plan and evaluate. She prepares us for what may lie ahead so that we are well equipped to make good decisions and respond well.

3. *A comforter* to encourage us when we fail or are hurt—someone who weeps with us, tends to our wounds, and helps us to get up and try again. This person understands our sorrows but doesn't let us drown in self-pity. She reminds us of God's goodness from Scripture and shows us how to keep going by faith when life gets hard.

All these strengths are seldom found in one person, and maybe not in one place. We have to get to know people and watch for these qualities in order to recognize these types of friends. Our local church is a great place to start seeking out teachers, advisors, and comforters. We should also try to discern which of these three roles best fit our own strengths. Then we can work on developing those strengths so we can reach out more effectively in friendship.

"Two are better than one, because they have a good reward for their labor. For if they fall, one will lift up his companion" (Ecclesiastes 4:9–10).

Talking Points: Pray and discuss the following with your leading friend.

1. Considering my past and present friendships, which do I consider as healthy, and why? Which ones are unhealthy, and why?

2. What aspects of friendship produce the most fear in me?

3. Read 1 John 4:18. How might God's love overcome my fear?

4. How do I typically test a relationship?

5. What are my expectations (what do I want for and from this person)? Are they healthy and reasonable?

6. Sometimes love cuts deep, but it is always good. Am I willing to risk being hurt, if God intends for me to learn how to love and be loved in a new or restored relationship?

7. What is my typical response when I am hurt by a friend?

8. Read Luke 22:39–61 and Matthew 26:56. How did Jesus' friends hurt him?

9. Read John 15:13 and 21:1–19. How did Jesus respond to his friends after they hurt him?

10. How can knowing and being loved by Jesus make a difference in how I respond to the challenges in my friendships?

11. Which of the three types of friends (teachers, advisors, comforters) do I have?

12. Which of the three types of friends describes me best?

13. How will I reach out to others with friendship today?

Who Are You, Then?

Relationships are beautiful and hard, designed to drive us to God for definition, unity, and purpose. As we drink deeply from the cistern of his love, we can reflect the character of the God who loved us and gave himself for us. As believers, we are his children, his family, here to reflect his character and extend his invitation to eternal life.

Amazingly, God's wisdom and grace can flow through flawed and frail beings like us, because his goodness and mercy has been freely given to us. Human relationships, built upon the law of love according to the principles of Scripture, enable us to weather the storms and find redemptive joy in the journey.

Treasure: Friends of godly character will strengthen our wisdom and faith.

Part VIII

WHERE DO WE GO FROM HERE?

Chapter 24

Looking Ahead in the Journey

Walking through the wreckage of sexual abuse is a gut-wrenching journey. You are a brave soul and God delights in you as you express your faith in his goodness and continue to trust him in spite of the horror you have endured.

Treasure in the Ashes has been written to acknowledge the hardships in our stories, to expose lies, and to embrace the hope of the gospel as we navigate the past and present pain of sexual abuse. We have been learning:

- To tell our story and why it matters,

- To view and pursue God in light of his true, good, and unchanging character,

- To be drawn to Jesus as our Savior, healer, and redeemer,

- To find our identity as a child of God, and

- To relate to others in a gospel-driven, biblically healthy way.

My Story Matters

Everybody has a story. Even those among us who seem to "have it together" carry a story deep within their souls: our testimony through time and experience. All of life is etched with pain, pleasure, joy, and sorrow. None of us escape the realities of living in a fallen world.

As we consider how our lives have been drastically altered by sexual abuse, we must begin to see our story as shaped by God's amazing history of redemption. We will never fully understand God's ways, but when we accept our good God for who he is, we can rest knowing that our story is being purposefully redeemed in him (Psalm 119:68; Isaiah 61:3; 2 Corinthians 1:3–6).

But where do we go from here? Some of us may be tempted to think that finishing this study means that we have accomplished our task and may finally file "sexual abuse" into some neatly organized drawer hidden deep within the file cabinet of our life. If we follow and love Jesus will all the questions vanish? Will all the pain go away? And will life be continuously easy and happy? Probably not. We do still live in a fallen world where hardship exists (John 16:33). The struggle continues, but in a new dimension, infused with hope and purpose as we walk with our Savior, the Prince of Peace.

God continues to write our stories, and we will continue to need Jesus. In the good days and the bad days to come, he will constantly be with us, and when we turn to him, we will be helped. But that is not all we can do. While on our journey home, God bids us to look for ways to share with others what he is doing in our lives. We can share the purpose, hope, and peace we are finding in him.

"Go home to your friends, and tell them what great things the Lord has done for you, and how He has had compassion on you" (Mark 5:19).

"Blessed be the God and Father of our Lord Jesus Christ, the Father of mercies and God of all comfort, who comforts us in all our tribulation, that we may be able to comfort those who are in any trouble, with the comfort with which we ourselves are comforted by God" (2 Corinthians 1:3–4).

"These things I have spoken to you, that in Me you may have peace. In the world you will have tribulation; but be of good cheer, I have overcome the world" (John 16:33).

From these passages …

Describe some ways that you have found peace in Christ, even during suffering.

Continuing on the Right Path

As we have journeyed together, we trust that your relationship with your local church has become deep and meaningful, so that you have established some lasting friendships and have become involved with ministries that will encourage spiritual growth. Stay connected to a gospel-centered church that teaches the Word faithfully.

And continue to search Scripture every day, to light your path as you follow Jesus. Periodic reviews of this book my help.

Talking points: Think through the following questions and discuss with your leading friend.

1. Discuss the process of your growth in Christ and how you might share with others the peace and help you are finding.

2. Talk awhile with our Good Shepherd and reflect on where you have been and where you might be going.

3. Look at the recommended resources throughout and the bibliography at the end of this book if you would like to do further study in areas we have not thoroughly covered.

4. Consider how to talk to a friend about what God has been doing in your life.

The Next Step

The written portion of *Treasure in the Ashes* has come to an end, but "you are our [letter] written in our hearts, known and read by all [people]… written not with ink but by the Spirit of the living God, not on tablets of stone but on tablets of flesh, that is, of the heart" (2 Corinthians 3:2–3). Your journey is a testimony of what God is doing in a life that is turned to him. The next step in your journey is to consider who else might need to hear the good news you have found in Christ. No, we have not arrived at our final destination, but we can show the Way, the Truth, and the Life to someone struggling to find the path (John 14:6). If you find it difficult to talk about your experiences, simply share what you are learning about Christ and then pray for those who are suffering. When you are ready, your leading friend may be able to suggest ways for you to reach out to others in need.

We have prayed earnestly for you, dear friend, that your journey in this fallen world would be illumined by our beautiful Savior who is leading you home. You will find the comfort, hope, and wisdom you have so desperately needed in the person of Jesus Christ. Life is hard in this valley of tears, but it can also be astonishingly and vividly beautiful when in faith we lift our eyes to him. Keep pushing back the darkness and embracing the light that shines so full of hope, healing, and redemption.

> … that the God of our Lord Jesus Christ, the Father of glory, may give to you the spirit of wisdom and revelation in the knowledge of Him, the eyes of your understanding being enlightened; that you may know what is the hope of His calling, what are the riches of the glory of His inheritance in the saints, and what is the exceeding greatness of His power toward us who believe …
> —Ephesians 1:17–19a

Additional Resources

Baker, Amy. *Getting to the Heart of Friendships* (Bemidji, MN: Focus Publishing, 2010)

Braddock Bromley, Nicole. *Breathe: Finding Freedom to Thrive in Relationships after Childhood Sexual Abuse* (Chicago: Moody, 2009)

Harvey, Dave. *When Sinners Say "I Do"* (Wapwallopen, PA: Shepherd Press, 2007)

Holcomb, Lindsay and Justin. *Rid of My Disgrace* (Wheaton, IL: Crossway Books, 2011)

Hubbard, Ginger. *"Don't Make Me Count to Three!"* (Wapwallopen, PA: Shepherd Press, 2003)

Jeffrey, Robert. *When Forgiveness Doesn't Make Sense* (Colorado Spring, CO: Waterbrook Press, 2000)

Lane, Tim and Paul David Tripp. *Relationships: A Mess Worth Making* (Glenside, PA: New Growth Press, 2008)

Miller, Wendell. *Forgiveness: The Power and the Puzzles* (Warsaw, IN: Clear Brook Publishing, 1994)

Morison, Patrick H. *Forgive! As the Lord Forgave You* (Phillipsburg, NJ: P&R Publishing, 1987)

Nicewander, Sue. *Help! I Feel Ashamed* (Day One Christian Publishers, 2012)

Peace, Martha. *The Excellent Wife* (Bemidji, MN: Focus Publishers, 1995)

Pryde, Debi. *A Biblical Approach to What to Do When Your Husband Abuses You* (www.ironwood.org), Iron Sharpeneth Iron Publications.

Tuggle, Brad and Cheryl. *A Healing Marriage* (Colorado Springs, CO: NavPress, 2004)

Welch, Ed, *Shame Interrupted* (Greensboro, NC: New Growth Press, 2012)

————. *When People Are Big and God is Small* (Phillipsburg, NJ: P & R Publishing, 1997)

Wilson, Jim. *How to Be Free from Bitterness* (Moscow, ID: Canon Press, 1999)

Younts, John A. *Everyday Talk* (Wapwallopen, PA: Shepherd Press, 2004)

Supplement:

TRAINING TO BE
A LEADING FRIEND

Preparing to Help a Learning Friend

Dear Leading Friend,

Your beautiful desire to comfort and strengthen one of your broken-hearted sisters or brothers reflects the heart of our Redeemer. Those who have been abused need to know Jesus Christ better, but they are often devastated by lies that blind them to who he truly is. May God use you to shine his light and share the truth that will set them free.

As a biblical counselor, I have met scores of women (and some men) who have been sexually abused. By reaching out to them I have learned that walking with a learning friend is not simply advocacy, but also a journey of faith. As my own motives, beliefs, thoughts, and actions have been revealed and tested along the way, I am learning day by day what it means to know and trust in Christ, to live as his representative, to be his hands and feet—even as I struggle with my own imperfections. He leads me to humility and greater faith in the process, especially as I see all the ways I serve myself instead of him.

As my learning friend and I discover and acknowledge our mutual need, we find companionship and hope in Christ. He shows me how good he is and invites me to come to him, bringing my friend with me. We fellowship around his Word, driven to his throne time and time again, to find him faithful in our frailty and desperation. Because Jesus is always good, we learn together to trust him for strength, wisdom, endurance, and hope.

My friend is needy, but so am I. Personally, I believe that God intended our journey to be as much for my growth as it is for Maria's. We shared our journey to encourage and challenge you to let God transform you as you walk with your friend. You are a leader, but never forget that you are also a learner.

Thank you for caring enough to help a hurting friend. May your own soul be helped along the way as you come together to the throne of grace.

For Jesus,
Sue

Bear one another's burdens, and so fulfill the law of Christ.
— Galatians 6:2

Introduction

Welcome, leading friend, to the journey of a lifetime. May God bless your servant heart richly as you help a hurting soul to find the way through a bewildering maze of powerful emotions and baffling questions about God, herself, [55] and relationships.

Treasure in the Ashes is a systematic tool to help you and your learning friend walk together biblically. It is not simply to ease emotions, but to think through significant questions, beliefs, doubts, responses, and relationship challenges so that your learning friend can grow and become fruitful in Christ. We cannot be exhaustive with this subject, especially because every experience is unique, but we do offer this book as a general guide. Please take your time when moving through this material, seeking additional resources using the suggestions provided.

At the end of chapter 14, we suggested that you take a break to read an additional book that we found to be important at that stage of the journey. Take whatever time you need together to accomplish that reading, and feel free to read Additional Resource books (on pages 270–271) at another point if you think that would be more helpful to your friend.

This supplemental section is intended to be a reference source for you. Please read it through, and then come back to relevant sections as you walk with your learning friend. Not every section will be equally important in your journey. Seek out additional resources when you need them. Remember that resources come in many forms, including other people. Please be alert for times to wisely ask your pastor or another biblical counselor to assist you.

The end of this chapter provides some summary sheets to keep close at hand for reference during your interactions and fellowship times with your friend. These handy references are provided to help you to stay biblically focused and purposeful during your time together.

---

[55] We have chosen to use feminine pronouns when referring to a learning friend because it avoids the cumbersome 'him or her' grammar and is in keeping with the authors' stories. We recognize and respect the devastation of male abuse and ask the reader to accept the feminine pronoun when a masculine one would have been equally appropriate.

Leading and Learning Together

Maria and I (Sue) met at church in 2008. In 2011 we started on an incredibly rich and terribly messy road of leading and learning together. (You'll hear more of our stories during the *Treasure in the Ashes* study.) At some points we rejoiced, while at other times we wept, struggled, and mourned. Parts of our pathway have been clearly marked, while other segments were shrouded in pain, darkness, and uncertainty. Our journey together has certainly not been easy, but we have found that the rewards of friendship, perseverance, and deepening faith have far outweighed the risks and hardships.

Throughout our way, we have sought the Light of life, Jesus Christ—often desperately! He has been consistently faithful, anchoring us in his strength and wisdom. We encourage you to join us in walking toward the Light that will give you and your learning friend freedom.

"But I'm Not a Counselor!"

You may not be professionally trained for formal counseling, but you are still a counselor. We all counsel every time we give advice, answer a question, or offer our opinion. We also counsel by example: our character and our choices say to others, "This is what to value. Here's how to live." So the question is not whether you will counsel; the question is whether your counsel is biblical or not. We're here to help with that.

Why Reach Out?

Have you ever been hurting and deeply in need of someone to help you by caring for you, listening to you, and praying with you? Have you hungered to see Christ reflected in someone's eyes, to feel his hand reaching out in someone's kindness, to hear his voice in someone's prayers? Godly tenderness makes tremendous impact. We urge you to reach out like that to someone devastated by sexual abuse. But to truly help, your outreach should follow a biblical approach.

How Your Church Can Help

God designed human beings as social creatures, created to interact and love one another (Genesis 2:18; Ephesians 4:15–16). God delights in believers who reach out as compassionate burden-sharers, walking in unity and exhorting one another in faith (Galatians 6:1–2; Psalm 133:1).

> *A biblical local church can be a safe, fertile environment for a learning friend to grow.*

We believe that godly believers like you are the Titus 2 lifeline for those who have been sexually abused. As the book of Titus exemplifies, your lifeline needs to be tethered to a local church that will provide you and your friend with the following:

- Consistent biblical teaching and preaching;

- Godly leadership;

- Helpful accountability;

- Personal support;

- Faithful human examples;

- Models of friendship and family relationships;

- Love and acceptance;

- Appropriate opportunities to serve.

In general, your local church is a safe environment where your learning friend can establish her relationship with God, know his Word, and relate better to others. You can encourage and assist your learning friend to regularly attend services and to get involved in church events such as fellowship meals, missionary groups, Sunday school classes or Bible studies where she can get to know God and his people.

The local church as teacher.

Your church can help your learning friend discover the meaning of the gospel and its application to her journey. Your learning friend may have had little real background in the Scripture or in building godly relationships. Your friend may also need help with basic life skills such as keeping a checkbook, using a credit card, organizing a kitchen, planning a menu, parenting children, making decisions, or keeping a calendar. As you walk together, seek to identify what instructional needs are present. Patiently teach life skills and engage others in the process as needed. As helpful teaching tools; use Scripture and its principles, read reliable literature, and perhaps perform role-plays. Within your local church there are godly people who are good examples to follow. Ask for help if you need it. See if life skills may be taught by someone else in your church; additional supportive relationships will be established in the process.

Local church fellowship.

You can help your learning friend to broaden her circle of friends and acquaintances by resisting the urge to be at her side all the time at church; she needs to know you support her, but she also needs to learn how to function independently from you. Engage others, for example, for transportation or other special help.

Watch your learning friend's interactions at church and identify one or two people that may become her good friends. If needed, guide her in how to introduce herself and start conversations. Provide reassurance that informal friendship and fellowship will develop social skills and often lead to joyful, godly human relationships. Caution your friend, too, that human relationships are always imperfect and "in-process." Your learning friend may be terrified of conflict, believing that relationship difficulties are always her fault and that they confirm her as a failure—neither of which is true. Perceived threats or insecurities may be met with anger or may tempt your friend to run away in fear. Reassure your friend that God is at work in hard relationships to reveal himself and our need of him, not to condemn (Romans 8:1; 5:3-6). Study how Christ handled relationships, and make a list of some practical ways to follow his example. Part 5: "Who are You?" is designed to help.

A godly local church can nurture and care for you as a leading friend.

To encourage your spiritual and social maturity, ask mature Christians in your church to pray and offer wise advice as you walk with your friend. Avoid gossip by using unnamed examples as you seek advice, or bring your friend (or get written permission) if you need to be specific.

A biblical local church is called to equip and protect.

A wise church will proactively equip leading friends to be ready when a need becomes known. Your church can also assist victims of sexual abuse by forming an advocacy committee to assist the sexually abused to find counseling and to report abuse, and by training godly church members to disciple and counsel. Be aware of the possibility of ongoing domestic violence and have a plan for intervention when necessary. In addition, check your church's constitution and policies to see whether a plan for biblical church discipline is stated clearly and thoroughly. [56] [57]

In the local church setting, people can meet together safely and biblically work together toward truth. This kind of interaction may be completely new to your learning friend, who has probably been living alone socially, and perhaps spiritually, since the abuse occurred. Isolation is not good. Instead, your friend needs to learn how to trust God and dependable people. She needs to know what a good relationship is, and how to navigate ever-present challenges God's way. Teach her how to reach out in meaningful ways to build a relationship with God and with you—perhaps the first healthy relationships your learning friend has ever known. This book is designed to help.

---

[56] Consult www.HisPeace.org for help to write a comprehensive plan for church discipline.
[57] For more suggestions, see 'Betrayal, Fear, and Faith,' *The Baptist Bulletin*, May/June 2013, July/August 2013, and September/October 2013 issues. www.BaptistBulletin.org Click on "About Us" to read past and current issues of the magazine.

Beginning Our Journey

A Word to Remember for our Leading Friends: <u>Patience</u>
"But let patience have its perfect work, that you may be perfect and complete, lacking nothing." —James 1:4

A Word to Remember for our Learning Friends: <u>Faith</u>
"Trust in the LORD with all your heart, and lean not on your own understanding; in all your ways acknowledge Him, and He shall direct your paths." —Proverbs 3:5-6

Establishing a Relationship

God will probably bring your friend to you, as he did with your two authors. However, if you are seeking someone to minister to, be sure to bathe your search in prayer. Talk to godly people, such as your pastor and his wife, or another church leader. Wait patiently. Once you find someone you think may be God's choice for you to lead, consider the following. None of the items on this list will necessarily qualify or disqualify you from working together, but you will have some idea what challenges and advantages may lie ahead as you work together.

- *Common interests:* A good local church can provide a solid base for mutual interests, so we recommend that you and your friend attend the same church while you are walking together. See Appendix A for a list of qualities of a good local church. [58] You may also find it helpful to share other activities to help you build trust and feel comfortable with one another (e.g., crafts, sewing, childcare, decorating, cooking, sports, volunteer work, music).

- *Compatibilities of schedule and location:* Will you be able and willing to spend time together?

---

[58] Another good resource when looking for a church is Jim Newheiser's *Help! I Need a Church* (Shepherd Press, 2016).

- **Character:** Is this person teachable? Are you able to instruct and find appropriate teaching resources? [59] Are both of you likely to persevere through the whole study? Is this person's heart drawn to wisdom (even if she currently lacks wisdom and needs a great deal of instruction) and willing to work hard (even if she currently lacks organizational skills or wise work habits)?

- **Personality:** Do you get along? You don't necessarily have to like each other right away, but you should believe that you can work together, grow together, and that you can learn to love one another biblically.

- **Faith:** Do you share belief in Jesus Christ, or do you share an interest in the things of God, even if she is not yet a believer?

- **Boundaries:** Are you able to set realistic boundaries for your relationship? Do you believe those boundaries will be respected?

- **Age:** Age difference does not have to prevent you from working together (e.g., the relationship between your authors spans two generations). Consider generational differences such as social experiences, relevant subjects, interests, and vocabulary.

Spiritual preparation

Treasure in the Ashes training will prepare you in part, but your greatest preparation will be in Christ. Your friend carries deep wounds that no human being can heal. Do not be alarmed or disappointed that you fall short of fixing what is wrong. You are not called to be the savior, but you do walk alongside them to point your learning friend to the real Savior. This book will guide you to address questions and life skills

---

[59] This book will suggest numerous resources you can use beyond the lesson materials to address her specific needs. If she requires counseling, we suggest that you talk to your pastor, your leader, or look for a biblical counselor in your area at the ACBC website: www.biblicalcounseling.com

with which your friend may need assistance. However, you will find your primary help from Scripture because God alone knows human needs and how to fulfill them. This book provides many Scriptural references as starting points to address specific needs. Speak Scripture's truth, and patiently walk together toward Jesus, seeking him in prayer, obedience, and trust. Both of you will feel bewildered along the way, but rest assured that he does not. By faith, let God lead you both. He will not fail, even when you do.

If you have suffered abuse yourself, *Treasure in the Ashes* presents a beautiful opportunity to share how the Lord is ministering meaningfully to your brokenness. By grace, God has equipped you (2 Corinthians 1:3–7), to recognize when someone is spiritually thrashing or silently drowning in despair. Share Scripture that has been helpful to you, and talk about how God has been good to you in your journey. Let nothing shake you from your Rock. As you reach out to your learning friend, may you grow in your personal walk with Christ to greater faith and understanding, not only for the unspeakable suffering you see in your friend, but also for his faithfulness to rescue both of you.

Praying for Your Learning Friend

Prayer is an essential ministry because you will experience lasting freedom and forward movement only in God's strength. You both need him. Connect with God through prayer every day. At the end of this chapter is a list entitled Praying Scripture Head-to-Toe. We suggest that you pray one section per day for your learning friend, opening your Bible and speaking to God directly from his Word. Pray, too, for your friend's salvation, faith, spiritual growth and wisdom, financial and material needs, self-image, work, family, health, relationships, and safety. Frequently ask your learning friend for prayer requests, and encourage her to share answers to prayer as well.

Your Role as a Leading Friend

The term leading friend was chosen because it defines your primary role as a leader (a guide) in the context of mutual friendship. Trustworthy guidance and faithful companionship are rare, especially in the wake of sexual abuse. As you patiently and kindly walk alongside one another, you will be living out the qualities you want your friend to learn. Let God use your Christlike love to teach her that God loves her.

Initially, your learning friend may react like a bird with a broken wing: fearful and resistant. Being self-protective, your friend may lash out, keep a "safe" distance, or even hide. Don't be surprised if you encounter skepticism and frequent testing in your relationship until your friend is sure you are genuine. However, as you patiently show your gentle goodwill and compassion, you may slowly be allowed to nurse that brokenness toward healing, to build courage, and to help your friend find the freedom to fly.

Your role in this journey is to patiently reflect the character of Jesus Christ in the context of true friendship. As you extend courtesy, thoughtfulness, patience, consistency, exhortation, and punctuality, your learning friend may be astonished to realize that faithful people really exist. Here are more ways to demonstrate godly friendship:

- Patiently hear your friend's experience of abuse (without overreacting), allowing your friend time to fully verbalize the story before you jump in to offer help. Listen without judging or critiquing what is said: take the story at face value without trying to correct what you hear. In so doing, you will find out about the experience. (See the appendix at the end of this chapter for more help to listen effectively.)

- Listen patiently, again and again, to identify: **beliefs about God, self, others, and life in this fallen world. What questions do you hear? What yearnings and themes?** Be careful not to judge or to get too emotional; instead, seek earnestly to understand.

- Where do her thoughts dwell or linger? Look for patterns of thought and what triggers them.

- What does your friend do? What constructive and destructive actions does she take (especially habitually)?

- How does she feel? Your learning friend may have learned to suppress her feelings out of self-preservation, and therefore may need help to identify emotions. Use defining words such as anger, fear, uncertainty, doubt, sorrow, etc., in your conversations.

- Pray patiently and consistently for your friend. Pray with her, too, to teach her how to pray in faith. If you need help, check the section at the end of this chapter entitled, "Praying Scripture Head-to-Toe." Choose a few of the more helpful categories and pray the Scripture with your friend.

- Comfort your learning friend (2 Corinthians 1:3-6). Verbalize your sorrow over what has happened, and say that the abuse was wrong. Weep together. Talk about God's love and your love for your friend. Express anger toward the horrible things that have been done. Reiterate your commitment to walk together.

- Keep your word.

- Be consistent.

- Contact your friend regularly to express your interest and care. But be careful not to encourage over-dependence on you. It's a delicate balance.

- Reinforce biblical truth and draw upon the resources God has provided—especially Scripture and prayer. Find specific passages that apply. The psalms are a good place to start.

- Encourage, model, and reinforce responsible living.

- Lead in thanksgiving and appropriate praise to God each time you talk.

- Set meaningful boundaries for your relationship.

* *Define an emergency, and let your friend know that strong feelings alone are not emergencies.*

* Talk about times of the day to call you in a non-emergency, and tell your learning friend the number of times you are available to get together during the week.

* When you feel smothered or distanced, be kind but honest about what you see and how it is affecting your relationship. Your honesty and wisdom may teach her how to build her other relationships with integrity.

* Set up a contingency plan. (See Contingency Plan on pages 297-298.)

As you set wise boundaries, a clingy, learning friend may loosen her grip and begin to trust you, an angry friend may relax, or an isolated friend may draw near to you and to God. Over time, with great patience and endurance, as you point to God by example and instruction, you may lead your friend to grow in faith and spiritual strength. At that point, you will begin to see more unity and give-and-take in your relationship. This is a good sign of growth in your friend and in her relationship with you. But be patient and resilient. Change is hard, it makes unexpected turns, and it takes time.

Preparing Your Mind

As a leading friend, we strongly recommend that you become familiar with the entire *Treasure in the Ashes* book before beginning the journey, so you will know what will be covered and what supplements you may need. And please read two of the following books before beginning *Treasure in the Ashes* with your learning friend. Both books will help you to understand your friend's struggle and to know what you can do for him or her.

* *Instruments in the Redeemer's Hands* by Paul David Tripp presents a biblical approach to helping others, something few Christians understand.

- *Rid of My Disgrace* by Lindsay and Justin Holcomb is another excellent source of biblical help for those who have been sexually abused. If your friend is not a reader, an alternate choice might be Debi Pryde's *Why Me, Lord?* (Debi Pryde www.ironwood.org or Bob Jones University Bookstore at www.bju.edu), a booklet explaining the experience of childhood sexual abuse in a way that helps victims to see that they are not "weird" or stupid.

We suggest that you also become familiar with *A Shepherd Looks at Psalm 23* by W. Phillip Keller, because it is a scheduled supplemental study in *Treasure in the Ashes*. This book will help your friend gain a more accurate understanding of God's benevolent and loving character, as well as his strength and protection, as her Good Shepherd.

A snapshot of the Treasure in the Ashes *study plan*

Treasure in the Ashes begins by introducing Sue and Maria's stories. Following that, our leading and learning friends are encouraged to share their stories and the personal impact of their experiences.

Then we wrestle with some difficult questions about God's character and the necessity of the gospel. Next, we meet Jesus Christ and learn how his sacrifice on the cross provides rich knowledge, compassion, and solutions for suffering.

Upon that foundation, we explore personal identity—past, present, and future, followed by a redemptive approach to relationships with others.

Each chapter is designed to bring your friend a step closer to freedom in Christ. Throughout the lessons, questions guide group or friend-to-friend conversations to help us get to know one another and to grow in biblical thought, action, and relationship with God, bringing spiritual growth, emotional stability, and personal strength.

We have tried to be as thorough as possible with this Bible study and its supplemental resources. However, every individual requires her own pace. You may find that you need to slow down or provide more intensive help at certain times so that your learning friend can absorb what she is hearing.

Other Resources

Everyone has a wealth of resources upon which to draw, maybe more than we realize. Below is a partial list to which you can refer to help your friend. Try to identify as many available resources as possible for each of you, using this list as your starting point. For example, identify the people who serve as teachers, protectors, and comfort-givers in your lives. Discuss and learn from one another how you might make the best use of your resources. Seek to develop further resources for your learning friend in areas that are lacking.

- *Spiritual*: Prayer, Scripture, encouraging music, obedience to clear commands and biblical principles, standing up to evil, exercising faith, wisdom and thanksgiving, biblical love, spiritual disciplines, personal devotion to God

- *Church*: Scriptural preaching and teaching, godly examples or models, fellowship, friendship, ministry opportunities, admonishment and reconciliation, praise. The church may have to serve as primary family for your friend.

- *Family*: Christian family members, supportive family (even distant relatives) who can help with material needs and life skills

- *Social*: Friends who provide good influence, goodwill, comfort and encouragement, material provision, good instruction, exhortation, and wisdom

- *Education*: Schools, tutors, and teachers present opportunities based on interests and potential, future plans.

- *Material*: Job, home, neighborhood, transportation, personal possessions, gifts, savings, retirement, insurance, people of wealth, banks (see also "financial")

- *Skills*: Memory, intellectual or reasoning, reading or research, artistic, music, discernment, job skills, personal abilities (or disabilities) to care for self, family, property

- *Financial*: Paychecks, savings, investments, selling possessions, borrowing, credit cards or other debts (see also "material")

- *Physical and Health*: Physical strength, safety, dexterity, and ability; contingency plan for physical safety; medical resources, health insurance

- *Vocational*: Work experience, educational background or potential, references, skills and interests

- *Community*: Local church, parks, library, events such as concerts or art fairs, holiday events, public assistance, crisis centers, social services

- *Government*: Laws and ordinances, judicial system, police, fire protection, 911, child protective services

- *Technology*: Computers (see public library for access), home and car alarm systems, phones, recorders, cameras, remote locks, entertainment systems, etc.

Understanding the Experience of Your Learning Friend [60]

If you have never experienced sexual abuse, you need to do some learning before you will be able to offer much help. Your reading assignments have already given you some knowledge to help you in your journey. Here are some further ways you can learn about your friend's experience of abuse. (We use the pronoun "she," but "he" could be used equally correctly.) The *Treasure in the Ashes* Bible study will touch upon as many areas as possible, but you will need to be sensitive to the individual needs of your learning friend so that you can fill in the gaps. Ask for help from your pastor or a biblical counselor if needed.

---

[60] Materials in this section have been adapted from notes taken at a workshop by Dr. Laura Hendrickson: "Helping Survivors of Sexual Assault," for the National Association of Nouthetic Counselors (now the Association of Certified Biblical Counselors), February 2009.

- Do not presume to know her experience of sexual abuse. Listen well, and ask good questions.

- Statistics: "One in four women and one in six men will be sexually assaulted in their lifetime. These numbers are probably underestimated...."[61] Every two minutes someone in the United States is sexually assaulted ... 88-92 percent are female; 8-12 percent are male.... As many as 1/3 of all girls and 1/5 of all boys have experienced incest...."[62] Two major studies show a strong correlation between childhood sexual victimization and subsequent adult sexual victimization. [63] ... a high percentage of offenders are acquaintances of the victim. Most sexual assault perpetrators are white, educated, middle-class men." [64]

- Abuse is an act of violence, power, and domination—a crime, no matter what the law says, and no matter how people have responded to the victim's story.

- Your learning friend probably accepts fault or blame to the core of her soul for the abuse, even if she doesn't articulate it. She may think she consented if she did not fight her abuser or report the abuse immediately. She may not realize that not objecting to her abuser or not reporting it is not the same as consent.

- Those who are children, or who are somehow impaired (verbally, cognitively, or physically) or who are unconscious (at any age) cannot consent to sex.

- If the abuse or assault was recent, your friend is probably still in shock. Memories of the abuse are probably fresh, powerful, disturbing, and usually interrupt sleep. Nightmares and flashbacks are common. She may respond by cry-

---

[61] Justin and Lindsay Holcomb, *Rid of My Disgrace* (Wheaton, IL: Crossway, 2011), 31.
[62] Ibid., 32.
[63] Ibid., 33.
[64] Ibid.

ing and trembling, or she may shove the memory aside and try to get on with her life. She is not okay. She is most likely feeling guilt (including self-blame), shame, anger (even hostility), and incredible fear.

- If the abuse occurred a few months or a few years ago, she is probably attempting to forget what happened to her, and to get over it and move on. She has stopped talking about the abuse and is trying to live normally. But eventually memories will again begin to trouble her, and she will realize that she needs to come to terms with what has happened to her and how it has deeply impacted her life. At this point, most victims—perhaps your learning friend—come for help.

- Your friend probably thinks something is wrong with her. She may seem unstable. She also may wrestle with her affections in present relationships (even healthy ones). Same-sex attraction may be a struggle for her.

- If she is married, she may have difficulty relating to her husband in areas of trust and intimacy. This struggle may lead to the temptation to find intimacy in other places.

- Common beliefs or thoughts with which she wrestles may include:

  * "It's my fault. Maybe I led him on. I should have known what he would do. Maybe I didn't really say no."

  * "I should have done something. I should have fought back. I should have stopped him."

  * "I'm stupid. I should have been more careful."

  * "I deserved it."

* "This only happens to bad women. I'm bad." (Sexually pleasant physical responses during the abuse add to this belief.)

* "Why didn't God protect me? Is he mad at me? Is he punishing me? Doesn't God love me?"

* "Can I trust God? He can't be good."

* "I am a mess! Who am I? I hate who I am!"

* "I am crazy. I am damaged goods. No one can help me." [65]

During Crisis

When your learning friend experiences crisis—emotional or otherwise—you can help by staying calm, assessing the problem, praying with her, taking her to Scripture, and giving wise advice. Be prepared for your patience and endurance to be tested, but steadily remain her friend. The emotional tide will rise and fall. Rely upon the Lord and continue in your role as a leading friend. She will greatly benefit from your consistent demonstrations of Christ's love, even when she seems unappreciative, out of control, or hopelessly lost.

You are not called to be her savior. You cannot rescue her, nor should you take her responsibilities upon yourself. Both of you will need to remind yourselves of that regularly, especially if she clings to you, floods you with her problems, or opposes you. Remember that you are called to reflect Christ and to point her to him. Recognize that your learner's greatest and most constant need is for Jesus the Great Physician, the Good Shepherd, the Wonderful Counselor, the Everlasting Father, the Prince of Peace—but she doesn't know how to find him. It's your job to pray for her, to love her enough to tell the truth, to listen to her struggles without letting her indulge in self-pity,

---

[65] See also Sue Nicewander's three articles on victims of sexual abuse by a church leader. Betrayal, Fear, and Faith, The Baptist Bulletin (Schaumburg, IL) May/June 2013, July/August 2013, and September/October 2013 issues. www.BaptistBulletin.org . Click on "About Us" to read back issues of the magazine.

to guide her knowledge of Scripture by example and instruction, to help her get up when she falls, and always to point her to the true Savior in meaningful ways, especially through his Word.

Remember that you are not the expert. Christ himself is your traveling companion, your guide, your strength, and your destination. He will be giving you many opportunities to trust in him as the two of you travel together. Take her to Jesus constantly and show her how to trust in him. Learn together.

Be sensitive to the intensity of your learner's struggle and to your capabilities, and get more help when necessary. However, when seeking additional assistance, be cautious to avoid violating your friend's trust.

Challenges You May Encounter

This section is intended to be used as a reference when challenges are encountered. Familiarize yourself by reading through it, and then go back to it as needed when difficulties arise.

Regardless of your intentions, preparations, or sincerity, expect to meet some perplexing challenges as you walk with your learning friend. Refer to the following list to help you with your journey. The textbook *Rid of My Disgrace* by Lindsay and Justin Holcomb provides more thorough discussions about these and other challenges.

Most of the items on this list are in alphabetical order. However, because "emotional pain" permeates everything, we present it first.

Emotional Pain

During this study, your friend will be asked to honestly attend to painful wounds so they may receive proper care. Powerful emotional responses may arise unexpectedly as those wounds are reopened. She may experience an overwhelming fear of risk, feelings of failure, discomfort, despair, confusion, and anger as she struggles to learn new responses to her abuse.

Emotions are *interpretive responses* to life events, fueled by our individual beliefs about God, ourselves, and our relationship to the world around us. Help your friend to understand that God's purpose for emotions is to affirm correct belief, behavior, and thought; and, conversely, to signal the need for correction. Your friend has interpreted her past, and her emotions are reflecting the nature of those interpretations. Therefore, it is important for you to understand her conclusions about her past so that you can help her to correctly inform her emotions with truth, establish accurate beliefs, and guide her to appropriate behaviors.

Your goal is not to make your friend feel better, but to seek her long-term well-being in a way that honors God. Just as a physician may have to break a crooked bone so that it can heal properly, you will have to help your learning friend to recognize how her responses are contributing to her emotional pain. She may have to break some powerfully destructive habits of thought, action, and belief. Only then will she be able to make lasting changes. For a while, your friend may feel worse before she feels better. However, barring purely physical causes, her emotional responses will become more manageable as her thoughts, beliefs, and actions become more Christlike.

Anger and Sabotage

Your learning friend may habitually or manipulatively exhibit anger, especially in new situations. Some of her angry responses may seem random and highly destructive. She may seem to intentionally sabotage your relationship. There could be any number of reasons for this behavior. She may be testing your relationship to see if you will remain her friend. Or she may be afraid of herself, her past, and the path she is taking with you. She may misunderstand the character of God in her confusion, and she may be overwhelmed by the clash of powerful emotions she is experiencing.

From Maria's Journal

"Lord, I am angry. Why do I continue to struggle so much in my perception and understanding of what relationships are for? Does it even matter why? I'm tired of needing anything from anyone, or my screwed-up past. I'm tired of not having enough faith, or not being "surrendered" enough. I'm sorry for my sinful responses to everything I have experienced. I want to submit to you. I know that you are good and kind, but I can't figure out how to muster up that kind of faith. How do I get outside of all this pain?

I want to not need. Lord, please—without your intervention I will ruin everything. I will run away."

Maria's form of sabotage is to abandon relationships. Others may sabotage in such ways as verbal attacks, physical violence, aloofness, lack of commitment—anything that might make you back off.

Your learning friend needs stability in the Rock of Ages. Guide her to that place when she isn't thinking right or understanding that Jesus is what she needs and craves. Avoid coddling her (which feeds clinginess and dependence on you) or lecturing her (which feeds her sense of condemnation and drives her away from God).

Respond with reassurance of God's acceptance and love. Lead her to express herself biblically for the purpose of identifying what is troubling her so that you can address the underlying problem together. [66] Talk to her about how far God has brought her, and encourage her to be in the Word and in prayer. Recall what she has learned, reinforce ways that she has responded well to God so far, and assure her that he will never abandon her nor condemn her. Using Scripture, remind her that she is safe in Christ. You will probably need to help her identify the emotions she feels, so that she can balance them with truth. Help her to find Scripture that speaks to her struggle. If sabotaging behaviors continue, biblical counseling may be helpful for both of you.

Check your own heart, too. Your learning friend's attempt to sabotage your relationship will test your motives for helping her. You must seek your fulfillment in Christ, not in this or any other relationship.

Chaos

Your learning friend may wear chaos like a protective cloak to distract her from facing the painful reality of what has happened to her. Her inner chaos may show up as disorganized thinking, bizarre behaviors, self-injury, eating disorders, painful shyness, frequent apolo-

---

[66] If you have difficulty with this, see a biblical counselor for help.

gies, embarrassment, nagging frustration, or anger. Inadequate life skills are common and may be reflected in a messy house, difficulty with punctuality, and disorganized finances.

Chaos is hard to overcome because every area of life is usually affected. You may become frustrated and overwhelmed if you try to fix everything. Remember, you are not the savior. Your friend's greatest need is peace with God. No amount of comforting or rescuing will suffice. God ministers through his Word, and he requires responding to him in faith. Until your friend exercises faith in God (including diligent—albeit imperfect—obedience), your progress will be very slow at best. Remember, the main problem is not behavioral. Your friend needs a change of heart and mind in Christ Jesus, available only through a regular application of Scripture. Assure your friend of that.

To help, be persistent and structured in your instruction and in your prayers. Encourage engagement with a reliable circle of helpers, preferably from your church or believers within her family. They should point her to Christ, teach her life skills, urge acceptance of responsibility, and pray for her. You may need to fast and pray for your friend during crisis periods. Pray and study for wisdom to discern when to instruct, when to help or to exemplify, and when to step back and exhort your friend to exercise faith and accept her responsibilities.

Contingency Plan

Physical and emotional pain magnifies our need of God for the purpose of driving us to him. However, your learning friend may not understand that pain was designed to drive us to God. Your friend may want you to serve as a savior instead, so he or she may cling to you, scold you, or make unreasonable demands on your time and energy. Your friend is experiencing deep emotional distress, which, at its peak, he or she may identify as an emergency. Your friend may want you to drop everything and run to them at a moment's notice. Belief in personal helplessness may lead to the expectation that God should serve his or her self-defined needs, absolving personal responsibility. This can be draining and frustrating for the leading friend, especially when the learning friend is ungrateful for the energies that have been expended on his or her behalf.

You can help your friend by setting some realistic boundaries in a contingency plan. These boundaries will consistently help your friend to move away from sinful habits, plan wisely, move ahead productively, and become more responsible and confident in his or her everyday life. Success encourages growth in hope, strength, and initiative.

Go over the contingency plan with your learning friend so that you both are aware of expectations. As you prepare the plan, pray with your friend using "Praying Scripture Head-to-Toe" at the end of this chapter. Discuss how each step in the plan can be carried out according to reasonable expectations based on her abilities. Write down what you decide and sign the paper together.

When your learning friend calls in distress, your first question should be, "Have you followed your contingency plan?" If there is no imminent danger, then arrange a specific time for them to call after the plan has been followed to step 4.

CONTINGENCY PLAN

List situations that commonly trigger emotional distress or danger for you:

1. *Ask God for help* immediately.

2. *Think through Scripture verses* that you have found helpful. If possible, have some verses already written on cards to help you when emotions are intense.

3. *Generate movement in a good direction.* Identify safe places and move to those places as needed (e.g., a comforting area of the house, or moving away from the television or the argument). Continue to pray and consider whether additional steps are necessary (see step 4).

4. *Get help if necessary.*

   * <u>Imminent danger</u>: *Write down emergency phone numbers (including 911) and emails for people to contact in case of immediate danger: that is, imminent physical threat to self or others.*

   * <u>Distress without imminent danger</u>: *Write down names, phone numbers, and emails for people to contact when in distress but not imminent danger. Write down appropriate boundaries for calling those people. For example, what time of day, how many times per day, time limits on calls.*

5. *Choose alternate activities.* List some things to do when in distress without imminent danger. Begin spending time talking to God: use the "Praying Scripture Head-to-Toe" list at the end of this chapter. Next, take care of your immediate responsibilities. Other examples might include caring for the children, writing a letter, balancing the checkbook, preparing a *Treasure in the Ashes* assignment, cleaning countertops,

washing dishes, doing laundry, grocery shopping, or reading a good book.

6. *Add to your thanks list,* and thank God for each item. Start writing a list of blessings to which you will add items when feeling distressed. For example, thank God that you can walk, read, play with the children, or for your home, a beautiful sunrise, the Word, your leading friend, etc.

Communication

Communication is an important key to building a relationship. Since 80 percent of communication is nonverbal, seeing one another is important. If you are unable to meet, then online video chats such as Skype or Facetime are the next best alternative. Telephone calls are less effective because you miss nonverbal cues. Avoid email or texting as a primary means of communication. Your learning friend can easily cloak her emotional and spiritual condition, depriving you of important information.

During your journey, help your friend to tell her story: urge her to seek God, read her Bible, keep a journal, and meet regularly with those who are committed to helping her. Communicate with your learning friend, and encourage her not to hide from the truth. She may think, "I should be okay. I shouldn't need anybody." Talk about the fact that we all get confused and sometimes need help sorting out the truth within the mess. Identify with her humanness. Don't assume that your friend sees things the way that you do. She does not. So be sure to ask lots of questions and listen carefully before you respond to her answers.

Denial and Minimizing

You and your friend may be tempted to think that faith means saying, "It's not so bad," when dealing with struggles associated with sexual abuse. Christ never minimized his trials. Instead, he remembered God's purpose for his human life. He recognized the enormity of our needs, and from that knowledge, he pursued the solution. Follow his example by being honest about the seriousness of abuse and its effects, but also about God's provision of hope in Christ (see Part 3: "Who Is Jesus?").

Your friend may have a tremendous desire to dismiss her pain in order to avoid facing reality. Watch for the ways she protects herself against vulnerability. For example, she may refuse any admission of need. She may deny her abuse or its significance. She may isolate herself—afraid of discovery, painful shame, physical harm, and rejection. Your friend may wear a veneer of superficiality or pursue pleasure-seeking distractions (some very destructive). On the other hand, she may lash out, become manipulative, or distance herself behind a wall of anger.

Your friend may not be in deliberate denial, but she probably knows or suspects that unpleasant memories are hidden in the recesses of her mind and she is unwilling to face them. She may wonder, "Why walk back into pain?" "What could possibly be worth the risk?" Gently urge her to face the truth. The Lord will bring her memories to the surface when she is ready to address them, and when he purposes to use them to accomplish good things in her life.

Fear and Shame

Shame, guilt, and overwhelming fear usually coexist and may leave a woman reluctant to seek help, even while she feels locked away in a suffocating prison. Fear and shame may be manifested in denial, emotional outbursts, self-injury (cutting, eating disorders, promiscuity, or chemical addictions), insecurity, panic attacks, isolation, anxiety, and avoidance. Your friend may fear that God is not who he says he is, or she may think he is like her abuser. She may avoid telling her story, even to herself, because she is terrified of renewed pain and crushing failure. Memories of abuse may have faded over time, and your friend may understandably feel hesitant to revisit them. She may seem paralyzed to take the next step, or angry that she is being asked to move out of her "safe place." She will probably find it difficult to share her journey with you—or even God—because it makes her feel vulnerable again. She may sabotage your relationship to escape the pressure.

When you recognize fear and shame in your friend, give her your acceptance, your patient ear, and your gentle encouragement. Find out specifically what she fears, and help her to seek physical safety if necessary. If you sense a fear of failure, then reassure her of your commitment to help her and of God's love for her, and encourage her not to lose heart. You may find it helpful to use the following illustration.

A two-year-old draws a picture of herself and gives it to Mommy. It is certainly not a perfect drawing, just a crooked circle with four lines for limbs, a wobbly mouth and two dots for eyes. But Mommy is absolutely delighted because she loves her child and knows that child has done what her capabilities allow. God loves us like that; he is delighted when we want to "draw him a picture." When your friend says, "I can't," then reassure her that God is pleased when she sincerely expresses faith, even in very flawed ways (Galatians 5:6). God empowers her faith with his wisdom, ability, and strength, to cause her to grow according to his timetable.

Recognize that fear may fuel much of your friend's life and her questions about her abuse, the perpetrator, and God himself. Use your *Treasure in the Ashes* lessons to patiently and consistently share the truth that will set her free. Help her to find additional counseling if necessary.

Gospel Extremes and Misapplications

Misapplications of the gospel usually (but not always) flow out of a misunderstanding of the nature of the gospel. Whole books have been written on this subject. We will summarize the extremes only briefly here, so that you can be looking for misapplications with your learning friend.

1. **Wrong views of sin**

    a. Behaviorism (good works misapplied).[67] In the area of sin, the first extreme is behaviorism, in which a person is expected to clean herself up and stay clean in order to merit God's acceptance. If you see frustration and constant guilt and shame, explore this possibility.

    b. Permissiveness (grace misapplied).[68] The other extreme is permissiveness, which presumes that God functions like a sentimental teddy bear who winks at sin, so people can live as they please with the expectation of God's approval because of Christ. The result is self-centered

---

[67] Jerry Bridges, *Transforming Grace* may be a good place to start to work on behaviorism.
[68] Erwin Lutzeer, *Winning the Inner War* may be a good place to start to work on permissiveness.

hedonism. If your learning friend is self-focused, pursues pleasure, runs from responsibility, is confused or repulsed by self-discipline, or thinks God is ineffective, explore this possibility.

2. Wrong views of redemption

a. Behaviorism (good works misapplied). Regarding redemption in Christ, the behaviorist believes her sins were forgiven at the time of salvation, but from that point until heaven she alone must keep herself "clean" or suffer God's wrath. Since Christ says, "without Me you can do nothing,"[69] expect to see frustration, bitterness, guilt, and shame that result from this approach.

b. Permissiveness (grace misapplied). The permissive person believes that redemption means she can do whatever she wants without consequences. She thinks that Christian liberty and God's grace absolve her of personal responsibility. If your learning friend acts foolishly and resents the consequences, or if she treats God flippantly or disrespectfully, explore this possibility.

Hopelessness

Victims of sexual abuse will often feel hopeless. Resist the urge to tell your learning friend not to feel like that. Instead, point to Christ as her ever-present hope. Look over her list of resources and thank God for the many ways he has blessed her. Talk about the blessings of the local church and her friendships there. Reassure her that God and you will not give up on her but will continue to love her no matter what happens. Share some psalms of comfort and strength, such as Psalm 10, 18, 37, 61, or 86. Pray for her, and teach her how to pray. Introduce her to those who have had victory after sexual abuse.

---

[69] John 15:5

Ongoing Abuse or Danger

Your learning friend may live with continuing oppression from her family and friends. Many victims do not recognize abuse because it has become a "normal" part of their lives from childhood. Help her to see reality, and teach her where she is able to make changes and what she must accept. She needs to discern truth and reject cruelty and manipulation.

Oppressors use mind-manipulation and emotional confusion to control their victims. In the case of domestic violence, we recommend Debi Pryde's book *A Biblical Guide to What to Do When Your Husband Abuses You,* available at www.ironwood.org, and Leslie Vernick's *The Emotionally Destructive Relationship.* Help her to take appropriate action to protect herself and her children. For example, set up a safety plan and an escape route to a crisis center or the home of a godly friend.

Secure assistance in extreme situations. Governmental authority is provided by God to oppose evildoers (Romans 13:1–2). Get help from the police or other authorities as needed to protect your friend's physical safety. Explore options such as a restraining order or a legal separation if a threat of physical harm is imminent. A crisis center may be able to advise your friend in these matters so that she can make an informed decision about her options. If your learning friend needs more help than you can reasonably or safely provide, go to your pastor or help her to seek a qualified biblical counselor.

Physical

If you suspect that your learning friend is suffering physically, recommend that she see a licensed medical doctor. Help her to write down her medical background along with a list of concerns and questions to discuss with her doctor. Go with her to the appointment if she would be more comfortable having you there. Afterward, help her to follow through with her doctor's advice. For example, schedule a follow-up appointment (or a second opinion consult), and write an exercise schedule and a diet plan.

Your learning friend may become resentful or bitter about the physical aftereffects of abuse, especially if she is now unable to have children. James Halla's book *Pain: Plight of Fallen Man* may be a good resource for her.

Scripture Misapplication

Again, patience is required during the messy process of unlearning wrong thinking and replacing it with correct thinking. When your friend misapplies Scripture, whether deliberately or not, take her directly to God's Word and kindly show her the truth. Be gentle but firm, assuring her of God's grace and love, but also of her responsibilities. Make careful applications using illustrations, examples, and role-plays. Encourage her to read good books or to watch instructional videos if the topic with which she struggles is complex or habitual. For suggestions, consult the Biblical Counseling Coalition website: www.biblicalcounselingcoalition.org

Self-Righteousness

Because the sins of the perpetrator are wicked, your friend may tend to think of herself as innocent and righteous in comparison. Lead her to recognize that Christ's obedience is the standard. She has neither innocence nor righteousness apart from Jesus. Rather than saying, "How could that person have done such horrible things to me!," lead her to recognize that Jesus could have said that of her, but instead he loved her enough to provide the solution for her sins and lead her to abundant eternal life.

Once she has embraced the gospel, gently remind her that in Christ she has been called to love her enemy, not to exalt herself in comparison with him. She will need to learn what that kind of love looks like. Patiently show her. Learn together. (See chapter 4 "Who is Jesus Christ?" and chapter 6 "Who Are You?")

Social Awkwardness or Inappropriate Social Behaviors

Your learning friend has been through trauma that has likely distorted her understanding of how human relationships should be developed and maintained. Her fears have probably made her self-conscious, skittish, and shy so that she avoids the risks of friendship.

You can help your friend by noticing when she withdraws from others and asking her privately what she is afraid will happen. In so doing, you may help her to identify triggers that she can counteract with Scripture to help her trust God, think appropriately about herself and others, and improve her social interactions. Love her by reassuring and complimenting her when she does things well.

Space

You will need wisdom to know when to give your learning friend some space to reflect and process, and when to urge her to take a step forward. She will probably need time to digest and apply what she is learning. She may abandon you for a while; do not take it personally, but see these pauses as part of the growth process.

Give her space, but gently and patiently keep in touch if she will let you. Gently walk alongside her as her leading friend, faithfully listen to her, identify her questions, pray with her, patiently give her Scripture that addresses her needs, and encourage her faith and her responsibility to think and act according to truth. Remember, this process is messy and you both will do it imperfectly.

Listen for what she finds threatening, and help to alleviate her fears with Scripture that encourages her to put her faith in God. You will have to trust that God will reach her; she is not beyond his love—ever! Remind her of that if you can. Keep praying: encourage those close to her to pray and reach out to her as they are able.

Unbelief

No matter what your learning friend thinks about God, she needs him. The two points of the gospel (I am a sinner, and Christ is the only Redeemer) are essential to her, regardless of how she responds to Christ. Unbelief results from wrong thinking about God, self, and others.

Look for incorrect perceptions of God's character, of herself, and the sins of others against her. Ask questions about how she reached those conclusions, and listen closely to her answers. Ask your learning friend, "If you were wrong about that, would you want to know?" If she says, yes, then look together for biblical answers, with a goal of leading her to Christ through the gospel. Review applicable lessons from this Bible study. Talk to your pastor for more help.

Victim Mentality

Childhood sexual abuse often fuels feelings of helplessness and self-pity. As a child, your friend was truly a helpless victim of an adult or an older child. However, unless she learns to reject the lies that her perpetrator told her, even now as a capable adult, she may consider herself to be helpless. Your friend's victim-driven beliefs are self-reinforced and self-fulfilling as she dwells in self-pity, despair, social anxiety, fear, bitterness, and frustration instead of the truth of Scripture.

Be careful not to indulge her negativity and self-pity, or you may find yourself being manipulated and used. Your friend needs to hear God's definition of her identity over and over again until she accepts who she really is in Christ (see chapter 5, "Who Am I?"). Teach her some Scripture verses and spiritual songs or hymns. Show her God's faithfulness and his acceptance of his children. You may also want to allow her to succeed by giving her small tasks that she can easily accomplish: include her in fellowship at church events, help her to write a daily list of the ways that God has blessed her life, and then lead her to thank God for those things. Remind her that God has given her a choice, to believe him rather than continuing to believe the lies she has learned in the past.

The Unteachable Victim.

You may encounter a woman who talks incessantly for hours about her suffering, but who will not listen to what you say or follow through on any of your suggestions. This woman probably wants affirmation but is unwilling to change because she sees herself as innocent in every sense. She may have rehearsed her victimization so often that she is blind to everything else, and tends to exhaust anyone who tries to help her. Beware of being drawn into her self-pity. You can't fix her; your advice will fall on deaf ears because she is interested only in using you as a sounding board. This person needs your prayers, a well-placed reflective question or two, relational boundaries that do not allow her to manipulate you, and a referral to a good biblical counselor.

Some Final Thoughts

By now, you may be thinking, *Why would I sign up for this?* The short answer: Because in Christ you can. First John 4:7–21 urges you to love your sister as Christ has loved you. While you will certainly feel inadequate for the job, at least you are seeking to be part of the solution rather than allowing a sexual abuse victim to suffer. Maria and I feel inadequate, too, but we all have a God who is abundantly able to lead us faithfully through our journey.

- God is your friend's primary need and her hope.

  As a believer in Christ, you have what your learning friend desperately needs, so you are in a position to offer hope. God's love is real and has been extended to each of us through the effectual gospel of Jesus Christ. This may be the first time in her life that anyone truly reaches out to her with the love of Christ. You can make an enormous impact simply by showing biblical concern for her well-being.

- Choose biblical hope no matter how she feels.

  Keep in mind that emotional empathy is not the same as biblical hope. Entering into her emotional state will not give her any security. Not only is emotionalism a temporary fix, but it tends to reinforce a belief that God has not really been good to her. Lead her to take refuge in God and speak truth into her emotions until they settle down. Certainly you should weep with those who weep and rejoice with those who rejoice, but do so as you point out that God is faithful, sufficient, and always there no matter how she feels.

- Avoid the savior mentality.

  Remember, too, that you are not her savior, so don't set yourself up in that role. God is her rescuer, and she needs to learn to go to him. Be consistent with that message.

- Pray.

  As you and your learning friend walk through *Treasure in the Ashes*, prayer must be a regular part of your daily life, and you must spend time in Scripture in order to discern the mind of Christ for the challenges of this relationship.

- Celebrate little victories.

  Different kinds of relationships hold different kinds of challenges and joys. Expect surprises, both delightful and difficult. You will struggle and fail, but get up and try again. Rejoice in every forward step by praising and thanking God. Review those forward steps frequently, so you don't forget how much God has done. "Rejoice in the Lord always. Again I will say, rejoice!" (Philippians 4:4).

- Lean into the pain.

  Expect to have to expend effort as you and your friend fight to make forward progress. Learn to fail and recover, and press on when you both feel like quitting. You may find yourself disillusioned with your friend along the way, and she may feel the same about you. It may help to think about working through past sexual abuse as something like having a baby: you will probably do better if you lean into the pain rather than resisting it. Accept pain as a natural part of the entrance of new life, with hope and joy in Christ.

- Exercise grace.

  Success won't be handed to you. However, God's grace says: "Humble yourselves in the sight of the Lord, and He will lift you up" (James 4:10). It's hard to know how to humble yourself rather than humiliate yourself for your shortcomings and sins. But the truth is that God's grace fully covers our sins in Christ. His wrath was completely poured out on Jesus, so that God will never use our sins against us. We must not use them against ourselves, either. Confess your failures and sins to God, asking him to change you into his image.

"But may the God of all grace, who called us to His eternal glory by Christ Jesus, after you have suffered a while, perfect [mature], establish [firmly stabilize], strengthen, and settle you" (1 Peter 5:10).

- Persevere.

  Processing this material can be exhausting and sometimes even discouraging. Some learning friends may want to quit when the discussions involve sensitive or painful subjects. Spend some time rejoicing, singing, thanking and praising God after you have studied a deep or troubling lesson. Encourage your friend to be patient with the process and to allow it to draw her closer to Jesus. Ultimately, our goal is to build a relationship with the God of the Bible.

If you need more help

If you and your friend need more help, find a qualified biblical counselor who can address her individual concerns. The Association of Certified Biblical Counselors has a list of counselors on their website.

When you feel discouraged, afraid, or angry, read Psalm 145:14–21 and take heart.

"The LORD upholds all who fall, and raises up all who are bowed down. The eyes of all look expectantly to You [the Lord], and You give them their food in due season. You open Your hand and satisfy the desire of every living thing. The LORD is righteous in all His ways, gracious in all His works. The LORD is near to all who call upon Him, to all who call upon Him in truth. He will fulfill the desire of those who fear Him; He also will hear their cry and save them. The LORD preserves all who love Him, but all the wicked He will destroy. My mouth shall speak the praise of the LORD, and all flesh shall bless His holy name forever and ever."

A Summary for Leading Friends

Important Main Points to Remember

Your role in this journey is to reflect the character of Jesus Christ in the context of faithful friendship. Your learning friend may be astonished to learn that godly people actually exist as you extend courtesy, thoughtfulness, patience, and consistency. Here are more ways to demonstrate godly friendship:

- Set meaningful boundaries for your relationship.

- Patiently hear her experience of abuse (without overreacting). Give her time (days, weeks, or months) to fully tell her story before you jump in to offer help. Listen without judging or critiquing what she says. Take her story at face value. It is her experience. Find out about it.

- Learn to ask good questions. Listen patiently, again and again, for the purpose of identifying what she believes about God, herself, others, and life in this fallen world. What questions does she have? Be careful not to judge; instead, seek to understand (Proverbs 20:5).

- What does she dwell on in her thought life? Where does she let her mind linger, and what triggers those thought patterns?

- What does your friend do? What constructive and destructive actions does she take (especially habitually)?

- How does she feel? Your learning friend may need help to identify the emotions that she feels.

- What does she feed: faith or doubt?

- Pray patiently and consistently for her and with her.

- Comfort her (2 Corinthians 1:3–6). Verbalize that you are sorry for what has happened to her. Reassure her of God's love and your love. Tell her that you will walk with her.

- Point to Christ as her Savior and Redeemer at every opportunity.

- Keep your word.

- Be gentle and consistent.

- Contact her regularly to express your interest and care for her.

- Remind her of biblical truth and the resources God has provided.

- Encourage and reinforce responsible living. Rejoice in her successes.

- Lead her in thanksgiving to God.

Before your first meeting, read the following:

Instruments in the Redeemer's Hands by Paul David Tripp (Phillipsburg, NJ: P&R Publishing, 2002).

Rid of My Disgrace by Justin and Lindsey Holcomb (Wheaton, IL: Crossway, 2011).

Familiarize yourself with *Treasure in the Ashes*. Read chapter 1 and answer the questions.

Acquire two copies of each of the following books (one for yourself and one for your learning friend). You will go through these books together during this study.

1. *Rid of My Disgrace* by Justin and Lindsey Holcomb (Wheaton, IL: Crossway, 2011) **or** *Why Me, Lord?* by Debi Pryde (avail-

able at www.ironwood.org or Bob Jones University Bookstore www.bju.edu .)

2. *A Shepherd Looks at Psalm 23* by W. Phillip Keller (Grand Rapids: Zondervan, 1970, 2007).

"Unto the upright there arises light in the darkness" (Psalm 112:4). "But seek first the kingdom of God and His righteousness, and all these things shall be added to you" (Matthew 6:33).

When Your Friend Tells Her Story [70]

1. Listen. This is most important. Let her lead the conversation.

2. Respond calmly, but with compassion. Let her know that she does not have to face her assault alone. Convey that you believe her. Reassure her of your love and care for her.

3. Affirm and ask open-ended questions. Listen actively and empathetically. Let her know it was not her fault. Ask broad, encouraging questions like "Then what happened?" or "Are you safe?"

4. Avoid leading or shaming questions, like "What time was it?" or questions that are too detailed, like "Then did he? … " can hinder healing.

5. Do not try to "fix" her or minimize the abuse. You are not responsible to fix her. Jesus is the only true Healer. Let her know that Jesus experienced assault; he identifies with her. Never minimize abuse; it is always significant.

What to say to support, empathize, and encourage

- I believe you.

- It wasn't your fault.

- It's okay to cry.

- Thank you for sharing this with me.

- I'm sorry this happened to you.

- I can't imagine how terrible your experience must have been.

- I'm glad you're safe now.

---

70 Uncopyrighted materials used with thanks to RESPOND at https://www.respondinc.org

- How can I help?

- Your reaction is not uncommon.

- I'm angry that this happened to you.

What NOT to say (to avoid unintentional harm)

- I know how you feel.

- Calm down; relax.

- Why didn't you _____?

- Try to be strong.

- You need to forgive and forget.

- Move on with your life.

- Tell me the details about _____.

- Good things can come from bad.

- Time heals all wounds.

- You're lucky that _____.

- It was God's will.

- Don't worry.

- It's going to be all right.

- I understand.

Helpful Scripture Verses:

- Psalm 34:18

- Galatians 4:4–7

- Hebrews 4:14–16

- Psalm 46:1–3

- Romans 8:31–39

- Colossians 2:13–15

- 2 Samuel 13

PRAYING SCRIPTURE HEAD-TO-TOE [71]

The following are suggestions for scriptural prayer. We suggest choosing a category each day and praying from a Bible for yourself and others. Add further verses as you read Scripture.

Mind:

Mind of Christ (Philippians 2:5)
Try me and know my thoughts (Psalm 139:23)
Obediently captivate every thought and imagination (2 Corinthians 10:5)
Fill me with all spiritual knowledge and understanding (Colossians 1:10)
Dwell on true, honest, just, pure, lovely, good, virtuous, excellent, praiseworthy things (Philippians 4:8)
Plan ahead and prepare well (Proverbs 6:6-8; James 4:13-17; Luke 14:28)
Remember God's Word to use it (Psalm 119:11, 16, 49)

Eyes:

Make blind eyes to see; open my eyes (John 9:25; I John 2:11; Psalm 119:18)
Set no unclean thing before my eyes (Psalm 101:3)
See from God's perspective and seek his ways (2 Kings 6:17)
Be watchful (1 Thessalonians 5:16)
Look to eternal goals (2 Corinthians 4:18)
Let my light shine before men to God's glory (Matthew 5:16)

Ears:

Hear the Word of God with understanding (Psalm 85:8; Matthew 11:15)
Be a doer, not just a hearer, of the Word (James 1:22)
Hear and follow God's wisdom, not man's (Proverbs 1:20–33; 11:14)
Take godly instruction (Proverbs 9:9)
Listen before answering (Proverbs 18:13; James 1:19)
Be careful what I listen to (Luke 8:18)

---

[71] Sue Nicewander, "Praying Scripture Head-to-Toe." http://www.bcmin.org .

Nose:

As Christ's representative, to be a sweet savor to God (Ephesians 5:2)
God would manifest the savor (fragrance) of Christ to others through me (2 Corinthians 2:14–15)

Mouth:

Speak and be silent appropriately (Proverbs 10:19; 17:27; 29:11; Mark 13:11)
Every word would honor God (Proverbs 15:7)
Know how to answer those who question or oppose (Titus 1:9; I Peter 3:15; Psalm 119:42)
Offer biblical advice (1 Thessalonians 5:14; Galatians 6:1–2)
Words would build up rather than tearing down (Ephesians 4:29)
Speak the truth in love (Ephesians 4:15)
Teach others about Christ (1 Timothy 4:11; 2 Timothy 2:2)
Offer praise and prayer to God (1 Thessalonians 5:17–18)

Neck:

Turn from a haughty (proud) attitude (1 Corinthians 13:4–5; Proverbs 8:13)
Humble rather than stiff-necked (stubborn and self-willed) (James 4:6; Acts 7:51)

Shoulders:

Cast cares (burdens) on the Lord (1 Peter 5:7; Matthew 11:28–30)
Bear responsibilities well (1 Corinthians 10:31; Colossians 3:23)
Persevere (Galatians 6:9; Hebrews 10:22–12:15)
Comfort others (2 Corinthians 1:4)
Bear one another's burdens (Galatians 6:2)

Arms:

Strength to do God's will (Psalm 18:12–22; 29:11; 119:28)
To recognize and rest in God's everlasting arms (Deuteronomy 33:27)

Hands:

Skill to complete today's appointed tasks (2 Corinthians 3:6; 1 Corinthians 10:13)

To do those tasks with an eternal focus (1 Corinthians 3:14; 2 Corinthians 4:18)

Lay up treasures in heaven (Matthew 6:19–21)

Establish the work of my hands (Psalm 90:17)

Hold onto what is good (I Thessalonians 5:21)

Heart:

Love God with all my heart (Matthew 22:37)

Worship God, not the things he created (Romans 1:25; 1 Corinthians 10:14)

Abide in Christ (John 15:1–10)

Seek God (Psalm 119:2; Matthew 7:7)

Serve God with all my heart (1 Samuel 12:20)

Purify the desires of my heart (Psalm 139:23)

Submit my will to God (James 4:7)

Deny myself, pick up my cross daily, and follow him (Luke 9:23)

Lose my life in his (Luke 9:24)

Be wise (Proverbs 2:6–7; Psalm 119:66)

Word of Christ indwells (Colossians 3:16)

Stomach:

Eat to nourish my body, not out of greed (Romans 14:23; Hebrews 13:9)

Be a good steward of my body (1 Corinthians 4:2)

Health to bring God honor, as he wills (2 Corinthians 12:7–10; James 5:14–16)

Desire the meat of the Word (Hebrews 5:12–14)

Provision for physical needs (Psalm 84:4; James 1:17; Philippians 4:19)

Loins:

Moral and sexual purity, living honorably (1 Thessalonians 4:2-3; 1 Corinthians 6:19-20)

Resist temptation (James 4:7; Hebrews 12:1–3)

Rightly use God's gift of sexuality in marriage (Song of Solomon 4:7; Psalm 128; Hebrews 13:4)

Godly parenting (Deuteronomy 6:4-9)

Honor my body as the Holy Spirit's temple (1 Corinthians 6:19–20)

Legs:

Walk in the Spirit, not in the flesh (Galatians 5:16)
Stand fast in Christ (Galatians 5:1)
Ready to go where God sends (Matthew 9:38; Isaiah 6:8)
Walk with godly companions (1 Corinthians 15:33)
Go in the right direction (Proverbs 3:5–6)
Walk in the Word (Psalm 119:105, 133)
Walk in safety (Psalm 138:3–8)
Walk as a faithful ambassador of Christ (2 Corinthians 5:20)

Feet:

Founded on the Rock (Matthew 7:24–27)
Stability (Psalm 119:38; 1 Peter 5:10)
Freedom (Psalm 119:45; Isaiah 61:1–2)
Seeking opportunity to share the gospel (Romans 10:15)
Feet shod with the preparation of the gospel of peace (Ephesians 6:15)

APPENDIX A
CHOOSING A BIBLICAL CHURCH

Involvement in a biblical local church is a vital part of our journey, teaching us truth about God to free us from the lies we tend to accept, introducing us to the true gospel, and inviting us to follow our gracious Lord. Relationships in a good church offer: nonthreatening and meaningful fellowship with God's people, opportunities to find a godly leading friend, observations of God's work in the lives of real people, development of healthy friendships, and a sense of belonging. In addition, a biblical church will facilitate spiritual growth, accountability, discipline, endurance, and hope.

Warning: Not all churches are biblical and spiritually sound. Look beyond friendliness, great music, and impressive buildings. Plenty of churches—large and small—may seem appealing but teach heresy and lack love. A weak church can undo much good. Here are some steps to finding a church that teaches truth and fits you well. Keep praying for God to lead you throughout this process.

A. Does the church follow truth, starting with the true gospel?

Find a church that teaches Scripture. Biblical teaching about believing and following Christ is the most important aspect of a church. Explore church websites for statements of faith (sometimes called doctrinal statements) to learn what each church believes. Read each one carefully for thoroughness and soundness. Try to detect what is missing as well as what is stated. If a church's beliefs about the gospel don't fully reflect the biblical concept, pass that one up, even if it's a popular place.

A biblical church believes and teaches the true gospel:

1. Scripture is fully reliable and authoritative because it is God-breathed. Almighty God authored the entire Bible—every word and every part of it (2 Timothy 3:16). It is complete and absolutely true (Revelation 22:18–19; John 17:17).

2. Jesus Christ is God the Son who came to earth as a man. He is fully God as well as fully man. He has always existed as God, and he always will be God (John 1:1; 20:31; 1 Timothy 3:16).

3. Christ shed his blood on the Cross to pay for our sins. Every person has sinned and has earned eternal death (Romans 3:23; 6:23). Jesus paid for our sins by dying for us. (Romans 3:24–26; Colossians 1:13; Hebrews 9:14–21; Revelation 1:5). He is the only Savior.

4. Christ arose bodily from the grave so we can have eternal life. Jesus raised himself from death, proving that he is God (Luke 24:1–12, 34–48; 1 Corinthians 15:1–20). He is the only Redeemer. He gives me eternal life when I put my faith (belief) in his sacrifice and resurrection. None of my good works contributes to my salvation: it is by grace alone through faith alone in Christ alone (Romans 3:23; 6:23; 10:9–13; 1 Corinthians 15:3–4; Ephesians 2:8–9; John 1:12).

If you need help to figure out if a statement of faith is biblical or not, pray for wisdom. Then ask for help from someone who knows Scripture well. (NOTE: Browsing the Internet is not usually reliable unless you know the source is a godly biblical scholar, not just someone offering an opinion.)

B. Do the people love God and one another in Christlike ways?

Visit a few churches.

After finding a few churches that are doctrinally sound, look at the geographical locations, service times, and other activities offered at those churches. Visit the most promising ones for a few Sundays, and really try to get a sense of the spirit of ministry there.

1. Were you welcomed when you arrived? Did you know where to go? Were people available to answer your questions? What is the overall attitude of the people? Are they friendly? Approachable? Joyful? Does the church appear to be well organized and follow good leadership?

2. Is the Word of God prominent in the preaching? Is prayer a significant part of the services? Did you hear the gospel? Did you see evidence that the church reaches out compassionately to a hurting and lost world? Does the church seem to care for its friends and members who are suffering? Did the people seem to worship God with sincerity? Were you asked to use your Bible throughout the service or lesson time? Was the core teaching directly from the Bible? What did you specifically learn about God? How were you encouraged or challenged to worship God and to follow Christ biblically?

3. Regarding smaller groups such as Bible studies or Sunday school classes: Were the topics age-appropriate, relevant, and clearly taught from Scripture? Were the teachers knowledgeable and enthusiastic about their classes? Did the audience or class seem engaged? Were their questions and comments wise and compassionate? Was everyone welcomed and appreciated?

4. Did you leave with a sense that you and your family could learn, grow spiritually, befriend others, and serve the Lord there?

Narrow your choices.

Pray and talk with any family members who will attend church with you, and narrow your choices to one or two churches.

C. Talk to the senior pastor.

Schedule an hour appointment to speak with the senior pastor at the most promising church. Ask him what he believes are the most important things about his church. Discipleship (teaching people to follow Christ) should be among the first things he lists. Ask him to explain the gospel. Were all the points there (see above)? Ask about the importance of Scripture, church leadership and staff, ministries and activities, and future plans. What is required in order to become a member? What opportunities does the church offer for individuals to serve the Lord? Does the pastor appear to love Christ? Did he pray with you? Do you think you would fit in there? Why or why not?

Get to know the church.

Take a little plunge. Attend your first choice for six to eight weeks to learn a little more about the church, carefully going over the list that follows. Also, go to worship services, a women's Bible study group, and a few family activities. If women or families offer hospitality, accept the invitation if it is offered appropriately. Take the opportunity to ask questions about what they believe and how they serve the Lord in their church. The content of the teaching is the most important thing, so be sure they are literal in their use of Scripture and accurate in their understanding of the gospel.

Do you see evidence of the following:

1. **The Bible is the authority for belief and action.** Do the people (as a whole) read, study, and rightly interpret Scripture? Do they seek to do what it says at every level? 2 Timothy 3:16–17

2. **Every believer is taught to follow Christ to bring God glory,** according to Scripture. Do believers seem to love Christ and

his Word, actively seek to avoid sin, share the gospel, pray, give, help one another, encourage prayer and discipleship, provide accountability, and teach truth in word and action?

3. **Two ordinances: the Lord's Supper and baptism.** Are these practiced as acts of obedience and devotion, but not necessary for salvation? Matthew 28:19–20; 1 Corinthians 11:23–32

4. **Saved, baptized church members.** Is church membership encouraged for every person who has received Christ according to the true gospel? Acts 2:41–47; 1 Corinthians 12:12; 2 Corinthians 6:14; Ephesians 4:3

5. **The fruit of the Spirit in leaders and the church as a whole**, using Scripture accurately and respectfully, loving and serving one another, with concern for unity and growth of the body. Galatians 5:22–23; 1 Corinthians 12

D. Take time to be sure, then join.

No church is perfect, so be realistic. But when you have found the church you believe God wants for you, then become a member so you can participate fully as part of the church family. Get involved.

APPENDIX B

SUGGESTIONS FOR GROUP STUDY

Group use of *Treasure in the Ashes* is best viewed as a vehicle for equipping and encouraging discipleship between leading friends and learning friends. This book provides an anchor in the Word of God and a starting point for discussions, while consistently pointing to Christ as our source of help. *Treasure in the Ashes* cannot be comprehensive, because everyone's experience is different. Group leaders and leading friends should be prepared to have long and frequent discussions in and out of meeting times as their learning friends wrestle with what has happened to them. These discussions are essential, and, when biblically directed, are necessary for learning friends to find their way.

Ideally, we recommend that you choose individuals to join your group so that you have an equal number of leading friends and learning friends present. Carefully pair up compatible members of your group, with the intent that leading and learning friends will continue to meet informally between sessions and after the group meeting is done. The goal is to encourage discipleship per Matthew 28:19–20, so if you are not able to pair people before the group starts, seek for good pairing as you go through the study.

Schedule a training meeting for leading friends before the regular group meetings begin, using the *Treasure in the Ashes* training supplement. Start a schedule for yourself and the leading friends in the group to read these recommended books:

- Start with *Instruments in the Redeemer's Hands* by Paul David Tripp

- Then read *Rid of My Disgrace* by Justin and Lindsay Holcomb.

A reading-record form can help to motivate leading and learning friends to complete the reading.

Treasure in the Ashes group studies may be structured by chapters (**24 weeks**) or parts (**8 weeks**), depending upon the needs of your group. Choose a few questions or talking points to discuss at the meeting. Stop to pray frequently. Do not hurry; be mindful of the pace needed by your group. Encourage your group to further explore the hard questions that trouble them, using this book and its suggested resources as a guide (not the Internet). During your weekly meetings, ask your group members to mark the questions they want to discuss further, and to contact leading and learning friends to talk about those questions as needed.

- The 8-week group provides an overview of the chapters in each part.

- The 24-week group will be able to talk in more depth about the themes of each chapter, but please encourage further discussion and prayer between meetings.

Further suggestions: Choose gospel-focused music to greet your group as they arrive and to set their minds in the right direction. Begin and end with prayer. Make eye contact as frequently as possible, and remember to smile.

Thank you for serving the Lord by reaching out to someone in need. May he bring healing through your efforts.

APPENDIX C
STUDY NOTES

A Shepherd Looks at Psalm 23
by W. Phillip Keller

Make 12 copies of this study sheet. Fill out one sheet for each chapter in *A Shepherd Looks at Psalm 23*.

Chapter # _____: Chapter Name _____
_____

1. How does this chapter describe *sheep* and their needs?

2. From this chapter, explain the ways a *good shepherd cares* for the needs of his sheep.

3. How does the author *compare Christians with sheep*?

4. How does the author describe our *Good Shepherd* (Jesus) and his care for his children?

5. Write something *personally significant* that you learned about the Good Shepherd and the sheep from this chapter.

6. Write some ways you can *apply* what you learned from this chapter. How does it make a difference to you, especially in your relationship with Christ?

7. Now, above the chapter name you wrote at the beginning of the study notes, write *another title* in your own words that reflects what the chapter says about you and your Good Shepherd (e.g., "The Lord is my Shepherd" could be renamed "God Owns Me: I Belong").

APPENDIX D

NEW LIFE IN CHRIST

"New Life In Christ" builds on our previous discussion of the good things that God gives to us immediately when we receive Christ. These things endure. In other words, we will never lose them because they are given to us by Christ and depend only upon his goodness rather than ours. Everyone needs to be reminded of these truths.

Scripture is clear that we only come to Christ once for salvation. Remember John 5:24: "Most assuredly, I say to you, he who hears My word and believes in Him who sent Me has everlasting life, and *shall not come into judgment [condemnation], but has passed from death into life.*"

John 17:11 tells us that he keeps us—we don't keep him. Ephesians 2:8–9 says we are saved by grace through faith, not of ourselves ... it is the gift of God, not of works. Therefore, we can't gain eternal life by doing good things, and we can't lose eternal life by insufficient works. Verse 10 tells us that we were created to do good things, but those things don't save us. Instead, they are evidence that we belong to God, and those things, by example, encourage others to come to him for salvation.

Immediately when we receive Christ, we have ...

1. **Forgiveness through new birth:** We used to be dead, but when we receive Christ our souls are brought to life. We are no longer what we were. Christ completely satisfies God's justice and anger over sin; we are utterly and fully forgiven. "And He Himself is the propitiation [wrath-removing sacrifice] for our sins ... "(1 John 2:2a). God is not mad at us. Where we were once characterized as sinners, we are now children of God, with the Holy Spirit dwelling inside us to guide us and keep our soul safe (John 1:12; 3:3–9; 2 Corinthians 5:15–17; Ezekiel 36:24–26).

2. **A new family:** Those adopted as his children are given a new identity in the family of God. "For you did not receive the spirit of bondage again to fear, but you received the Spirit of adoption by whom we cry out, 'Abba, Father!' The Spirit Himself bears witness with our spirit that we are children of God, and if children, then heirs—heirs of God and joint heirs with Christ" (Romans 8:15–17a). God becomes our Father. Unlike our earthly fathers, God is a completely good and perfect parent who loves us wisely and purely. He gives us the local church as our new family of believers. He guides our way (if we will follow) and teaches us how to live in our new relationships (Proverbs 3:5–6; 1 John 4:7 – 12).

3. **A new life:** We are recreated in the righteousness of Christ. Our identity is in him. He now calls us beloved. "Therefore, my beloved and longed-for brethren, my joy and crown, so stand fast in the Lord, beloved" (Philippians 4:1). Our Father is pleased to teach us through his Word how to be transformed into the person he has created us to be (2 Corinthians 5:17; Ephesians 1:3–21; 4:24; Philippians 3:9; Romans 8:28–29; 2 Timothy 3:16–17).

4. **Acceptance:** We never have to wonder if God loves us or if we are acceptable to him. We are accepted in Christ (Ephesians 1:6). Because Christ is the basis of our acceptance, and he never changes, we never have to fear that God will reject us—Ever! (Hebrews 13:8; Matthew 9:20–22).

5. **A new purpose:** We are becoming like Christ in character, thought, and living. This purpose arises from our new identity in Christ, so that when we exercise faith we do not have to be hindered by our past or present circumstances (2 Corinthians 3:18; Romans 8:28–29).

6. **A new home:** Heaven. We are promised a home with him forever in heaven. "Now, therefore, you are no longer strangers and foreigners, but fellow citizens with the saints and members

of the household of God" (Ephesians 2:19). Our citizenship has changed, so that we live with our eye on our real home (Philippians 3:20–21).

7. **New spiritual covering:** Our shame has been removed in Christ and replaced with white linen of purity provided for us by God. When God looks at us, he does not see our sin or our past; he sees the righteousness of Christ that has been given to us regardless of the sins we have committed or the evil that has devastated us. Nothing can take that covering away (Matthew 22:11–12; Romans 10:11; Revelation 4:4; 19:14).

8. **Nearness to God:** God promises never to leave us nor forsake his children. We can draw near to God because of Christ, and he promises to draw near to us when we draw near to him. He will hear our prayers when we pray in his name, according to his will (John 9:31; Ephesians 2:13; James 4:8).

9. **A living Person:** We are not alone. When we receive Christ, we receive a real person unlimited by time, one who is tireless, all-knowing, good, always present and powerful, who leads us and forever stands in our defense. We will never again be alone (John 10:27–30; Hebrews 7:25; 1 John 2:1–2).

LIVING IN CHRIST

From the moment of our salvation until we go to heaven, God intends for us to spend our earthly lives learning what it means to be who he created us to be: "But grow in the grace and knowledge of our Lord and Savior Jesus Christ. To Him be the glory both now and forever. Amen" (2 Peter 3:18). Although we will not be perfect until we get to heaven, in this world as we grow spiritually and get to know God, he makes us more and more like himself. Scripture says we are transformed into his image when we seek him wholeheartedly (Romans 8:28–29; 2 Corinthians 3:18). For the rest of our lives the Lord will teach us what that means.

APPENDIX E

GOD'S WORD TO THOSE WHO SUFFER

Read the following verses and mark the ones that express your suffering especially well. Copy those passages and keep them nearby to read when your suffering is particularly intense.

- **Psalm 55** —Give ear to my prayer, O God, and do not hide Yourself from my supplication. Attend to me, and hear me; I am restless in my complaint, and moan noisily, because of the voice of the enemy, because of the oppression of the wicked; for they bring down trouble upon me, and in wrath they hate me. My heart is severely pained within me, and the terrors of death have fallen upon me. Fearfulness and trembling have come upon me, and horror has overwhelmed me. So I said, "Oh, that I had wings like a dove! I would fly away and be at rest. Indeed, I would wander far off, and remain in the wilderness. *Selah*. I would hasten my escape from windy storm and tempest." Destroy, O Lord, and divide their tongues, for I have seen violence and strife in the city. Day and night they go around it on its walls; iniquity and trouble are also in the midst of it. Destruction is in its midst; oppression and deceit do not depart from its streets. For it is not an enemy who reproaches me; then I could bear it. Nor is it one who hates me who has exalted himself against me; then I could hide from him. But it was you, a man my equal, my companion and my acquaintance. We took sweet counsel together, and walked to the house of God in the throng. Let death seize them; let them go down alive into hell, for wickedness is in their dwellings and among them. As for me, I will call upon God, and the LORD shall save me. Evening and morning and at noon I will pray, and cry aloud, and He shall hear my voice. He has redeemed my soul in peace from the battle that was against me, for there were many against me. God will hear, and afflict them, even He who abides from of old. *Selah* Because they do not change, therefore they do not fear God. He has put forth his hands against those who were at peace with him; he has broken his covenant. The words of his mouth were smoother than butter, but war was in his heart; his words were softer than oil, yet they were drawn swords. Cast your burden on the LORD, and He shall sustain you; He shall never permit the righteous to be moved. But You, O God, shall bring them down to the pit of destruction; bloodthirsty and deceitful men shall not live out half of their days; but I will trust in You.

- **Psalm 56** —Be merciful to me, O God, for man would swallow me up; fighting all day he oppresses me. My enemies would hound me all day, for there are many who fight against me, O Most High. Whenever I am afraid, I will trust in You. In God (I will praise His Word), in God I have put my trust; I will not fear. What can flesh do to me? All day they twist my words; all their thoughts are against me for evil. They gather together, they hide, they mark my steps, when they lie in wait for my life. Shall they escape by iniquity? In anger cast down the peoples, O God! You number my wanderings; put my tears into Your bottle; are they not in Your book? When I cry out to You, then my enemies will turn back; this I know, because God is for me. In God (I will praise His Word), in the LORD (I will praise His word), in God I have put my trust; I will not be afraid. What can man do to me? Vows made to You are binding upon me, O God; I will render praises to You, for You have delivered my soul from death. Have you not kept my feet from falling, that I may walk before God in the light of the living?

- **Psalm 57** —Be merciful to me, O God, be merciful to me! For my soul trusts in You; and in the shadow of Your wings I will make my refuge, until these calamities have passed by. I will cry out to God Most High, to God who performs all things for me. He shall send from heaven and save me; He reproaches the one who would swallow me up. *Selah* God shall send forth His mercy and His truth. My soul is among lions; I lie among the sons of men who are set on fire, whose teeth are spears and arrows, and their tongue a sharp sword. Be exalted, O God, above the heavens; let Your glory be above all the earth. They have prepared a net for my steps; my soul is bowed down; they have dug a pit before me; into the midst of it they themselves have fallen. *Selah.* My heart is steadfast, O God, my heart is steadfast; I will sing and give praise. Awake, my glory! Awake, lute and harp! I will awaken the dawn. I will praise You, O Lord, among the peoples; I will sing to You among the nations. For Your mercy reaches unto the heavens, and Your truth unto the clouds. Be exalted, O God, above the heavens; let Your glory be above all the earth.

- **Psalm 10:2-18** —The wicked in his pride persecutes the poor; let them be caught in the plots which they have devised. For the wicked boasts of his heart's desire; he blesses the greedy and renounces the LORD. The wicked in his proud countenance does not seek God; God is in none of his thoughts. His ways are always prospering; Your judgments are far above, out of his sight; as for all his enemies, he sneers at them. He has said in his heart, "I shall not be moved; I shall never be in adversity." His mouth is full of cursing and deceit and oppression; under his tongue is trouble and iniquity. He sits in the lurking places of the villages; in the secret places he murders the innocent; his eyes are secretly fixed on the helpless. He lies in wait secretly, as a lion in his den; he lies in wait to catch the poor; he catches the poor when he draws him into his net. So he crouches, he lies low, that the helpless may fall by his strength. He has said in his heart, "God has forgotten; He hides His face; He will never see." Arise, O LORD! O God, lift up Your hand! Do not forget the humble. Why do the wicked renounce God? He has said in his heart, "You will not require an account." But You have seen, for You observe trouble and grief, to repay it by Your hand. The helpless commits himself to You; You are the helper of the fatherless. Break the arm of the wicked and the evil man; seek out his wickedness until You find none. The LORD is King forever and ever; the nations have perished out of His land. LORD, You have heard the desire of the humble; You will prepare their heart; You will cause Your ear to hear, to do justice to the fatherless and the oppressed, that the man of the earth may oppress no more.

- **Psalm 82:1-4** —God stands in the congregation of the mighty; He judges among the gods. How long will you judge unjustly, and show partiality to the wicked? *Selah* Defend the poor and fatherless; do justice to the afflicted and needy. Deliver the poor and needy; free them from the hand of the wicked.

- **Psalm 91:9-11** —Because you have made the LORD, who is my refuge, even the Most High, your dwelling place, no evil shall befall you, nor shall any plague come near your dwelling; for He shall give His angels charge over you, to keep you in all your ways.

- **Psalm 86:1-7** —Bow down Your ear, O LORD, hear me; for I am poor and needy. Preserve my life, for I am holy; You are my God; save Your servant who trusts in You! Be merciful to me, O Lord, for I cry to You all day long. Rejoice the soul of Your servant, for to You, O Lord, I lift up my soul. For You, Lord, are good, and ready to forgive, and abundant in mercy to all those who call upon You. Give ear, O LORD, to my prayer; and attend to the voice of my supplications. In the day of my trouble I will call upon You, for You will answer me.

- **Psalm 107:39-43** —When they are diminished and brought low through oppression, affliction, and sorrow, He pours contempt on princes, and causes them to wander in the wilderness where there is no way; yet He sets the poor on high, far from affliction, and makes their families like a flock. The righteous see it and rejoice, and all iniquity stops its mouth. Whoever is wise will observe these things, and they will understand the lovingkindness of the LORD.

- **Psalm 103:1-19** —Bless the LORD, O my soul; and all that is within me, bless His holy name! Bless the LORD, O my soul, and forget not all His benefits; Who forgives all your iniquities, Who heals all your diseases, Who redeems your life from destruction, Who crowns you with lovingkindness and tender mercies, Who satisfies your mouth with good things, so that your youth is renewed like the eagle's. The LORD executes righteousness and justice for all who are oppressed. He made known His ways to Moses, His acts to the children of Israel. The LORD is merciful and gracious, slow to anger, and abounding in mercy. He will not always strive with us, nor will He keep His anger forever. He has not dealt with us according to our sins, nor punished us according to our iniquities. For as the heavens are high above the earth, so great is His mercy toward those who fear Him; as far as the east is from the west, so far has He removed our transgressions from us. As a father pities his children, so the LORD pities those who fear Him. For He knows our frame; He remembers that we are dust. As for man, his days are like grass; as a flower of the field, so he flourishes. For the wind passes over it, and it is gone, and its place remembers it no more. But the mercy of the LORD is from everlasting to everlasting on those who fear Him, and His righteousness to children's children, to such as keep His covenant, and to those who remember His commandments to do them. The LORD has established His throne in heaven, and His kingdom rules over all.

- **Psalm 118:5-9, 13-14** —I called on the LORD in distress; the LORD answered me and set me in a broad place. The LORD is on my side; I will not fear. What can man do to me? The LORD is for me among those who help me; therefore I shall see my desire on those who hate me. It is better to trust in the LORD than to put confidence in man. It is better to trust in the LORD than to put confidence in princes.... You pushed me violently, that I might fall, but the LORD helped me. The LORD is my strength and song, and He has become my salvation.

- **Psalm 94:16-19** —Who will rise up for me against the evildoers? Who will stand up for me against the workers of iniquity? Unless the LORD had been my help, my soul would soon have settled in silence. If I say, "My foot slips," Your mercy, O LORD, will hold me up. In the multitude of my anxieties within me, Your comforts delight my soul.

- **Psalm 59:6-10** —At evening they return, they growl like a dog, and go all around the city. Indeed, they belch with their mouth; swords are in their lips; for they say, "Who hears?" But You, O LORD, shall laugh at them; You shall have all the nations in derision. I will wait for You, O You my Strength; for God is my defense. My God of mercy shall come to meet me; God shall let me see my desire on my enemies.

- **Psalm 62:5-8** —My soul, wait silently for God alone, for my expectation is from Him. He only is my rock and my salvation; He is my defense; I shall not be moved. In God is my salvation and my glory; the rock of my strength, and my refuge, is in God. Trust in Him at all times, you people; pour out your heart before Him; God is a refuge for us. *Selah*

- **Acts 2:25-26** —"For David says concerning Him: 'I foresaw the LORD always before my face, for He is at my right hand, that I may not be shaken. Therefore my heart rejoiced, and my tongue was glad; moreover my flesh also will rest in hope.'"

- **John 16:33** — "These things I have spoken to you, that in Me you may have peace. In the world you will have tribulation; but be of good cheer, I have overcome the world."

- **Mark 9:42** — "But whoever causes one of these little ones who believe in Me to stumble, it would be better for him if a millstone were hung around his neck, and he were thrown into the sea."

APPENDIX F
INFORMING POWERFUL EMOTIONS WITH TRUTH

The only truly effective and lasting way to respond to emotions is to dwell on biblical truths. Over time, as we diligently inform emotions with truth from Scripture, those feelings become less and less troublesome, even when our emotions have a physical component. The following list contains examples of some common emotions and a few of the thoughts or beliefs that instigate them, followed by statements of truth that can moderate them.

At a time when you are feeling emotionally stable, look at this appendix (perhaps with your leading friend). Consider which of these emotions tend to trouble you the most, and whether your mind dwells on inflammatory thoughts or on what God says in Scripture.

Choose a few of the truth statements and write them on a card. Look at the card each morning and evening to help you dwell on truth instead of on destructive thoughts. As you learn from God's Word, add more truth statements to your list.

Notice how your attitude is affected when you do this, and talk to God about those results.

ANGER

Lies: Dwell on injustice

- "I deserve better!"

- "I shouldn't have to go through this!"

- "My will be done."

- "God isn't good to me."

- "People stink."

- "If I were in control, things would be better."

Truth: Dwells on God's goodness and justice.

- "As a sinner, I deserve nothing good. Even so, God has done an amazing number of good things for me by his grace. (Name some examples; such as friends, breathing, sunshine, a good meal, eyesight, a biblical church, a safe place to live: _____)." (Hebrews 12:14–15; John 3:16; Psalm 84:11; 1 Thessalonians 5:18)

- "Everyone has trouble. God has not singled me out for punishment. Suffering is part of living in a fallen world; I am called to endure with hope" (1 Corinthians 10:13; John 16:33; James 5:11).

- "God is in control—I am not, and that's okay. For me, control is only an illusion that prevents me from yielding to God. If I were in control, I'd make a mess" (Psalm 62:11; Psalm 57:1–3; Romans 7:18).

- "Jesus is my boss (Lord). His will be done. He is all-wise, all-loving, and all-powerful, so I can trust him to do right and good things" (Philippians 2:9–11).

- "God loves sinners, and so should I. Love is not simple, fluffy, or easy, but in Christ I can learn to love people the ways he does" (John 3:16; 1 John 4:7–12; John 15:9).

- "I choose to trust and submit to you, God. Not my will, but Thine be done, O Lord" (Proverbs 3:5–6; Luke 22:42; James 4:15–16).

- "I must distinguish between sinful and righteous anger, so that my anger is not focused on me (selfish anger). I will talk to God, admitting my selfish anger, and turn away from it.

Instead, I will seek what God wants (holiness) and trust him to help me." (Psalm 7:11; James 1:19–20).

FEAR

Lies: Dwell on bad things that have happened or might happen

- "I'll never measure up. I'm anxious and insecure, with a knot in my stomach most of the time. That's just who I am."

- "I'm unlovable, always afraid you don't like me. Either I will do whatever it takes to please you, or out of fear, I will withdraw from you."

- "I'm afraid to risk making a friend because I might get hurt again."

- "God can't be trusted. He doesn't keep me safe."

- "I just want to be secure; to know that I am safe. Therefore, I will control as much of my world as I can."

- "Shame overpowers me; my faith is wobbly. I feel guilty and condemned."

- "These feelings are unbearable. I wish I could get off this emotional roller coaster."

Truth: Dwells on the certainty of God's presence and provision.

- "I choose to trust God with my whole heart, thanking him for creating me as he did, no matter what may happen or what people may think or do." (Proverbs 3:5–6; Psalm 139:14; Romans 8:21–39).

- "God allows only what he will use for my good: to make me more like Christ. I need not fear, but even if I feel afraid I will trust him" (Psalm 23:4; 27:1–14; 56:3; Romans 8:28–29; 1 Corinthians 10:13).

- "To allow the opinions of people to control me is to give them too much power over me. My identity, my hope, and my abilities are in Christ, regardless of what people may think or do" (Ephesians 1:1–14).

- "When I live for the approval of people, I am not free to love them (to seek their well-being) because I'm too busy needing or trying to get something from them. This drains and suffocates my relationships. Fear is overcome by mature love for God and people" (1 Corinthians 13:1–8; Romans 14:19; 1 John 4:18).

- "Anxiety and fear can be replaced by trust in God. When I am afraid, I will choose to trust God. I will pray with thanksgiving and think about the things he says to think about" (Psalm 56:3; Philippians 4:6–8).

- "My hope is not in people; it is in God" (Psalm 42:5).

- "I am completely forgiven in Christ. Christ's example teaches me to look beyond my feelings of shame to his higher purposes and his better ways" (1 John 1:9–2:2; Hebrews 12:1–3).

- "There is no condemnation to those who are in Christ Jesus. I am deeply loved by God. His grace covers me completely so that I have no fear of his rejection or anger." (Romans 8:1a; Ephesians 2:4–10; 1 John 4:7-12)

- "Rather than fearing that I won't have enough of something, I will be grateful for what I have and will trust God for what I need" (1 Thessalonians 5:18; Ephesians 5:20; 1 Peter 5:7).

DESPAIR

Lies: Dwell on negatives and hardships

- "No one understands my struggles and my pain."

- "No one can help. Nothing helps."

- "No one cares."

- "There is no hope. It's no use trying. I might as well give up."

- "The pain is too great for me to bear. I can't go on.

- "God has forsaken me. He doesn't like me, is mad at me, and is punishing me."

Truth: Dwells on God's sovereignty and good purposes

- "God is near. He understands my struggles and my pain, and he will hear me when I call out to him" (Psalm 139:23–24; 120:1; 121:1–8).

- "God is sovereign (in control) over everything, and he helps those who turn to him" (Psalm 46:1; 1 Corinthians 10:13).

- "My feelings don't tell the truth. God's Word does. I may not feel great all the time, but I don't have to follow my feelings. I will follow God and choose to believe in his faithfulness no matter how I feel" (Psalm 42:5, 11; Psalm 91).

- "God cares for me, and so does his true church. I can faithfully fellowship with God and his people." (1 Peter 5:7–10; Hebrews 10:25)

- "Hope is found in God, not in anything on this earth. Have I been hoping in the right things?" (Psalm 43:5; Colossians 3:1–4).

- "God says not to give up. Giving up (or losing heart) means I have stopped putting my faith in God. Faith is something I choose, not something I feel" (2 Corinthians 5:7; Psalm 119:30; Hebrews 11).

- "I can choose to trust God for everything, including the results that I cannot see at this point" (Psalm 135:6; 71:14–16; 56:8–11; 57:1–11).

- "Thank you, Lord, for … " [Give thanks for specific things you have or appreciate today.] (1 Thessalonians 5:17–18).

- "I will sing a hymn or a spiritual song wholeheartedly, paying careful attention to the words" (Colossians 3:16–17). "I will do this constructive thing for someone else, and I will encourage someone else in these ways: _____" (Romans 12:10–13).

GUILT AND SHAME

Lies: Dwell on self, to condemn, berate, and pity

- "I'm worthless. I'll never amount to anything."

- "I've done too many bad things. I'm condemned because of _____."

- "I'll never be good enough for anyone to love me."

- "I'm bad, a slut, a liar, an idiot, and there's no way out."

- "People tell me I'm stupid, guilty, or bad. They are right."

- "I can't change, so I'm doomed."

- "I'm a miserable failure."

Truth: Dwells on God's love and forgiveness in Christ.

- "God loves me deeply, because he is good. His love is endless and it doesn't depend on my merits" (John 3:16; 1 John 4:7–19).

- "There is no condemnation for those who are in Christ Jesus" (Romans 8:1a).

- "Love seeks the well-being of the one loved, not because of personal merit, but because that's the nature of love. Therefore, even though I do not deserve God's love, I can learn to accept God's love and to love God and other people in the way that God loves me" (John 3:16; 1 John 4:7–19).

- "I am a sinner like everyone else, but rather than beating myself up over that, I will accept Christ's complete and freely offered forgiveness on my behalf. He alone is the key to freedom from guilt and shame. But I must accept this truth in order to experience the freedom that is mine in Christ" (Romans 3:23; 6:23; 1 John 1:9–2:2).

- "I choose what to dwell on. I will dwell on the good things from Philippians 4:8: the things that are true about God, noble, just, pure, lovely, good, virtuous, and praiseworthy."

- "People and experiences do not define me. In Christ I have a new identity as described in Ephesians 1. I am blessed, chosen, holy, blameless, adopted, accepted, loved, redeemed, forgiven …" (Ephesians 1:3–14).

- "Throughout my life since I received Christ, God has been transforming me into the image of Christ, little by little each day. Although I'm not yet perfect, he does not regard my failures, because he has already overcome them in Christ. One day I will stand before Jesus and will be like him, perfect in every way" (Psalm 103:10–14; Romans 8:28–29; 2 Corinthians 3:18; 1 John 3:2).

IMPULSIVENESS

Lies: Dwell on self, to fulfill passions and desires

- "I want it now. I shouldn't have to wait, especially considering all I've had to go through."

- "I was made this way, so I can't help it. People should be more understanding."

- "I can't trust God. There's never enough."

- "I want more, right now. So I will go after what I want, whatever it takes."

- "You owe me."

- "Why can't we just have fun? Life is short, so I'm going after some pleasure."

- "Let somebody else do the work. I've had enough hard stuff in my life. I deserve some relief."

Truth: Dwells on God and others, to become more like Christ.

- "God's timing is always best; waiting is part of his plan so that I can learn the character of Christ, which includes patience" (Galatians 5:22–25; James 1:2–4; Romans 5:3–4).

- "Everyone, including me, naturally bends toward sin, but that doesn't mean I have to continue that way. In Christ, I can seek to overcome that tendency" (Luke 9:23–24; Philippians 4:13).

- "Others can often see me more clearly than I can see myself; I should listen to those who speak wisely" (Proverbs 8:33; 10:17; 13:18; 14:7–8).

- "I am called to trust God as my provider. He is more than enough and he gives me good things. My own heart deceives me to think that I can find anything truly good apart from him" (John 15:5; Proverbs 3:5–6; 14:14).

- "What I need is more of Christ, not more of the things of this world. This world will ultimately disappoint and then pass away, but Christ remains faithful and good forever" (Matthew 24:35; 1 Peter 1:24–25; 2 Peter 3:10–14).

- "No one owes me anything. Using people to meet my felt needs will only damage my relationships. Instead, when I live by faith in Christ's love for me, I am able to learn to love others" (Galatians 5:13–15; 1 John 4:7–19).

- "Pleasure is empty in the end. It isn't the same as joy, which is found only in the Lord" (Ecclesiastes 2:1–11; Galatians 5:22–24).

- "From the very beginning, people were designed to work. Work is deeply satisfying and brings joy when approached with determination to do well, to the best of my ability" (Genesis 2:15; Ecclesiastes 3:11–13; 2 Thessalonians 3:10–13).

- "Live for Christ, not selfishly for relief from suffering. Relief from suffering is fleeting; Christ is eternal" (Colossians 2:9–10; 3:1–2).

APPENDIX G

Building Relationships with Believers and Unbelievers

Relationships with Believers

Delighting in God together: The LORD delights in our unity and love (Psalm 133).

- Building relationships, as in everything we do, should be done for the glory of God (1 Corinthians 10:31).

- God created us in his image. The Father, Son, and Holy Spirit talk with each other (Genesis 1:26). We are good image bearers when we relate well to other believers.

- God's love is demonstrated in relationships.

- Healthy relationships express the glorious character of Christ our Redeemer.

Entering in: Companionship and enjoyment (Genesis 2)

- Selflessness, humble self-disclosure (being honest and vulnerable wisely)

- Commitment to another person's well-being

- Forgiveness and reconciliation in conflict and adversity

- Prayer and giving

- Recreation and joy

Reaching to one another: Teaching and supporting
(Galatians 6:2, Titus 2)

- Discipleship (mentoring, teaching, sharing)

- Compassion and comfort

- Help and care (the hands of Christ in one another's lives)

- Reaching out together: serving and accomplishment
  (Nehemiah)

- Serving together creates unity and knits together the body of
  Christ (Colossians 2).

- Teaching others to serve and teach (Titus 2)

Testimony: Declare the gospel; glorify and magnify God
(1 Corinthians 10:31).

- Reflect the character of Christ in our responses to life's
  situations.

- Share the gospel (our story of salvation and the ways God is
  teaching us to grow in our relationship with him).

Relationships with Unbelievers

An unbeliever's greatest need is to hear and see the gospel lived out. It
is crucial for us to understand that unbelievers are completely incapable
of loving others with pure motives. Apart from Christ, an unbeliever's
best attempts to serve and love others are drawn out of a heart that
seeks its own good. Consider these truths:

- Each unbeliever needs to know that there is a marvelously
  kind, merciful, and good God; that he is the almighty Creator who is worthy to be feared and trusted.

- Each unbeliever is a slave to sin. Without Christ, we are all drawn away and enticed by our own desires. Even nice people need to be rescued and redeemed.

- Each unbeliever regardless of their belief system, is accountable to God. Jesus Christ offers the only way to God and eternal life, and the unbeliever needs to receive him (John 1:12).

Relating to Unbelievers

Delighting in God:

- Express the love of God to them in word and deed

- Reflect the good character and wisdom of Christ in word and deed.

Entering in: Companionship and enjoyment (Genesis 2)

- Selflessness, humble self-disclosure when appropriate and wise

- Commitment to primary relationships

- Forgiveness and reconciliation during conflict, allowing for trust to be earned

- Pray for them

- Recreation and enjoyment in biblical ways that reflect the character of God

Reaching to one another: Teaching and supporting (Galatians 6:2, Titus 2)

- Compassion and comfort with the gospel

- Help and care (extend the hands of Christ)

- Reaching out together: serving and accomplishment (Nehemiah).

- Community service

- Hobbies

Testimony: Glorify and magnify God (1 Corinthians 10:31).

- Talk about the character of Christ in our responses to life's situations. Encourage belief.

- Share the true gospel (our story of salvation and the ways God is teaching us to grow in our relationship with him). Invite them to a relationship with Christ.

BIBLIOGRAPHY

Books and Booklets

Allberry, Sam. *Is God Anti-Gay?* Croydon, UK: The Good Book Company, 2013.

Anonymous. *Principles of Love, Sex, and Dating.* Lafayette, IN: Faith Resources.

Baker, Amy. *Getting to the Heart of Friendships.* Bemidji, MN: Focus Publishing, 2010.

Bancroft, Lundy. *Why Does He Do That? Inside the Minds of Angry and Controlling Men.* Penguin Publishing Group, 2002. (Note: Some vulgar language).

Berg, Jim. *God Is More Than Enough: Foundations for a Quiet Soul.* Greenville, SC: BJU Press-JourneyForth Books, 2010.

Bridges, Jerry. *The Joy of Fearing God.* Colorado Springs: Waterbrook Press, 1997.

Bromley, Nicole Braddock. *Hush: Moving From Silence to Healing After Childhood Sexual Abuse.* Chicago: Moody Publishers, 2007.

————. *Breathe: Finding Freedom to Thrive in Relationship After Childhood Sexual Abuse.* Chicago: Moody Publishers, 2009.

Delk, Ruthie. *Craving Grace: Experience the Richness of the Gospel.* Chicago: Moody Publishers, 2014.

Fitzpatrick, Elyse, and Carol Cornish. *Women Helping Women.* Chicago: Harvest House, 1997.

Harvey, Dave. *When Sinners Say "I Do."* Wapwallopen, PA: Shepherd Press, 2007.

Henderson, John. *Abuse: Finding Hope in Christ.* Phillipsburg, NJ: P & R Publishing, 2012.

Holcomb, Justin, and Lindsey Holcomb. *Rid of My Disgrace: Hope and Healing for Victims of Sexual Assault.* Wheaton, IL: Crossway, 2011.

Hubbard, Ginger. *"Don't Make Me Count to Three!"* Wapwallopen, PA: Shepherd Press, 2003.

James, Carolyn Custis. *When Life and Beliefs Collide: How Knowing God Makes a Difference.* Grand Rapids, MI: Zondervan, 2001.

Jeffrey, Robert. *When Forgiveness Doesn't Make Sense.* Colorado Springs, CO: Waterbrook Press, 2000.

Jones, Beneth Peters. *Mount Up on Wounded Wings: For Women from Hurtful Home Backgrounds.* Greenville, SC: BJU Press, 1994.

Kellemen, Robert W. *Sexual Abuse: Beauty for Ashes.* Phillipsburg, NJ: P&R Publishing, 2013.

Keller, W. Philip. *A Shepherd Looks at Psalm 23.* Grand Rapids, MI: Zondervan, 2007.

Lane, Timothy, and Paul David Tripp. *Relationships: A Mess Worth Making.* Greensboro, NC: New Growth Press, 2008.

Lewis, C. S. *The Joyful Christian.* Nashville: Broadman & Holman Publishers—Simon and Schuster, Touchstone Edition, 1996.

Lucado, Max. *When God Whispers Your Name.* New York: Thomas Nelson Publishing Group, 1994.

Mack, Wayne. *Your Family God's Way.* Phillipsburg, NJ: P&R Publishing, 1991.

McLaren, Brian D. *Finding Faith.* Grand Rapids, MI: Zondervan Publishing House, 1999.

Miller, Wendell E. *Forgiveness: The Power and the Puzzles.* Warsaw, IN: Clear Brook Publishing, 1994.

Morison, Patrick H. *Forgive! As the Lord Forgave You.* Phillipsburg, NJ: P&R Publishing, 1987.

Nicewander, Sue. *Help! I Feel Ashamed.* Wapwallopen, PA: Shepherd Press, 2017.

O'Donnell, Rosie. *Find Me.* New York: Warner Books, 2002.

Patrick, Crough. *Seducers Among Our Children: How to Protect Your Child from Sexual Predators—A Police Investigator's Perspective.* Eureka, Montana: Lighthouse Trails Publishing, 2012.

Peace, Martha. *The Excellent Wife.* Bemidji, MN: Focus Publishers, 1995.

Powlison, David. *Recovering from Child Abuse: Healing and Hope for Victims.* Greensboro, SC: New Growth Press, 2008.

———*Sexual Assault: Healing Steps for Victims.* Greensboro, NC: New Growth Press, 2010.

———*Why Me? Comfort for the Victimized.* Phillipsburg, NJ: P&R Publishing Company, 2003.

Powlison, David, Ed Welch, and Paul David Tripp. *Domestic Abuse: How to Help.* Phillipsburg, NJ: P&R Publishing, 2002.

Pryde, Debi, and Robert Needham. *A Biblical Perspective of What to Do When You Are Abused by Your Husband.* Newberry Springs, CA: Iron Sharpeneth Iron Publications, 2004.

Pryde, Debi. *Why Me, Lord? Help for Women Who Have Been Sexually Molested.* Newberry Springs, CA: Iron Sharpeneth Iron Publications, 2012.

Smith, Robert, M.D. *Biblical Principles of Sex.* Hackettstown, NJ: Timeless Texts, 2003.

Spurgeon, Charles. *Faith: What It Is and What It Leads To.* Norhaven, Denmark: Christian Focus Publications, 1987.

Tautges, Paul. *Counseling One Another.* Wapwallopen, PA: Shepherd Press, 2016.

Tozer, A. W. *The Knowledge of the Holy.* New York: HarperSanFrancisco, 1961.

——— *The Pursuit of God*. Middletown, DE: Mockingbird Classics Publishing, 2015.

Tracy, Steven R. *Mending the Soul: Understanding and Healing Abuse*. Grand Rapids, MI: Zondervan, 2005.

Tripp, Paul David. *Broken-Down House*. Wapwallopen, PA: Shepherd Press, 2009.

——— *What Did You Expect?* Wheaton, IL: Crossway, 2012.

Tripp, Tedd. *Shepherding A Child's Heart*. Wapwallopen, PA: Shepherd Press, 1995.

Tuggle, Brad, and Cheryl Tuggle. *A Healing Marriage: Biblical Help for Overcoming Childhood Sexual Abuse*. Colorado Springs, CO: NavPress, 2004.

Van Stone, Doris, and Erwin W Lutzer. *No Place to Cry: The Hurt and Healing of Sexual Abuse*. Chicago: Moody Publishers, 1992.

Van Stone, Doris. *Dorie: The Girl Nobody Loved*. Chicago: Moody Publishers, 1979.

Viars, Stephen. *Putting Your Past in Its Place: Moving forward in Freedom and Forgiveness*. Eugene, OR: Harvest House Publishers, 2011.

Welch, Ed. *When People Are Big and God Is Small*. Phillipsburg, NJ: P&R Publishing, 1997.

Wheat, Ed, M.D., and Gayle Wheat. *Intended for Pleasure*. Fleming H. Revell, 1977.

White, John. *Daring to Draw Near*. Downers Grove, IL: InterVarsity Press, 2007.

Wilson, Jim. *How to Be Free from Bitterness*. Moscow, ID: Canon Press, 1999.

Younts, John A. *Everyday Talk*. Wapwallopen, PA: Shepherd Press, 2005.

Articles

Bauder, Kevin. "In the Nick of Time." *Church Accountability and Sexual Abuse,* October 2013.

Powlison, David. "'I'll Never Get Over It': Help for the Aggrieved." *Journal of Biblical Counseling* 28, no.1 (2014): 8-27.

Unpublished Notes

Barnes, Kristen. "Helping People Hurt by Abuse." Lecture at Bob Jones University, Greenville, SC, August 21, 2015.

Hendrickson, Laura. "Counseling the Sexually Abused." Notes from National Association of Nouthetic Counselors, Annual Conference, Spartanburg, SC, 2009.

Higbee, Garrett. "Writing a Personal Psalm to God." Notes from Solace Conference, Dallas, TX: Association of Biblical Counselors, 2013.

———. "Helping the Sexually Abused." Notes from Biblical Counseling Training Conference, Lafayette, IN, February 15, 2012.

Lelek, Jeremy. "Psalm 88: A Psalm of Lament, A Prayer of Faith, A Faithful God." Notes from Solace Conference, Dallas, TX: Association of Biblical Counselors, 2013.

Pryde, Debi. "Sexual Abuse and The Church." Session 6, Bob Jones University Seminar, Greenville, SC, November 7, 2012.

Smith, Robert. "Communication." Notes from Biblical Counseling Training Conference, Faith Church, Lafayette, IN, February 1998.

Online Resources

Author Unknown. "Carrots, Eggs, or Coffee: Which are You?" http://www.heavensinspirations.com/carrots-eggs-coffee.html

Holcomb, Justin. "What Does the Bible Say About Sexual Assault?" http:biblicalcounselingcoalition.org/ blogs/2013/08/28what-does-the-bible-say-about-sex

Maria's blog: www.strugglingwell2gether.weebly.com

Moore, Russell. "Moore to the Point: What Should the Duggar Scandal Teach the Church?" Ethics and Religious Liberty Commission of the Southern Baptist Convention. Accessed July 13, 2015 http://www.russellmoore.com/2015/05/22/ what-should-the-duggar-scandal-teach-the-church.

Pryde, Debi. "Dealing with Child Protective Services." http:// www.debipryde.com. Accessed May 31, 2010.

Poetry Card

Chaplain, John. "He Leadeth Me." Bible Truth Publishers, poetry card 7962-50.

HELP! I FEEL ASHAMED

Sue Nicewander

LifeLine mini-book, 64pp
ISBN 978-1-63342-057-1

Do feelings of shame baffle you or hold you hostage? Shame can overwhelm us, leading to confusion, fear, and desperate behavior. This mini-book uses case studies and practical examples to examine the true causes of shame and present hope through Jesus Christ, the Savior who loves you and can restore you, regardless of your past. Learn to answer shame his way and find victory.

"I love the LifeLine mini-books! You can trust these resources to provide accessible, practical, and Bible-saturated help with many of the most common and perplexing problems found in our fallen world."
—**Dr. Heath Lambert,** First Baptist Church, Jacksonville, FL, Executive Director the Association of Certified Biblical Counselors (ACBC)

"These mini-books are exactly the kind of books you'd want to have available to you at church—short, biblical and inexpensive enough to give away."
—**Tim Challies,** Blogger

LIFELINE

DISCIPLING THE FLOCK:
A CALL to FAITHFUL SHEPHERDING

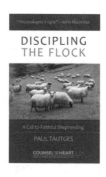

Paul Tautges
Trade Paperback, 96pp.
ISBN: 978-1-63342-142-4

Here is an urgent appeal to return to authentic discipleship; here is a call to shepherds to be tenacious in their preaching of the whole counsel of God, and tender in their application of its truth to the lives of God's sheep through personal ministry.

Author Paul Tautges has been in gospel ministry since 1992 and currently serves as senior pastor of Cornerstone Community Church (EFCA) in Cleveland, Ohio. Paul is the author of many books including *Comfort the Grieving, Counseling One Another*, and *Pray about Everything*, and serves as the series editor for the LifeLine mini-books. He is also an adjunct professor and he blogs at CounselingOneAnother.com.

"Here is an anchor for authentic ministry that will stimulate real spiritual growth in God's people." **—Dr. Steven J. Lawson**

"... this book gets it right." **—John MacArthur**

"... a biblically faithful, practically helpful guide to find the important balance between the public and private ministry of the Word of God ..."
—Brian Croft